THE EXPLODING SELF

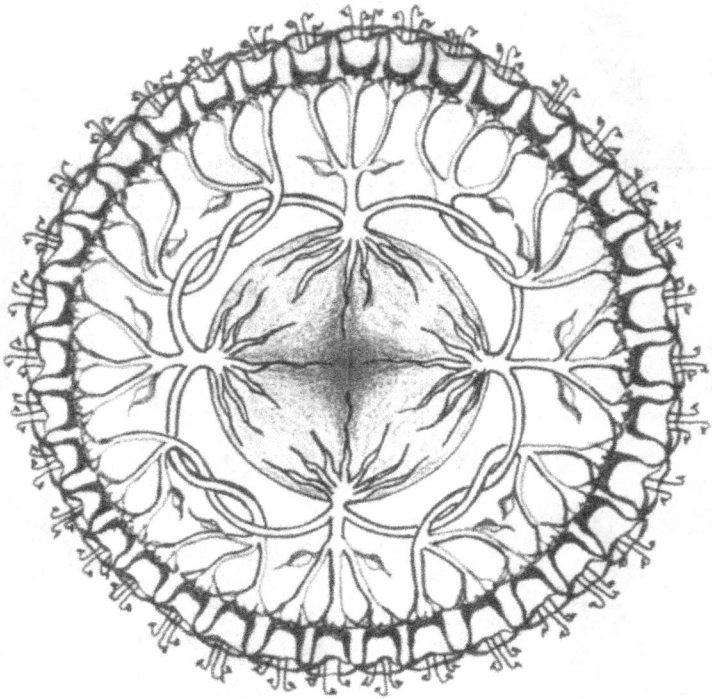

THE
EXPLODING
SELF

The Creative and Destructive Nucleus
of the Personality

Joseph Redfearn

Chiron Publications • Wilmette, Illinois

Library of Congress Catalog Card Number: 91–38084

Printed in the United States of America.
Editing and book design by Siobhan Drummond.
Cover design by Michael Barron.

Library of Congress Cataloging-in-Publication Data:

Redfearn, Joe (Joe W. T.)
    The exploding self : the creative and destructive nucleus of the personality / Joe Redfearn.
       p. cm.
    Includes bibliographical references and index.
    ISBN 0–93029–60–8 : $16.95
    1. Good and evil – Psychological aspects. 2. Aggressiveness (Psychology) 3. Self-destructive behavior. 4. Projection (Psychology) 5. Conflict (Psychology) I. Title.
    BF789.E94R43 1992
    155.2′32 – dc20
                                                                                    91–38084
                                                                                    CIP

    ISBN 0–933029–60–8

To my analysands herein, my family,
and my friends at the S.A.P.

"It is conceivable that Art and Science, bravery and points of honour, life and property could one day explode as a result of some incalculable error. Once our peaceful prosperity has gone up in smoke, a time of general famine will surely follow, a time of death prepared for slowly and yet with blind infallibility. And so we should once more find ourselves standing at the point from which World History first set out, and might indeed receive the impression that God created the world in order for the Devil to take it."

Richard Wagner, *Art and Religion*

Contents

Contents

Foreword

Dr. Redfearn's thoughtful, valuable book is the product of his many years of experience as a Jungian analyst. Since nuclear weapons have made it possible for man himself to eliminate the human species, it is vital that we understand and come to terms with our potential for destructive behaviour.

Redfearn points to the intimate connection between destruction and creation. Using many illustrations from history and from individual cases, he demonstrates that potential destruction can often be transformed into new and fruitful change *provided that the urge to destroy can be contained for long enough.* In individuals, aggressive behaviour is often a thoughtless substitute for accepting painful experiences and resentful feelings which are unacknowledged by the individual and projected upon "enemies." Acting out aggression by attacking others brings temporary relief but no insight; whereas containing aggression and reflecting on its cause makes possible the development of new attitudes.

Redfearn believes, with good reason, that most of us go through life acting out our own myths. Our picture of reality is so deeply distorted by subjective prejudice that we often act against our own best interests. Believing that we ourselves are the carriers of good and that our enemies embody evil is a dangerous myth which leads to our own destruction as well as to the destruction of our enemies.

The beginning of wisdom is the realization that the conflict between good and evil is an internal battle going on within ourselves, not Superman versus the Evil One or even President Bush versus Saddam Hussein. It is when we feel ourselves torn apart by outrage that we are most likely to attack others explosively. When we are possessed with "righteous anger," our attempts to destroy the Evil One result in unforeseen disasters, as Vietnam and the Gulf War vividly demonstrate. But, when we learn to contain the opposites within ourselves, we realize that wisdom comes by way of pain, and that negotiation can and must be the only way to avoid destruction of our world.

Dr. Redfearn wears his learning lightly, and his allegiance to Jung is never doctrinaire. His gift for clarity of exposition ensures that his book will appeal to a wide general readership. His message is timely, urgent, and profound. I hope his book will have the success which it so eminently deserves.

Anthony Storr

Preface

In 1988, when I was getting on well with the first draft of this book, my doctor told me that my blood pressure was "dramatically high." At that time, therefore, I began to worry about my person exploding before the world did so. Early one morning, while not yet fully awake, I felt my heart thumping and my head banging away in a frightful fashion, and I embarked on a vicious spiral of panic and its somatic consequences. On this occasion I tried to "go with" my fears and submit myself to whatever was to happen. I was rewarded by a visual image of myself bursting like a rocket (a firework, not a missile) over the world and scattering a beneficent shower of light. So I assume that my fear of bursting produced this wish to burst fruitfully over the world, which I have turned into this book. The evident desire of humanity, in like manner, to blow itself to pieces is its subject matter. Let us hope that this explosion, too, has a creative outcome.

Clearly, as I write, neither I nor my world have yet exploded. Indeed, for all I know, we may be a little further away from the abyss because of medical and political revolutionary changes respectively. But the danger of a false sense of security is obvious. I do not feel it necessary to modify the thesis of this book, concerning the almost inherently explosive nature of the human individual and, correspondingly, of our spiritual need for the divine thunderbolt of truth to shatter repeatedly our cosy narcissistic illusions and false sense of harmony and security. The current explosion of change in the countries beyond the erstwhile Iron Curtain is indeed a powerful case in point, let us hope of the creative kind.

From this it is clear that my thesis in one sense consists of fancifully projecting my own inner wishes and fears onto the world scene. All we human beings are doing this all the time, although not many realise it. That is the nature of great historical and social changes, as the reader will explore further in this book. We shall see that in the human being all energy is potentially explosive as well as potentially creative. My purpose is to indicate the sorts of background and attitudes which can help to ensure a creative outcome.

Acknowledgments

I am extremely grateful to both my son Andrew and my friend Corinna Peterson for reading the draft manuscript very carefully and making valuable suggestions.

Coline Covington and Rosemary Gordon read the manuscript and gave encouragement when I needed it. I also wish to thank Rosemary in her capacity as Editor of the *Journal of Analytical Psychology* for permission to quote passages from articles of mine in the *Journal*. These are incorporated mostly in chapter 9.

Andrew Samuels read both early and later drafts and was very generous and helpful in advising on textual matters and on publication.

My colleagues on the committee of the Library of Analytical Psychology have been very helpful as this book has progressed.

The views expressed here have arisen out of the teaching and discussions I have had during my training and membership in the London Society of Analytical Psychology. Of course, I do not hold them in the least responsible for these views nor for the sometimes slightly overstated manner in which they are expressed.

CHAPTER 1

Introduction

In this chapter I present my basic thesis in several related ways:

(1) The vision of world apocalypse is an ancient one. However, it can now be enacted literally, and moreover, most human beings know this for a fact.

(2) The apocalyptic vision symbolizes the clash of opposing drives within the individual human personality. In practice this amounts to deep moral conflict (the conflict between good and evil). Experiencing this clash can be a bombshell, but facing the moral conflict can lead to a creative outcome with moral deepening and enrichment.

(3) Real warfare, and particularly nuclear warfare, allows the personal conflict to be avoided or bypassed in the grand cosmic or international scenario in which the fantasy is made real. Moral impoverishment is the price of this outer enactment.

This chapter, not meant to convince the reader, is simply an introduction to the concepts which will be elaborated later. Nonacademic readers may omit chapter 11 without losing the sense of the book as a whole. It gives a fuller historical background to the notions of the conflict of opposites elaborated in the rest of the book, using Pavlov, Freud, and Jung as exemplars of these basic notions, which are very ancient indeed.

Unconscious Destructive Wishes in Individuals and Groups

Forty years ago, when I was learning psychiatry, visions and fantasies of world destruction brought to mind a diagnosis of schizophrenia. Now this insane fantasy has been made into a realistic possibility by our leaders and scientists, acting on our behalf, and we all feel we can do nothing about it. Collectively, while seeking security, we behave in a self-destructive manner. If we were planning world destruction, the present cornucopia of world-destructive forces, exploitation of paranoid fears, doubtful control and safety measures, cover-ups, and lies would be the ideal scenario out of which we would achieve our baneful purpose.

Apart, possibly, from a few religious fanatics who believe that the Apocalypse is a necessary prelude to a higher state of being, I do not believe that anyone wants or plans world destruction. But as a psychotherapist I see every day how ordinary, sane, decent people like myself are, without being fully aware of it, actively bringing about self-destructive results as if they unconsciously intended to do so. Our behaviour so often runs counter to our conscious intentions and, even more, counter to our professed ideals that I feel I need not labour the point. Even if the reader cannot believe this of himself, he will readily observe it in his neighbour.

In psychotherapy, the patient cannot be helped to change a pattern of habitual disastrous behaviour until he realises that part of himself— one of his subpersonalities, as one might say—actively wills the destructive act. "I can't help doing it" has to be replaced by "I realise that part of me wants to do this destructive (or self-destructive) thing" before the patient is able to choose between doing it and not doing it. The self that *wants* to do the destructive or self-destructive thing is usually a hurt or angry child part of the personality that has been split off from the normal, grown-up part. Being split off from normal conscious awareness and control, for the simple reason that our normal self is ashamed to "own" or be responsible for the subpersonality in question, this hurt or destructive self behaves like a suppressed person and bides his time until a suitable circumstance presents itself. When conscious control is exhausted or weakened or when a crowd of fellow human beings, or the authorities, encourage it, the hurt, explosive, or savage subpersonality in us may be unleashed or may burst through our normal restraints as if an alien personality were in possession of us or of our social group.

Unconscious, Omnipotent, Destructive Wishes Behave as Malign Deities

Granted that no individual person is planning or working for world destruction, it is nevertheless clear that, collectively speaking, a powerful although unconscious portion of our total selves is working toward it. It is as if we were blindly carrying out the plan of a dark and omnipotent God who was intent on the destruction or replacement of mankind.

Could there be such omnipotent, destructive forces at work in mankind? Or (framing the same question differently) could God have such a dark and malevolent side? Whether we like it or not, the answer for all practical purposes must be yes. Man is so unaware of his infantile, destructive wishes that they are quite outside his responsibility, outside his capacities for choice. These unconscious destructive wishes or impulses therefore act on us in precisely the same way as the workings of an outside agent such as some omnipotent, evil God or aspect of God. Collectively, it seems that we have no more effective knowledge of or control over our sociopolitical behaviour than if an alien, often hostile divinity were at work on mankind.

For collectively, did we not slaughter millions of our brothers and sisters and their children in two great wars in the past seventy years? Did we not till our fields while hundreds of our fellow human beings were being gassed or otherwise slaughtered on the other side of the barbed wire? Did we not cheer as squadrons of our bombers passed over us at sunset on their way to drown our neighbours' cities in fire and flood in order to liberate ourselves and them from their satanic leaders? We did it all for the good of our parentland or for humanity as a whole. Even now we cannot be certain that it did not, on the whole, turn out for the good of mankind. Historical forces are not subject to black-and-white moral judgments, any more than are real human individuals. Yet these same historical forces are usually powered, or at least fueled, by genuine convictions of moral or religious rightness. Certain values, certain traditions, certain people, certain places in the lives of each of us are judged to be worth dying for or risking death for. I hope to demonstrate that this courage, this loyalty, this selflessness, this all-that-is-best-in-us naturally tends to feed the apocalyptic fires of world destruction in the hope of a better world.

Awareness Must Be Morally and Emotionally Involved

In the bizarre world of today it is probable that most of our schoolchildren do not fully believe they will reach adulthood, because the world will be destroyed before then. The morally degenerative consequences of this probable fact deserve reflection. We know in our minds that their fears are reasonable, but full awareness in our hearts of what we are doing to them is too much to face. This book is aimed not merely at the intellectual awareness of the reader, but at the kind of emotional realization which, following or even preceding mere mental awareness, alone can change our behaviour and make it responsible.

Knowledge with our minds alone about how we are actually behaving would not mean that we were in effective contact with or in control over what we are *in fact* doing. This statement is as true of our leaders as it is of ourselves, judging by behavioural criteria, over the generations. We must try to remember that wishing to avoid disaster, especially when fear or panic grip us, while at the same time moving inexorably toward it, is the sort of human behaviour with which we psychotherapists are very familiar in our patients, and it is plainly to be observed in the group behaviours of mankind.

The enormity of the risk and danger, the very frightfulness of that apocalyptic abyss on the edge of which we are teetering, would cause such fear and revulsion in us, if we allowed ourselves to become fully aware of what we are doing, that in order to keep our heads we have to turn away from the emotional reality. We employ psychological defences which, again, the psychotherapist encounters daily in his consulting room:

(1) "It is so frightful, so insane, that it can't possibly happen."

(2) "No one could be so suicidal as to start an atomic war."

(3) "It couldn't happen to me."

(4) "Even if it happens, I shall survive somehow."

(5) "There's nothing to be done about it so one may as well carry on as usual."

(6) "If it happens, as seems likely, let us enjoy ourselves in the meantime and make full use of the time left to us."

(7) "What is the point of anything?"

(8) "If it happens, I can always commit suicide."

And so on. These are some of the ways in which we try to ward off either the factual reality of impending disasters of our own making, or more still, the emotional impact of the facts.

The Nonchalance of Self-Destructiveness

Every few weeks in my work I am alarmed by some apparently stupid, careless, or accidental act done by one of my patients. Traffic accidents or near accidents are the commonest examples nowadays. In such patients I have usually plenty of evidence of unconscious violence and fears. But it is usually the case that the patient is unaware of the violence and fears that are within himself and which are producing these "accidents." Several narrow escapes, even when repeated, are still shrugged aside with a nonchalance which is itself quite disturbing to me, and even to the friends and relatives of the patient. Only when the patient can become appropriately aware of and alarmed by the reality of the "carelessness" or of the risks being run can a start be made toward responsibility for what is being enacted and for the self-destructive feelings involved.

Every psychotherapist, of whatever persuasion, meets such unconscious self-destructive behaviour in his patients. Freud, in his classic book *The Psychopathology of Everyday Life*, drew attention to these apparent accidents and their possible unconscious motivations. One does not have to agree with all Freud's overprecise and in most cases oversimplified interpretations of the particular motivations operating behind these "accidents." But one has to admit that self-destructive behaviour usually is unconsciously motivated and that the person so behaving has split off the realization of violence within in some way. For a cure, the split-off feelings of anger or fear have to be repossessed, recognized, even validated.

We may be sure that what is manifestly true of many individuals may well be true of groups of people, particularly when they are acting as masses. In fact, self-destructive behaviour (as seen by the outsider) may possess groups even more readily than individuals. I do not expect the sceptical reader to be convinced of this at this stage, but merely ask him to take note of this hypothesis.

Most Interactions Have Both Creative and Destructive Aspects

The self-destructive behaviour of individual persons, including suicide, is much more frequently unknowing and unintentional than it is knowing, let alone intentional. Conscious anger or violence is noticeable for its absence much more than for its presence. Only when a self-destructive outcome is repeated does the pattern of unconscious self-destructive behaviour begin to be discernible. Before corrective therapy can be successful, at least in psychoanalytic therapy, the hitherto unknowing violence and anger against the self (often displaced from anger against a parental figure or some other loved/hated figure) and the wish to hurt or destroy has to become conscious and morally grappled with ("accepted" is too simplistic a word for "the assumption of responsibility for"). It is then that the anger can be put to good use.

Just as a group contains different and differing individual persons, so an individual person is not a simple unified whole but consists of many more or less distinct "persons" which I have termed *subpersonalities*, some of which relate with each other in destructive ways and some in more creative ways. For example, in my personality, because of a bad relationship with my father in the past, a continuous or intermittent war may be being waged between my "father" and my "child" subpersonalities. Indeed, it is often a matter of fine judgment as to whether, on the whole, the total effect on the individual of such a particular interaction of subpersonalities is creative or destructive. A clash may be the result of my "child" subpersonality striking a blow for freedom, integrity, non-compliance against my "parent" subpersonality, with superficially disastrous results from an external, material, or commonsense point of view, but with some long-term benefits. Many apparent failures in achievement or competitiveness are of this sort, for example, in the academic sphere. Similarly, the individuals in a human group each tend to behave to some degree like subpersonalities of the self. Thus, in a therapy group, one person will tend to take on a good-father role, another will tend to take the role of mother, or of good child, or of scapegoat, or rebel, and so on. Of course, roles are interchanged and reversed, but always the groups acts as a larger self for each individual within it. Too much conflict and alienation within the group may break it up. Sometimes we may agree that a certain eventuality could be considered self-destructive from the point of view of the group as a whole.

If, in a family, rivalry between brothers reaches such murderous intensity that they destroy each other and the family business, and if as a result the parents and the grandchildren starve, we might justifiably talk about the self-destructiveness of the family considered as a group. Much self-destructiveness in larger human groups, such as nations and ethnic families, is of this sort. The internecine conflicts of the semitic nations and factions are cases in point today which are heartrending to witness. Yet rivalry and competitive pressures between subgroups are essential prerequisites for a healthily evolving society.

The Explosiveness of Fixed Rigid Boundaries in the Individual and in Society

Subgroups within larger human groups also behave as subpersonalities of the self. For example, we have rulers and ruled, powerful and weak, oppressors and oppressed, parentlike and childlike, and so on within the larger groups of society.

If one subgroup is always, and rigidly, the ruler, and another group the ruled, the human potential of each group is stunted. We are taking here the view that life is fullest when all one's constituent subpersonalities are lived out fully, and that this applies to subgroups within a community just as it does to the individual person. We know that an individual may be crippled if his neurosis, or a neurotic family or cultural upbringing, prevent him from living out all the diverse parts of himself. He is crippled who always has to be top dog, or always has to be underdog, or always has to be child, or protector, or teacher, or learner. Habit, rigid social roles, and neurosis can all bring about these rigid boundaries, by storing up and blocking energy flow along energy gradients, may produce an explosive situation in an individual. Rigid boundaries between subgroups in society may create potentially explosive conditions, in the same way.

But all energy in the human is both ˜potentially explosive and potentially creative. The main purpose of this book is to indicate how therapy—individual or social—can help toward the creative use of the energy of conflict, confrontation, and containment.

Magnetic Effect of Fears

Our lemminglike movement toward apocalypse suggests that a magnetic effect of the fearsome image may be at work. In some circumstances, certainly in individuals and no doubt in groups also, a fearful fantasy or preoccupation can bring about its own fulfilment, either in a nearly exact, concrete way or in some sort of symbolic sense. Psychoanalysts might perhaps say that, underlying each fear in us, a wish may well be operating, producing the fear and unconsciously bringing about its own fulfilment. The overanxious mother who is repressing her hostility toward her child may produce either a fearful and/or reckless child, who would be more prone to accident than the average child. Protestant hellfire preachers know how to terrify their congregations and lead some of them through fear, individually and collectively, to a sort of apocalyptic crisis which is the basis of this type of religious conversion. Fear and excitement produce an orgiastic rupture of normal consciousness, for which a volcanic eruption or a nuclear explosion might be an appropriate metaphor.

Intrapersonal Conflicts Avoided by Focusing on Universal Catastrophe

The present world situation allows every human being to displace his personal fears and unthinkablenesses onto the real universal nuclear threat. Nowadays the bomb is an appropriate symbol for the unthinkably terrifying thing in ourselves which we are avoiding facing. This may be the very part of ourselves that we most need to explore and know. I shall give examples in the next chapter to show what I mean by this. If the bomb can symbolize such a potentially creative clash within the person, which that person needs to experience but dare not, then it follows that the atom bomb of the outside world will provide a sort of excuse or easy way out for everyone, for it can focus our fears away from the personal moral conflict which is engaging us, or rather *should* be engaging us. A declaration of war performs a similar displacement. It reduces doubt, internal conflict, and the incidence of the neuroses in a population – but by the same token it reduces the beneficial, personal, moral conflicts in the individuals of the population at war. Moral crippling then results.

The Psychological Uniqueness of the Present Nuclear Situation

The present world situation is unprecedented, in that for the first time the human race can destroy itself in reality, and for the first time most of us know it. Hitherto we could all have private versions of the unthinkable catastrophe; now we have one we can all use. We can all displace our personal fears onto one realistic fearful possibility, and we can all help in our small ways to realize it. In other words, we have one huge common magnet for our apocalyptic yearnings for the first time in the history of humankind. It is not just the dream of one oppressed nation, or people, or class, or crazed minority. It is not just the explosive fantasy of the breaking of one rigid moral or traditional boundary in glorious revolution. But it can use the energies of all these things in its one fearsome, compelling image, an image representing an even more terrifying reality.

Dreams and Myths Enact Themselves Concretely and Symbolically

In psychotherapy we come to a partial, although limited, understanding of the dreams and fantasies which provide and power the leading motifs of our lives. It is as if each one of us has his own personal myth or fairy tale which underlies, motivates, and explains the major patterns and quirks of our individual lives. Through psychotherapy or other avenues of insight, we learn what our personal fairy tales, our unconscious fantasy themes, are. Only then do we realize how we have been continually enacting those prevailing fantasies without having previously realized it. Working on a dream, we realize days or weeks after the dream that we are in some vital sense enacting that dream, and probably have been doing so for years. To the psychotherapist it is obvious that the same is true of mankind. Myths can be eddies, whirlpools, or great tides of energy sweeping peoples along, often toward one excess or another, followed by reaction generated by compensatory countermyths. Our myths will determine our laws, our way of bringing up our children, the kind of people we admire, how we use our energies, and in short how we deal with our instincts.

What are the myths which motivate Western man, for example? I shall not list them at this point for fear of inducing the reader's wrath. One man's mere myth is another's universal truth. The most powerful are the least spoken of. But the fantasy (some would say vision or revelation) of apocalyptic universal destruction has been part of the mythology of mankind for many thousands of years, the most familiar being the Judeo-Christian versions of this recurrent theme. Myths are not noticeably subject to conscious rational control. It is probable that even if people no longer believe in hellfire, or in the apocalyptic triumph of good over evil, some such belief or fantasy will simply go underground into the unconscious of peoples, only to reemerge in an altered form more compatible with the altered style or flavour of the times. If the myth were to be relegated to the unconscious, owing to nonbelief, it would be all the more likely to motivate collective sociohistorical tides of human behaviour than if present in consciousness as a belief. I say all this on the assumption that the findings of psychotherapy in individuals and small groups apply also to large groups of people and to large-scale human interaction. "Dead" myths, "dead" dreams do not become entirely ineffectual but tend to go underground and energize concrete behavioural forms of themselves. Later, the "dead" myth or dream is resurrected in a transfigured form. What is true of Christ in the Christian myth of death and resurrection is also true of myths in general.

The Apocalypse Myth

In the Judeo-Christian type of apocalyptic vision there is a titanic struggle between the forces of good (the forces of light) and the forces of evil (darkness). In the course of this clash, the world is to be destroyed. The forces of good triumph, the followers of untruth are annihilated, and a new world arises from the ashes of destruction, in which the good inherit the blessings of a new earth. The present danger of concrete historical enactment of the apocalyptic fantasy is different in an important respect from this black-and-white moral/military conflict between the forces of good and evil in which the good conquers the evil. Perhaps nowadays the most sane people foresee a cold and empty world of no triumph and no survival in the event of a nuclear war. This absence of hope of victory and of the triumph of righteousness might paradoxically be the most hopeful aspect of the present situation. It would obviously be utterly disastrous if one side or the other truly believed that it had omnipotent righteousness on its side and hence that triumph was therefore inevitable, in this world or the next. However, it seems that some religious and political groups believe something perilously close to this, even today.

The "Personal Apocalypse"

On the other hand, as distinct from the *collective* apocalyptic myth, or the danger of collective enactment of the myth, I shall show in this book that the *personal* apocalyptic experience of the individual, in which the conflict and clash of opposing psychic and moral forces is suffered and faced squarely as moral conflict within the individual concerned, results in a strengthening and an enrichment of the person. Our psychological health demands that the defences and the cosy illusions of our narcissistic selves be periodically shattered by the awareness of the conflict of opposing forces within ourselves. But this entails taking one's share of responsibility in moral conflict, in a place where right and wrong are not black and white, not cut and dried. Failure to feel morally conflicted means clinging to a blind and delusory feeling of wholeness and harmony within the self. It is this regressive clinging which plants the seeds of explosive disruption of the individual self, and also of any society collectively experiencing or worshipping this defensive, morally unconflicted wholeness, harmony, or bliss.

In so far as each one of us clings to an experience, even a hope, of conflict-free wholeness and harmony in ourselves, I believe we are contributing, albeit minutely and certainly unintentionally, to the catastrophic, historical, concrete enactment of its opposite, the opposite of social and historical unity and wholeness. We are bringing down on ourselves the thunder and lightning of God's balancing retribution in concrete form.

The inner image of the monstrous reality which confronts us belongs in the same region of the personality as the omnipotent destructive fantasies of the psychotic level in ourselves (and "ourselves"

11

includes therapists, patients, and "normal people"). It is the sort of vision which can be produced in "normal" people by means of sensory deprivation, sleep deprivation, or hallucinogenic drugs. Fantasies or dreams of titanic struggles between great armies or forms of nature, of wars and clashes between light and darkness, good and evil, etc., may occur in psychotherapy when deep levels of the psyche are being reached.

Jungian analysts often refer to the "wars of the opposites" which occur in these penetrating analyses, when opposing forces and emotions within the psyche are invading consciousness simultaneously. The important opposites are love and hate, goodness and evil, light and darkness, inner and outer (relative to the "self"), large and small, male and female, omnipotent and impotent, parent and child, and so on – we could all make up our own lists. Out of the awareness of the deeply conflicted and essentially paradoxical nature of the self a stronger yet more tolerant and responsible self may emerge, with a corresponding healthily pluralistic rather than destructively schismatic social grouping of such individuals.

Psychotherapeutic and Religious Views Contrasted

It seems to me that in the *religious* apocalyptic vision good is seen to triumph over evil. This certainly applies to the Christian version, when the second coming of Christ will wipe away all tears. Whether this represents a higher synthesis emerging out of conflict squarely faced, or a mere reversal or turning of the tables, either in the present world or the next, depends on the maturity of the person concerned. In practice we know that the truly religious person is not exempt from moral conflict. As therapists we know that disaster always seems to happen when one side of the personality triumphs over its opposite, either in the dream lives or the waking lives of our patients.

Whether we take a religious or a psychotherapeutic view of the *nature* of these visions, the fact of the experiences, the power of the visions, and their potentially transformative value are not in doubt. I am simply saying what everybody knows, namely, that the naive, concrete approach to these ancient truths can be very dangerous.

A superficially nonreligious view of the apocalyptic vision was taken by the psychologist Stanislav Grof, whose LSD-based therapy was documented in his book *Realms of the Human Unconscious* (1976). He ascribed these apocalyptic experiences occurring in the course of LSD therapy to memories of the birth experience, of passage through the birth canal, when the foetus is experiencing a struggle to survive, with great mechanical crushing pressures and, frequently, a degree of suffocation. Grof says:

> The most important characteristic of this pattern [i.e., this phase of the birth experience] is the atmosphere of titanic struggle frequently attaining catastrophic proportions. . . . The visions typically accompanying these experiences involve scenes of natural disasters and the unleashing of elemental forces, such as exploding volcanoes, raging hurricanes . . . and various cosmic cataclysms. Equally frequent are images of similar events related to human activities . . . explosions of atomic bombs, thermonuclear reactions. . . . Some individuals describe complex catastrophic events such as . . . the destruction of Sodom and Gomorrah, the biblical Amageddon. (1976, p. 124)

So we must add analysis, meditation, and drug experience to the religious and mythological experience that can take us to these levels of the psyche. Christians are most familiar with the apocalyptic visions of St. John described in the book of Revelation. Here Christ, the sacrificial Lamb of God, is transformed into the Sword of the triumph of good over evil, the bridegroom of the mysterious marriage with the New Jerusalem, when God shall wipe away all tears, but the fearful, the unbelieving, the abominable, the murderers, the whoremongers, the sorcerers, the idolaters, the liars, shall be cast into the lake of burning brimstone (Rev. 21).

But the apocalyptic vision, interpreted concretely by the early Christians, was not confined to Christianity. We now see Christianity as arising out of a powerful current of Jewish apocalyptic movements of the century or two before the Christian era. The book of Daniel is an apocalyptic vision. The prophet Elijah is surrounded by apocalyptic mythology (Mal. 4:1–5). The Apocrypha has several references to a prophesied apocalypse, and the first Dead Sea Scroll is, in an important sense, a war manual for the apocalyptic army of the Essenes, the Sons of Light, in their vanquishing of the Sons of Darkness and in bringing about a world ruled by the righteous. The second scroll is a doctrine of the two spirits, truth and error, light and darkness, good and evil, purity and impurity, together with a statement as to how the sect is to be organised and disciplined along the lines of this doctrine. The third scroll uses passages from the Old Testament book of Habbakuk and rereads them to refer to the Maccabean Age in which the scrolls were written (Campbell 1964, pp. 282–285). I have thought it worthwhile to mention the Dead Sea scrolls because they illustrate the primitive, concrete, and political nature of these apocalyptic scenarios, without causing too much offence to present-day believers.

Whereas the Essenes were looking forward to the Messiah, the early Christians believed that the Messiah was come, and the Good News was interpreted literally in apocalyptic terms (e.g., Paul, Rom. 13:11–12: "Salvation is nearer to us than when we first believed: the night is far gone, the day is at hand").

The emphasis on light and dark may derive from Mithraic influences, where we encounter the divine fiery thunderbolt of illumination which features also in the aspect of Buddhahood known as Vajradhana, "bearing the bolt." Vajra means both "Thunderbolt" and "Diamond." Zeus's thunderbolt, and the thunder-god of the Aryans and the men of the North, reflect the psychological profundity and forcefulness of the image of the shattering and (we hope) delusion-dispelling shock of God's illumination. The atom bomb image is closely allied. If enacted objectively, literally, and concretely, this image could destroy mankind. If it were interpreted subjectively and as a psychological truth, mankind might not merely survive but take a step forward in awareness and vitality.

In my patients I find that the atom bomb *image* (not, we pray, to be confused with the *actual* world-destroying *use* of the atom bomb *in fact*) can represent an unfaceable psychic situation or confrontation which, when actually faced, leads on to further development of the personality. In this sense the atom bomb image functions like that shattering aspect of the divine which may have great moral and spiritual effect. It is like that "epileptic" experience of the divine that St. Paul had on the road to Damascus. The danger seems to me to be that because of the deeply numinous validity and power of the image, an irreligious humanity may be in danger of enacting the fantasy underlying the image in a concrete way, much as the psychotic patient enacts fragments of deep religious and mythological themes in a broken-up, literal (i.e., nonmetaphorical, concrete) manner.

The "Personal Apocalypse," Which Is Different for Each Person

For my patients, for myself, and no doubt for virtually all the individuals comprising that considerable proportion of mankind which is aware of world events, the nuclear catastrophe means or represents the unthinkable, nightmare clash of world-shattering forces. If we try to enquire as to the meaning or the deep significance of this nightmare image, we are dealing with the apocalyptic fantasy, which is a deep and powerful force within each of our personalities. But when we try turning the question into "What is the unthinkable which I am unable to think about?" or "What is the unfaceable conflict in my life which I am unable to face?" we come to personal moral or ethical matters, practical and humdrum perhaps, which are in most cases not grand or apocalyptic, but petty and demanding. As we shall see in the next chapter, one of us may be evading marriage, another may be avoiding clashing with a person on whom he depends in an infantile way, another may be avoiding the truth about her life's love. These are the materials with which each of us is engaged in manufacturing his or her own personal bomb. It is a relief and a catharsis when our leaders can be pressured into declaring war, thus massively enabling each of us to sidestep his or her personal moral conflicts. More, it transforms these personal moral conflicts, petty as they may seem, into grandiose historical struggles and explosions. What could be more grand, more final, more of a complete solution than a world-destroying nuclear exchange? The collective drift of billions of individuals resolves – yet, of course, does not in fact resolve – the differing personal evasions of each individual.

I am not proposing that each, or indeed any, individual would, if asked, prefer the world to be destroyed rather than face his or her individual, unfaceable, internal situation or conflict. The choice is not presented to any individual in this form. Both the collective suicidal drift and the evasion of personal conflict on the part of each individual occur unconsciously *for practical purposes*, i.e., there may be some degree of awareness on the part of most people. By emotional awareness in this case I mean the horrified realization of what we as human beings are doing to ourselves and to each other, and the facing of our own personal moral conflictedness.

The Paranoid Defences of Primitive Selves and of Nations

As primitive selves, we take in the good and impute it to ourselves; on the other hand, we project the evil outward and impute it to the bad outside person. We build up our self-respect in this way. The various parts of our selves are projected onto different people, different social roles, different social groups, different nations. Our internal conflicts are fought out in the form of external conflicts. We project the villain onto someone and behave villainously toward him, thereby forcing him to project the villain onto us. The primitive self is like a fortified city under siege, or a modern nation. The nation is a projection of the primitive self. Realization of the enemy's goodness or humanity is a bolt from the blue; it threatens our self-respect and our view of ourselves and the world. It is a bombshell. Our primitive selves prefer to avoid this kind of bombshell and to concretize the bomb, thus externalizing the evil within ourselves.

The Psychological Momentum of Material Objects

There is a reciprocal relationship between the concretizing primitive self and the self-aware self who can be aware of the evil aspects of his own nature and of the conflicting drives in himself (his different subpersonalities). Correspondingly there is a sense in which concrete behaviour, and the blind enactment of mythology, fantasy, or instinct, are all alien to the wholeness of the person. Of this I hope to say more later, but in the meantime it is necessary to mention also the momentum and the alien nature of material objects. In the course of history and in the competition to survive, weapons have become more efficient, more complicated, and have required more kinds of specialists for their manufacture and maintenance. It is true that our primitive instincts still long to use our fists, our sticks and stones, our skins, our shelter and homes in these battles. However, of necessity, we have to use hooligans and professionals partially to enact these primitive aspects of ourselves. But the really serious business of mass destruction employs millions – millions of people depend on our armaments to feed them and keep them in interesting occupations. Material objects have their own momentum, their own needs, their own willing servants, and they behave as alien wills for that reason. They command votes in a democracy and represent power in a dictatorship. The peacemaker is a pitiful amateur in the face of these forces. And he is vastly outnumbered, in terms of those whose vested interests (apart from survival) depend on fear and on armaments and on the hope of security through strength. But now perhaps we are beginning to see sheer survival on the peacemaker's side.

The Internalization of Conflict Is Indivisible

The professional therapist is one of a type which has a vested interest in peacemaking of a sort, although it is the peace of internal personal conflictedness. He brings not peace to the individual but the awareness of potentially shattering conflict. Similarly, the industrial peacemaker brings conflicting motivations out into the open, so that both sides have to grapple with the problems within themselves. The same may be happening in some international areas, where primitive defences are having to be abandoned and the pain of moral conflict within ourselves suffered. This would be to the long-term benefit of the individuals comprising the nations who succeed in working together in this way, providing that our primitive selves are neither forgotten nor despised. The latter eventuality could pave the way for other historical cataclysms such as religious wars or other conflicts in which primitive defences can disguise themselves as conflicts of omnipotent convictions.

The ability to suffer moral conflict supersedes, but only overlies, the primitive paranoid self, which feels a sense of healthy well-being when it is succeeding in projecting the bad and the evil outside itself. But the projection of evil makes it so much more difficult for the projectee to behave well and face moral conflict in himself. Moral conflictedness, therefore, like international peace, tends to be indivisible. It is the individuals who succeed in going against the social gradient in whom we vest our hope.

CHAPTER 2

The Bomb in Dreams
Unfaceable Aspects of the Self

The bomb in our feelings is close to the bomb of our dreams—a metaphorical bomb in fact. We might hope though that metaphorical world destruction does not get itself enacted in reality as so many dreams do, at least partially. The word *bombshell* is used in the English language to describe an event or a piece of news of shattering intensity or unexpectedness. What does the metaphorical bombshell shatter? I suggest that it shatters our illusions; our comfortable, mistaken preconceptions and expectations; our established patterns of conduct or outlook; our normal, habitual ways of seeing ourselves or others.

In all the great religions the god sometimes becomes manifest as one armed with the thunderbolt and the discharge of lightning. Order is destroyed, structure is crumbled by overwhelming force. If the god is held to be good, a good reason for the manifest destructiveness is found. The thesis here entirely agrees with this view in that the metaphorical atom bomb is or could be the source of boundless potential creativity in mankind, shattering our illusions and forcing us to face reality. How this can happen is explained by some actual cases in psychotherapy, but psychotherapy is, of course, not essential for us to be able to observe similar phenomena in life.

In the New Testament of the Christians, God first manifests Himself to St. Paul as a blinding light that throws him to the ground. We are entitled to speculate whether St. Paul suffered from epilepsy, and the conversion resulted merely from a fit. We may then have to come to terms with the possibility that epileptic seizure may be one of the more shattering ways in which God breaks or rather crashes into our consciousness. One aspect of the overwhelming power of God is clearly the overwhelming of normal consciousness by virtue of an excess of experience. Indeed, the direct, unprotected, and unfiltered exposure to God is commonly felt to be lethal, or nearly so, and this is why it is sometimes supposed that He is understood, or creatively experienced, only through indirect means – symbols, signs, portents, intermediaries, messengers, representatives, parables, and similar attenuated forms.

That having been said, I have to remark that in the experience of my patients, at least as reported to me, God is usually experienced as comforting and reassuring and as a kind person by nature. Explosions, earthquakes, floods, fires, wars, and titanic clashes, on the other hand, have an impersonal nature, although the clash of armies and the atom bomb itself are obviously human in origin, and these catastrophes are common in the fantasies and dreams of my patients.

My patients' dreams and fantasies seldom contain any person or being referred to as "God." Supernatural creatures and objects may be featured, even divine beings, certainly, but not often God; when someone called God appears, it is usually a surprisingly ordinary person, a grandfatherly figure or an administrator, for example. Often the ordinariness seems to be the point of the dream.

If this were the general dream experience of, say, Western persons (and at the moment I have no reason to presume otherwise), then it could mean that our notion of God – not merely intellectually but at depth – is of a basically simple and childlike sort. The dark, terrible aspects of reality and of our deep selves are split off from the personal and are projected, as it were, onto images of nature and impersonal physical forces. These are felt to be very remote from the responsible, personal I. It might mean that however much we preach to ourselves or each other, we are simply not at present capable of assuming personal responsibility for the more destructive feelings and wishes in ourselves. This being the case, we project our destructiveness into elemental forces of nature, like volcanoes or storms at sea. We thus abandon any pretence of control or responsibility for the impersonal, destructive power in ourselves.

One way of looking at dream images or dream figures is to regard them as parts of the self – subpersonalities. A person who is very dependent on his wife may, after a quarrel with her, dream of a volcano erupting. The volcano could then be regarded as having to do with a part of himself, a volcano self, which had erupted or had wanted to erupt or had been felt in danger of erupting (the dream details and other associations might help sort out which of these was the case). We also have to admit that the volcano to some extent would represent his wife or how he experienced her, and that how he experienced her and how he himself behaved would be determined by past and other present factors. He might also be worried about something else erupting, of course. The

19

point is that the dream image of the volcano indicates to the therapist that the anger or passion is being felt to be related to the responsible I in the same way as a volcano is, a massive underground force of immense heat and of permanent potential danger, something so mighty and powerful that the ego feels minute and helpless in relation to it.

Later in therapy, perhaps, or in a different situation, the person concerned would be much more in contact with his personal angry feelings, so that the angry subpersonality would not be a volcano but an angry person, for example, an angry old woman or an angry child. An intermediate degree of powerlessness would be conveyed by the dream image of a dangerous or unruly animal. Supposing we were in more effective contact with our feelings, then we would, by the same token, tend to experience natural forces and objects – volcanoes, for example – at least in dreams, as persons. The primitive, animistic view of nature in terms of persons and personalities is the sign of a feeling contact. An erupting volcano would be felt as an angry person – "The Earth-Shaker (Poseidon, for example) is at it again." This personalization of impersonal forces is quite the opposite of the splitting off and depersonalization of one's own repudiated and alienated feelings, which occurs in Western or alienated man, ourselves, that is.

Bodily impulses, and parts of the body, may become repudiated or feared or for some other reason alienated from our feelings. They may then be depersonalized and appear in dreams and fantasies in a mechanical, abstract, or "scientific" form. For example, a young scientist who was suffering from a mild anxiety neurosis dreamt of a clock. The dream caused him acute anxiety. This was because it was a sort of human clock, half alive. The mechanism of the clock was one with which he was not familiar in the real world, and it was this mechanism that seemed or felt frighteningly obscene to him. The escapement mechanism, instead of being controlled by a pendulum moving to and fro, side to side, was controlled by a pistonlike object on a spring moving up and down between the clock's "legs," now inside, now half outside the "body" or "torso" of the clock – like a baby being born, then going back inside; or a turd being extruded, then returning inside the body; or a penis moving in and out of the clock's "vagina," all natural, vital images of bodily oscillations against which his childhood fears had caused him to defend himself by means of a mechanical and scientific displacement of interest (and no great harm in that, one might think). The anxiety was caused by the breakdown of these long-standing defences and marked a healthy reconnection in feeling with his own body and that of the object of his love. The mild nervous breakdown turned out to be a break-through of the natural, feeling part of himself which had been split off and converted into scientific and mechanical thought images because of anxiety in the first place, in the latency period of childhood. The natural, oscillatory time of the body had been converted into linear, scientific, Western-man time by means of the alienation of the bodily, the affective, the frighteningly incestuous and "obscene" aspects of himself and the world – alienation followed by obliteration from consciousness.

During therapy, natural feelings tend to return because they become tolerable again. This is the reason for the dream I have just mentioned. Another patient of mine, an engineer who was in therapy following a suicide attempt and was also getting into contact with his feelings and natural impulses, dreamt of a furry little animal escaping out of a machine that was not working very well.

In summary, then, the atom bomb in our feelings or dreams is characterized by (1) its tremendous power and (2) its mechanical, scien-tifically miraculous nature. The former may compensate for our experi-ence of powerlessness in the face of our own destructive impulses. The latter is often a measure of our alienation from our feelings, from our bodies, and from our bodily feelings and biological interests. Prior to these dreams, the scientist and the engineer had been living machine lives to the detriment of their biological selves.

Another important general point I wish to emphasize here is that our dreams are being lived out by us continuously. We do not have to remember our dreams for this to be the case. Often in the course of therapy it becomes clear to the patient, after working on a dream, that he has been living that dream unawares not only during the days since he had the dream, but for a long time before this, perhaps for as long as he can remember. The dream, and the work on it, signal a potential aware-ness of this, and thus make it possible to some degree to choose whether or not to continue to enact the dream; it is sometimes propitious to repeat an old behavioural pattern or emotional habit, and sometimes better not to. For example, in some circumstances it is advantageous to explode when angry, and in other circumstances not.

To accomplish any great engineering, scientific, or military project some of our humanity may have to be sacrificed (see chapter 9). In Neolithic times and certainly until the Bronze Age, this had to be done concretely before the necessary motivation for the enterprise could be worked up in the people concerned. Humans or animals had to be sacrificed in a concrete, physical way, although they were soon replaced by pottery figures or other substitutes.

The Homeric Agamemnon had to sacrifice his daughter in order to produce favourable winds for his fleet's expedition to Troy. In dreams a wind often represents an unconscious motivational spirit, sometimes so strong as to be difficult to struggle against. No doubt the actual Mycenaean kings were often forced to make sacrifices of this sort before propitious motivating drives in their subjects became sufficient to mount one of their overseas raids.

Let us suggest that in a sense our engineer in his childhood had had to sacrifice the furry little animal in order to develop his interest in the machine of that dream. But the little animal had clearly not *really* been killed once and for all, irrevocably. The sacrifice of feelings had proved reversible, unlike a concrete physical killing such as the supposedly concrete killing of Iphigenia with all the hideous consequences of that act. Actual human sacrifice is not reversible, whereas the repression of our humanity, which is often necessary but can be a dangerous habit, particularly if unconscious, is mercifully often reversible. The man who spends all his time and energy at the office or the laboratory represses his feelings into his unconscious and "kills" only in this sense. His humanity may be projected, embodied as it were, onto his beloved or his children or pets, which become an addiction because they embody part of himself, another, better "half." Only if these psychological projection mechanisms fail does he strike disaster or need to recover his humanity-in-himself, as did the two men whose dreams I have mentioned.

The sacrifice of feelings and their relegation to the unconscious, "dead" world in ourselves may generate energy which is like a wind, a tide, a volcano, or an explosion (and there are many other energy symbols). This energy can be for good or ill; it may be creative and it may be destructive. Whether it is one or the other (it is usually both, in different aspects) is not at all accidental but depends on factors we only partly understand and which I will deal with later. The concept of "bottling up" feelings conveys the image of the process I am discussing. The stronger the feelings, and the stronger and more rigid the bottle, the greater the explosion if it eventually happens.

Extrapolating from my empirical observations of people in therapy, I assume that images and fantasies of explosion have occurred in people ever since feelings have had to be bottled up, contained, killed off, sacrificed, and so on. In a sense, the explosion would be a natural, restorative, or compensating image which, if realized, might be supposed to effect some sort of restitution or balance within the personality. If the image were of a natural explosive event, natural or divine forces would be felt to be at work and the corresponding measures taken. If the image involved social repression, tyranny, the bottling up of human feelings by political or administrative means, the corresponding explosive images would be relevant to attempted political solutions. We have already seen how the apocalyptic visions of the Jews of the time of Christ were felt to be about social, religious, and military events or hopes.

Immersed as they were in their chemical images of transformation, salvation, creation, and redemption, it was inevitable that chemical explosive images would occur in the lives and work of the alchemists, and that in the course of their studies real man-made chemical explosions would become possible. This is the case whether chemical explosions were invented by the irascible alchemist Roger Bacon or some other. From then on, the chemical explosion and the psychological explosion have been differentiated from each other in the human mind. To confuse the two thereafter would be superstitious nonsense. Chemistry, and later physics, have their own world, their own laws, their own fascination, and provide their own worlds of escape from the corresponding underlying human or emotional problems. They also have their own isolated alembics or vessels within which solutions to eternal problems can be envisaged and worked on, for in fact the chemical or physical solution and the psychological resolution are never completely divorced from each other in the human unconscious. Just as there are many roads to Rome, so there are many worlds in which one can work toward one's salvation.

And also one's destruction? For as we have seen in the vision of the apocalypse, destruction and salvation are the opposite sides of the same coin. They go together, presided over by the same god or goddess. If the explosion image represents the destruction of the self or the subjective world, then there are clearly dangers, and an ambiguous outcome. The actual outcome will depend on all sorts of factors, such as timing, the strength of the container, rigidity, ultimate optimism or faith, intelligence, and so on. *Reparative forces* is a term that therapists use; the word *love* might suffice here.

If the human psyche could split only at a superficial level, not at these deep levels, then the atom bomb could not have been dreamt of, conceived, and worked on until we were ready to conceive of manipulating immense world-destructive power, power which only a few generations ago could only be felt by the same individual to be in the hands of God, or possibly human beings of godlike nature. Democracy, irreligion, and psychology have contributed to our usurping of omnipotent power with the danger of psychological inflation and world destruction. One cannot help hoping for the creative leap forward which is potentially within our grasp, provided that we assimilate our external and internal omnipotence and see the other side of it as the infantile, impotent, and compensatory manic fantasy that it is.

As a psychiatrist I used to ponder on the antidepressive effect of the epileptic fit, especially the man-made one called ECT, electroconvulsive therapy. Consciousness is massively obliterated in the simultaneous excitation and discharge of the nerve cells, a level of excitement that is too much for the individual to experience consciously. I was reminded of the shattering, overwhelming, and unfaceable face of God in one of His aspects. When the atom bomb came into our lives, I reflected that man was envisaging and manipulating and, like the sorcerer's apprentice, inviting destruction by the ultimate convulsion of the divinity.

Electroconvulsive therapy may or may not be beneficial on the whole to particular patients, and I am not competent to make a balanced evaluation of its clinical effectiveness in different types of depressive and psychotic patients. My work has been entirely psychoanalytic in the past thirty years, and I used convulsive therapy only as a trainee psychiatrist. It cannot be said unequivocally that the experiences of ECT patients, or of St. Paul, Dostoyevski, and Moses, and the convulsions of people who are experiencing conversions and overwhelming flooding of consciousness in evangelical groups prove that fits are a good thing. However, it is clear that fits, breakthrough experiences, conversion experiences, revelations, inspirations, and therapeutic abreactions, birth and rebirth experiences, and the psychic (as opposed to the purely physical) orgasmic and ecstatic state, all have something in common, and all can be very powerful and profoundly therapeutic under the right circumstances. Undoubtedly the explosive dream or fantasy also comes into this general category of excitatory psychic events – powerful discharges of the nervous system accompanied subjectively by blinding or otherwise intense experience.

In the course of psychotherapy patients may go through periods of suffering, darkness, and loneliness as they repeat former unhappiness. They may feel hopeless about the possibility of change or as they realize that their previous notion of themselves consisted mostly of idealization and wishful thinking. Before they find their way out of all this darkness, they may have dreams of flashing lights or explosions or other signs of changes in the darkness. Recovery then is not too far away, and this is especially true if dark objects or the darkness itself begin to have their own luminosity. There are many ways out of the darkness of the soul, some of which are artificially induced or induced from outside and some of which are transformative and profound, resulting from staying with the darkness until it itself changes.

Of course, life is not simply a repeated cycle of clouds and silver linings, of deaths and rebirths. One need not remain bound by this cycle, any more than by other alternations of opposites. But swings, reversals, explosions, and breakthroughs at least show the "other side" of life or of experience, the previously unknown or unexplored side. And they at least demonstrate that something is alive and moving in the character of the person concerned.

The Atom Bomb Image in Psychotherapy

For the whole of my psychiatric and psychotherapeutic career, I have been aware of the paradoxical aspects of the therapeutic, one might say the paradoxical nature of God or psychic wholeness, or rather of that which leads in this direction. The therapeutic can be blinding or over-whelming as well as uniting and harmonizing. What seems ultimately evil, or terribly frightening, may prove to be the way forward if it is faced or suffered in the right spirit, as we all know. Ever since the first use of the atom bomb and my early psychiatric speculations about the com-mon ground between the experience of God and the experience of epilepsy, I have been noticing dreams and other material concerning the atom bomb and the apocalypse, and the experience of the truth as a "bombshell" or as a shock. I shall now describe some typical examples of atom-bomb dreams and their significance in cases where the signifi-cance seems clear enough. This case material indicates that, in psycho-therapy, an atom-bomb dream image signifies a conflict or confrontation of opposing drives or parts of the self which, *in the context of a secure, supportive therapeutic partnership*, tends to lead to a resolution of the conflict and a higher synthesis, with a corresponding deepening of the personality.

I should like to describe typical examples of such a development.

From any clinical material it can never be asserted that a dream about atomic warfare means this or means that. Clinical observations naturally cluster around what is most meaningful to the clinician making them; this is why I have first described the point of view or clinical bias which undoubtedly played some role in selecting the dreams which were observed. What is observed, what is meaningful when observed, and what meaning is gleaned from the observations, all depend on the bias and prejudice of the observer. A further limitation is imposed by what can be explained and described in a reasonably concise and interesting way in a book of this sort. I shall give a range of "meanings" for the atom-bomb dream which seem to me to cover the great majority of such dreams and to point to a single underlying meaning which is hard to put into words, but which the reader will be in a position to formulate for himself or herself.

The Atom-Bomb Image and the Primal Scene Fantasy

My first case history concerns a young man for whom the atom-bomb dream image signified simply marriage, which for him until that time had been unfaceable. I hope it will become clear what marriage meant to him and why he had not until that time managed to go through with a marriage.

This young man, Peter, had had a close and loving relationship with his mother and a much more distant one with his weak and unsuccessful father. He had had many girlfriends and these included close and affectionate relationships, but he had always avoided marriage when it became an issue, and two relationships had foundered on this particular hurdle, which he had not been able to surmount. He had an elder brother whose first marriage had been unsuccessful but who was now marrying for a second time. The night before his brother was to marry, Peter dreamt of an atom bomb exploding and destroying everything around, and he awoke in a state of some anxiety, which he associated with the dream rather than his brother's wedding. But it seems reasonable, in view of his own history of anxiety preventing marriage, to assume a connection between the unfaceability of the atomic explosion and the unfaceability of marriage, now being embarked upon by his brother. Peter's anxiety must have proved faceable on this occasion, because within three months Peter was himself able to marry his current girlfriend, with whom he had been very much in love in any case. The marriage proved as happy and successful as he could have wished.

Peter loved this elder brother, in whose shadow he had lived except for the fact that Peter was the one preferred by the mother. How much identification and how much rivalry there was in connection with the marriage cannot be assessed here. His brother's successful second marriage clearly helped Peter face marriage, and it is clear that this marriage was symbolized, before the event, by the explosion of an atom bomb. We cannot know whether his brother's marriage, and the marriage he himself both feared and wanted, represented the forbidden incestuous union with his mother, or the unfaceable union of his parents, or whether the jealousy of his brother or even of his future sister-in-law were the most important factors. All these formulations or interpretations are no doubt valid, but in a sense they are mere words attempting to describe something mightier, more explosive, less consciously faceable than any of these emotions.

For the psychoanalyst, the term *primal scene excitement* conveys the unfaceable, violent excitement involved. We no longer see this simply in terms of the represented memory of witnessing the parents' sexual intercourse. The actual, physical witnessing experience, if indeed it takes place at all, is usually not connected with the fantasy image or the excitement, the world-shattering, unthinkable, titanic, monstrous clashing union of the event in the child's or adult's psyche which would be of sufficient magnitude and grandeur to be expressed by the atom bomb or apocalyptic symbol. If we can think of the envy, the jealousy, the longing to destroy and the longing to merge with, the horror and the holiness of incest with mother and incest with father which are the energies bound and stored in the "primal scene fantasy" (as opposed to the mere witnessing of parental sex), then I think we can begin to see that the coming together and the facing of such feelings might be sufficiently intense to be expressed by means of the atom-bomb image. And we have not even included the intensity of the split-off feelings of sibling rivalry – repressed jealousy, envy, competitiveness for the mother's love, for the brother's achievements, for the joint parents' approval, all these underground feelings for the beloved brother – feelings that we all know can by themselves reach explosive and murderous levels.

The energy derives from keeping apart the various parts of the self – family feelings from incest, love from cannibalism, love from jealousy, mother from father, etc. It is the pressure for these parts to come together which is felt as the threat of the unthinkable. The subjective experience of the explosion, the blinding light, can potentially lead on, paradoxically, to the healing of the splits concerned.

Another way of looking at this subjective explosion is in terms of the rupture of defences. If an excluded part of the self, a "not-self" part succeeds in penetrating the ego defences (the Freudian term), the penetration is experienced as intense excitation of the type I have described. These boundaries separate not just the self from the outside objects, but also, to some degree, any two objects in the psyche giving rise to differing responses. The energies are the very gradients between the excitatory and the inhibitory properties of the myriad objects and responses of the psyche, if you prefer to express it in pseudo-physiological terms. It is in a sort of simplistic, shorthand way, therefore, that I refer to the subjective bombshell as the subjective aspect of the healing of psychic splitting defences, the coming-together of hitherto kept-apart parts of the self.

The basic idea I am trying to put forward is that the healing of splits and dissociations within the personality, the coming-together of parts of the self which are normally kept apart (always for good reasons), can be feared or experienced as a cosmic shattering explosion or disintegration of either the subjective self or the world, or both.

We all have to learn to distinguish good from bad, friend from foe. When an analyst talks of splits, he is not denying this. But we have no neutral, nonprejudicial word that includes both this perfectly normal differentiating and the pathological splitting between good people and bad people, which is at its most extreme and bizarre in some schizophrenic patients. At the atom-bomb level of the psyche to which I am referring here, Nature has not yet learned to differentiate between normal and pathological splitting.

The work of establishing these major differentiations is largely achieved in infancy. The agony of learning that the beloved mother is also (at a higher, realistic level, but more importantly, at an emotional level) the mother who sometimes abandons, hurts, or deprives is work done in childhood to some extent. The work of separating the incestuously longed-for mother from the everyday mother is also achieved largely in infancy. To interpret atom-bomb dreams in infantile language does little violence to the psychic facts, however ludicrous and inappropriate this seems on the surface to the layman.

The Matricidal Bomb

For my second patient, whom I call Henry, the atom bomb symbolized the imagined ego-shattering effect of confronting his unconscious murderous impulses toward the mother figure, the idealized, dominating mother figure of his childhood as projected onto his wife and onto me as mother/analyst.

I saw Henry for about three years when he was in his late thirties. He had been referred by an older female colleague who had become exhausted by him. He suffered from severe depressions and self-destructiveness. He had made several suicide attempts and had had horrifying motorcycle accidents, in one of which he had lost a foot. Two of his children had died from SIDS (sudden infant death syndrome). He idealized, and was dominated by, his wife and suffered from uncontrollable rages and moods. He was the most gentle and the most violent man imaginable.

At that time, I was working in a town some distance from London, and it was becoming clear that for various reasons I and my family should move to London. Three or four months before this was to take place, I told him of my decision. He came about 30 miles each way to see me and seeing me in London would have meant a round trip of about 120 miles instead of sixty. He said he would discuss with his wife the matter of continuing or terminating analysis; after doing so, he told me he had decided to bring our work to a close when I moved.

A few days later he dreamt of two adolescent boys manufacturing an atom bomb. In another scene of the dream, his wife was shopping in London. This dream ushered in a phase of intensely angry, murderous dreams. The chief target for murder in these dreams was the mother figure, and the murderer was himself or a shadow aspect of himself. During the ensuing weeks he became more in touch with his anger, both in the past toward his mother and in the present situation toward his wife and toward me as the mother person who was failing him. An important observation was that his depressions improved dramatically at this time. Ten years later, I learned that he had decided to divorce his wife.

In Henry's case we could say that the atom bomb symbolized the dreaded confrontation with the unconsciously hated aspects of the consciously idealized, dominating mother (with the restitution, incidentally, of the undervalued and despised father). The unfaceability of this confrontation could only be appreciated if one knew him and knew how gentle, polite, and underneath how violent and angry, he was, so I will not labour the point. It may help convey the energy involved if I again stress the violence and murderousness in both his dreams and his feelings in the weeks after this atom bomb dream, which happened when his wife persuaded him to terminate his analysis with me, for I was the father who was despised and ineffective as well as the abandoning mother in that situation.

Both of these very brief case histories illustrate the existence of a confrontation, even a clash, which at a deep level was felt to be destructive and, indeed, perhaps unthinkable; but when the emotions involved were actually confronted and felt, no doubt with the help of the atom-bomb dream, a forward movement was possible – marriage in the first instance, confrontation with a dominating, idealized partner in the second.

The Patricidal Bomb

In my third example, the unfaceable, as symbolized in the atom-bomb dream, seemed to be confrontation with me, the analyst, and that meant facing both homosexual feelings and aggressive phallic impulses.

In this psychotherapeutic relationship I represented for the patient mostly his father but also partly a brother figure. This patient was a young professional man who had married after several years of analysis with me and had had his first baby, a boy. He had come from a family of several brothers and had had close and, on the whole, affectionate relationships both with his brothers and with his father. We had worked well together in his analysis. He had used the couch most of the time, lying supine and never looking at me, although he could easily have done so. He had had an occasional dream in which I had made romping, homosexual advances toward him which he had repulsed, but there was no conscious homosexual feeling. Just before his baby was born, his father died, and although he was able to do some mourning, he was disappointed at not experiencing more grief than he did.

By the time his child was a toddler and becoming more independent, he himself started talking of ending his analysis, although I felt aware of our relative failure to confront each other in aggressive posture or to work through the homosexual transference. At this time, he had a dream of atomic warfare starting, and very shortly afterward he dreamt of shooting an elderly man in the face. When he came the next time after this shooting dream, he said he wanted to sit in a chair, so that we could talk to each other man to man in the normal way and confront each other. When he did this, he found himself able to feel both the clashing and disagreeing and the warm feelings toward me that had been avoided before in his rather impersonal and workmanlike approach to analyzing, before he was able to sit up and face me. The final phase of the analysis began and a more satisfactory ending was achieved.

Confrontation Between the Desirable and the Detestable Faces of the Self

In my next example, an atom-bomb dream again seemed to symbolize a feared confrontation, but this time with a shadow aspect of the analysand's own personality. This instance occurred in the analysis of a single woman in her fifties who worked very successfully in a therapeutic profession. Her profession and her philosophy were to do with caring for others, although she had never been able to marry or be really close to anyone, man or woman. Perhaps partly for this reason, we had never been able to have more than one session a week. For several years, we had talked a great deal about her hated, selfish, and sadistic father and her rather feckless mother and about negative authority figures in her everyday working life. Her feelings toward me were mostly positive and rather the opposite of her very negative feelings toward her late and unlamented father, although there was not, perhaps, much warmth or closeness between us—it is hard to say. She had several dreams of extreme cold. In one of these, she was in a group of people who were dying from the cold in Russia. One day she brought a dream in which the world nuclear war that we all dread, between America and Russia, had begun.

At this point I would like to mention the surprising distance that all of these dreamers experienced in relation to the atomic explosion and the nightmarish horror which the actual thing would be. Of the dozens of atom-bomb dreams I have noted in analysands, none had the horror, the hideous mutilations, the searing flames, the acute or chronic suffering and dying that radioactivity can actually bring, or the darkness and death of nuclear winter. A distant explosion known to be nuclear, the bombing raid known to be nuclear, the declaration of nuclear war, the black cloud that carries radioactive poison, these are the usual images in the series of dreams I am reporting. This distancing of affect is obviously important, if only because it is similar to the distancing, the denial, and the other defences we all seem to erect against the real nuclear threat.

To resume my patient's story, like the other atom-bomb dreamers she did not experience any great anxiety in the dream or on waking. When we tried to discuss the dream, the only association she produced was that, for her, the Russian political system used people for its own ends and that the conflict between the world powers might mean for her a conflict between treating other people as persons and using them for one's own political or ideological purposes, so that people become statistics or the recipients of one's "do-gooding" impulses and wishes. This cold, impersonal aspect of her personality was *the* important element in her shadow and disturbed her greatly in view of her conscious, completely opposite persona and ideals. So the dream ushered in an important confrontation with the shadow in her case.

The Moment-of-Truth Bombshell

Perhaps for all of us, certainly for most of us, our death, the end of our world, the end of the whole world maybe, symbolizes *the* moment of truth when our false hopes, our pretences and self-deceptions have to be finally shed. It often symbolizes having at last to abandon our illusions and wishful dreams and face the truth about ourselves and others. My fifth patient exemplifies this. She was a woman in love who had harboured unrealistic wishful fantasies and plans in connection with herself and the man she loved. One day she dared to express some of these hopes to him, and his reply was brutally honest and disillusioning. That night she dreamt of a distant atomic explosion with a plume of smoke that reminded her of an ejaculation. In a second dream the same night, there was a reference to death and mourning. Again the dream seemed to usher in a positive development in which she was able to experience and face her anger about being left out and rejected and about the gap between wish and reality. In a very real sense, the atom-bomb image, like the image of one's death, may signify the moment of truth, analogous with God's thunderbolt of revelation or illumination.

In the context of a successful ongoing analysis, the atom bomb image may *stand for* things that are *potentially* therapeutic:

confrontation with the bad mother or the bad father;

confrontation with latent homosexual feelings;

confrontation with the shadow side of one's personality;

the loss of cosy delusions of oneness;

the working through of primal scene material.

However, there is something fundamental, something in common, linking all these meanings. From our earliest infancy we learn to make differentiations. To differentiate I from non-I, love from hate, good from evil, eating the beloved from not eating her, these are some of the main differentiations accomplished in the first weeks and months of life. So the corresponding parts of the personality are separated out or differentiated. Yet these compartments are constantly wanting to break their bounds, and for a healthy person who wishes to question himself and the values of his culture, these barriers within the self must be mutually permeable, even shatterable, even though the shattering threatens one's subjective self and world. The atom-bomb image in this context would be a modern version of the divine thunderbolt which carries punishment and revelation and can transform one's life.

It will be quite clear that I am not arguing that the real atom bomb is a good thing, any more than I am arguing that the real bomb can take our minds off the spiritual need to be shattered, to have one's emotional habits changed, which I take to be the meaning of the bomb in the deepest levels of the mind. In short, the atom-bomb image may represent that conjunction of opposites which is the essence of the consciously aware self and the way toward self-realization. The corollary of this finding, it seems to me, is that in so far as each of us seeks to deny internal conflict and to promote harmony, integrity, and perhaps even "goodness" in his subjective state, each of us is guilty of helping the concrete acting-out, in projected form, of these intrapsychic forces. These intrapsychic forces may be destructive but are often destructive in a good sense with a potential for the enrichment of life.

If we try to make a rounded, well-defended whole of ourselves, we avoid the healthy shattering of our narcissistic defences, and this might encourage the emergence of material explosive forces in the outside world. These outside realities are merely expressing a denied inner necessity.

The demagogic and shoddily entrepreneurial boosting of individuality and the dethronement of God and the Devil as psychically real figures, while of potential long-term benefit, may in the short term be contributing to this concrete enactment of omnipotent destructiveness.

This is not meant to absolve any one of us, least of all myself, from interpreting as helpfully as possible these psychotic or archaic defence mechanisms where and when they occur. But it should teach us to listen to others when they "accuse" us of such psychoticlike defences, for our defences themselves preclude self-diagnosis.

CHAPTER 3

From Concrete Behaviour
to the Ability to Use Metaphors and Symbols in Therapy

The dream image of the bomb in my patients would seem to represent a clash of opposing forces within the personality. The conflict is subjectively almost unfaceable, like the atom bomb. But if faced, the conflict can usually be seen in more human proportions.

The capacity to experience the conflict consciously, leading to some sort of resolution, entails treating the dream image and the dream itself in a metaphorical way, rather than, for example, as a concrete prophecy about an actual historical event or as a divine revelation warning humanity of an imminent apocalypse. Religious interpretations, like psychological ones, may vary from the very superficial to the most profound.

Of course, if the dream is taken as prophecy or as divine warning or instruction, we are presented with the possibility of concrete fulfillment or enactment of the dream. A prophecy if interpreted concretely tends to be self-fulfilling. However sophisticated or civilised we are, this possibility always exists to a certain extent. In therapy we are constantly learning to our astonishment that when we understand a dream we also understand how we have been enacting that dream, in a metaphorical way, of course, for days, weeks, months, or years, in fact, often since childhood. The dream elucidates our previous nonreflecting emotional habits of relationship and affective behaviour.

In other words most of one's affective behaviour can be understood, in a poetic way, as the enactment of a dream as yet undreamt or, if dreamt, not remembered or understood. In this sense the unconscious is our behaviour (learnt, habitual, taken-for-granted, natural behaviour). Only when the unconscious pushes its way into consciousness as religious revelation, creative act, artistic work, or dream, do we stand a chance of becoming aware of what we are doing, of beginning to reflect on it in a symbolic way, and of moving from concrete enactment to metaphorical use of the symbol, with concomitant progress from unreflectingly choiceless affective behaviour to conscious choice between competing affects.

As Jung has pointed out, the dreams we constantly and unknowingly enact are not based only on learned behaviour or conditioned reflexes, but also on the instinctive behavioural and perceptual patterns of the human being as a biological species. The unlearned component of our behaviour corresponds to the biological notion of instinct and to Jung's notion of the collective unconscious. Of course, we can never observe either purely instinctual or purely learned behaviour – the two components interact from early in our intrauterine lives.

One of the aims of psychotherapy is to replace blind, instinctive, or habitual behaviours or feelings, especially when they give rise to insoluble problems in the patient's life, with conscious awareness of the conflicts involved, leading to conscious choice between alternative solutions. Freud verbalized the aim of therapy as "Where id was, there shall ego be." Patient and therapist labour together to replace "It is so" with "It is as if this were so." To take an actual example, a frigid young woman behaves as if the act of lovemaking is a violent rape. After her young man tries to kiss her passionately, she dreams of a bull goring a helpless victim. Gradually, with help from the therapist, she realizes that her sexual fears are based on a feeling about making love that it is as if she were being gored by a bull. How that feeling comes to be so is a matter of the personal history of the patient – perhaps of a violent father who often frightened her by shouting at her and bullying her. The patient and the therapist find that when the therapist makes an interpretation or when he speaks sharply to her, she feels bruised or hurt, as if she were being stabbed or gored. Patient and therapist work together on the meaning and the feelings surrounding the symbol of the goring bull and its victim. In the course of time, the image of intercourse or interaction is modified or even transformed, and different feelings occur. This sort of change is commonplace in therapy. The habitual avoidance behaviour begins to be modifiable once the image is experienced and understood. The pathological behaviour corresponds to the unsaid statement, "Human intercourse, including sexual interaction, is a gory, violent act which has to be avoided." Only when the image is experienced can the statement eventually be made, "I behave and feel as if human intercourse were the same as being gored by a savage bull." There is therapeutic potential in this, because there is the beginning of a possibility that the frigid behaviour can be given up.

The same transition from the primitive and literal to the metaphorical, "as-if" attitude can be seen in the progress of civilisation. Concrete, unaware behaviour, the helpless blindness of pure nature and instinct, can be replaced by cultural progress and moral choice.

In the lands around the Mediterranean, for example, the myth of the dying, yet immortal, sacrificed vegetation god-king is almost as old as agriculture itself, although not as old as the mother goddess and her fertility rites. In early times, these myths were literal truths, enacted concretely as part of indispensable agricultural practice, necessary to ensure that the crops grew. Individual human beings played separate and preordained roles in the enactment of the myth, including the willing sacrificial victims. The history of Western civilisation has been the history of the gradual deconcretization of this myth. The real human god-king was eventually replaced by other, lesser human beings, then by animals or dolls. At the same time, ideas about death and resurrection are originally (as in Egypt) very literal and concrete. Food is carried daily for the immortal corpse to eat in his afterlife, for example. In time, such practices become more symbolic. It is probable (for example, in Crete) that the concrete funerary practices were supplemented, then replaced by funerary rituals, even games, and that these games (at Cnossos, for example) were the precursors of the Greek games and the Greek theatre.

In the Christian version of the sacrifice of the god-king, the god-king is believed to have already been sacrificed, a willing victim not only for the sake of the crops but to take away the sins of the whole world. This one historical sacrifice is held to be sufficient, but each believer partakes, by identification, following the Way of the Cross, figuratively in the death and resurrection of the god-in-oneself. The change from concrete, bloody sacrifice to inner change and transformation is thereby complete.

The Reciprocal Relationship Between Behaviour and Mental Experience

The gradual raising of an element of behaviour from choiceless concrete enactment to the symbolic plane and to moral choice is a cultural achievement for society. The same is true for the individual. The achievement can be lost much more easily than it has been won, and this is just as true for human societies as it is for individuals.

But first I draw attention to the fact that affective behaviour can discharge the affect in question before it reaches awareness as affect. We all find it easier to enact our faults rather than to become aware of them. Even a violent criminal act may be committed *instead* of, rather than *because* of, feeling angry.

Weakness, fatigue, drugs, and regressions all make it more likely that behaviour occurs rather than awareness at the critical moment. One of the chief causes of regression to primitivity or infancy is the acquisition of wealth or other forms of power. The rich and the powerful tend to enact their infantile and primitive part-selves on others.

Suppose, for example, I am an employer when employees are plentiful, and I am in a position of great power. If one of my employees underproduces or otherwise frustrates my plans, I might dismiss him without the least feeling of anger—I might even indulge myself in a feeling of sympathy for his plight, or that of his family.

But suppose my dismissing behaviour is blocked by legislation, public opinion, economic forces, or even by my humanity. Then the shortcomings of my employee as a productive unit may cause me considerable anger, and a quite complex mental experience will occur instead of the simple, unfeeling, unthinking act of dismissing him. Only if I am not allowed to satisfy my needs by dismissing him will I become incensed or forced to reflect on my feelings. I think we can agree that dismissing is some kind of hostile or angry *behaviour* in the important sense that it inflicts real damage on the individual. So the angry *behaviour* can occur *instead* of the *experience* of anger, and vice versa. This is the reciprocal relationship between behaviour and mental experience (usually feelings or emotions, but also images and thoughts).

If I have been taught as a child to be gentle and loving, I may have difficulty being aware of any angry feelings which normally occur as a result of frustration. These angry feelings are not allowed to reach the light of day. They are part of the dark, unconscious aspects of myself that I do not know about. If I am kind and gentle, I may have an angry unconscious self. If I have such an angry unconscious self, I may falsely attribute anger to others or I may be subject to fits of anger or angry behaviour which are alien to my normal character ("I was not myself when it happened"). This would be a state of possession by an alien subpersonality, albeit temporary possession. All these situations are examples of the reciprocal relationship between behaviour and awareness. This is what I mean when I say behaviour is the unconscious. Our unconscious is simply our behaviour. In the last example, the angry subpersonality is repressed but can be projected onto others or can explode forth at times.

But I am not simply asserting that we often do not wish to know what we are really like and that this often includes a disinclination to acknowledge fully, in a feeling way, what we are actually doing. That is true. But I am of the opinion that there is an even deeper, more fundamental sense in which behaviour and mental experience do not go hand in hand, but occur in a mutually reciprocal fashion. Awareness of what we want to do is at a maximum when what we want to do is being blocked. Conversely, when we are doing what we want to do without any hindrance, external or internal, we are relatively unaware of what we are doing. This seems to be true whether the behaviour is simply habitual or deeply instinctive or a combination of the two. If we are aware of what is happening, it means that *new* learning is taking place.

Much of our everyday behaviour is habitual and is performed without awareness, even though it is complicated and cannot possibly have been performed in exactly the same way before. A simple act like crossing a room and opening a door, if there is no difficulty or unaccustomed obstruction, will be performed largely unconsciously. Only in case of difficulty or of a conflict about whether or not to do it will some sort of image arise in consciousness.

One kind of habitual behaviour that gives rise to much conscious awareness and feeling when blocked or frustrated is addictive behaviour. This is again true whether the block is external or internal. I have already given an example of the way angry *feelings* arise when, and only when, angry *behaviour* is blocked. The same applies to other emotions and drives, for example, sexual, parental, and dependent drives and feelings. The image or feeling arises when the impulse or drive cannot be enacted or cannot be enacted without some difficulty or unusual feature.

What we call our feelings and our attitudes are for the most part bodily actions or postures not actually acted out or taken up in a concrete form. For example, muscular impulses occur but they do not reach a magnitude sufficient to cause actual muscular movements. In the course of our long cultural evolution, we have learned to inhibit our snarling and our warlike threatening posturing to a certain extent and instead have feelings that are the conscious mental experiences arising when the primitive, instinctive muscular and vegetative responses are not fully enacted. The same applies to positive and submissive attitudes, which are also subthreshold bodily postures.

Dreams and the Forgoing of Behaviour

I am trying to give up smoking. I may, of course, have many images and fantasies of having a lovely smoke. Certainly many more thoughts and feelings about smoking occur than if I am simply indulging my addiction. I may also dream of smoking. I shall only do this if the forgoing of cigarettes is a really serious matter for me and the forgoing of the satisfaction is happening at a level where it counts and where creative substitute satisfactions – creative forgoing – is possibly about to occur. Cultural activity, including art, myths, and religions, results from these creative forgoings and creative substitute satisfactions. The dream is a sign of the beginning of this sort of mental activity. The unconscious in the sense of the source of dreams and cultural phenomena is a very busy and creative part of the personality.

A dream about smoking, then, is very likely to occur in a person who is *seriously* engaged in giving up smoking. Dreams occur at the boundary between mindless behaviour and the possibility of becoming aware of the particular behaviour referred to in the dream, even of taking up a relationship with it such as an attitude toward it, forgoing it, controlling it, or using it in some other way. What sort of behaviour is an atom bomb to do with? Exploding behaviour no doubt, whatever that means exactly. Let me explain further by contrasting the dream symbol of a bouncing ball with the dream symbol of a bomb.

Anger with someone I love can produce muscular tensions in me that make me hard, resilient, and self-sufficient. I become a ball, as it were, rather than a soft, human, cared-for infant. The circle is a two-dimensional version of the ball in this context. The ball is a closing-up, self-sufficient reaction to being hurt. Or rather, it is often successful in preventing my getting hurt. The closing-up and resilience keeps out the hurting person or event. If I cannot close up and repel the hurting person, I *feel* hurt or ill or I may even *become* ill.

If the hurt cannot be kept out and the invasive, hurtful person or personlike representation penetrates one's defences, the resulting clash between the opposing external and internal forces may be experienced mentally as a flash or explosion, or it may be enacted in explosive behaviour. The latter would be an extroverted response, the former an introverted one.

So a hurt may cause a hurt feeling or an illness; in other words, it can be experienced in the body as a sensation or emotion. Or it may produce a resilient, closing-up effect. Or it may produce a mental experience of illumination or of a shattering explosion, or behaviour of an explosive sort. The individual may even refer to it as "going through the roof" or "blowing his top." *The bomb dream tells us that explosive behaviour is now coming into consciousness and that there is a possibility of forgoing it.* But as we have seen, explosive behaviour is a feature of groups and individuals who cannot absorb hurt and who know they are right.

Acts seem to be precursors of mental experience in the sense that they express instinctual or previously learned behaviour in the infant, in the less-evolved stage of history, in the mental patient, or when no frustration or opposing drive is involved. We are fully entitled to describe a destructive act as angry and hold the agent legally responsible, even though no conscious anger was experienced, because the angry act may have actually been a way of avoiding the discomfort of angry or hurt feelings. In law, individuals are rightly held responsible for their actual behaviour, although some allowance has to be made for awareness of the rightness or wrongness of what they do.

In therapy also, many angry acts are committed, at first without any awareness of anger. The *feeling* of anger which eventually *replaces* the angry act may be a very important step forward in therapy. For example, a patient may repeatedly turn up late for therapy or even forget to come without feeling the least bit angry with the therapist. Eventually, as therapy proceeds, he is able to feel angry and to know why, and this happens at the same time he becomes able to stop being late.

The therapy may advance to a point where we see some creative, symbolic use for the anger. This is often encountered in the therapy of children, when the therapist plays with the child as a major part of the therapeutic work.

Let us suppose the therapist is trying to help a little boy who is prone to outbursts of violence at particular times or in particular circumstances. A study of the times and circumstances will give clues. The therapist may also find ways of talking to and playing with him, for example, with toys which in play can be taken to represent people or circumstances that elicit the anger. At the same time, as the boy feels more secure in the situation and in his relationship to the therapist, he may have spells of the violent behaviour toward the therapist.

If the child and his therapist are progressing successfully, we find two concomitant changes occurring:

(1) As the child gets to know and care for the therapist, the real violence is replaced by "pretend" violence.

(2) Images and symbols emerge during the play, usually of the therapist as some sort of witch or "baddy," and of the boy as hero, soldier, aggressor, or punisher, or of an aggressive beast, ghost, magic being, etc.

The images and symbols are woven into the play, into some sort of story or repeated play ritual. The play or play ritual goes through a stage where it constitutes a vital part in the relationship with the therapist and with the containment and eventual transformation of the violent part (subpersonality, behaviour, complex, or whatever) of the child responsible for the pathologically fixed and symptomatic behaviour.

If we reflect on this sort of creative transformation of violence in our therapy clients, we can see not only that such changes take place at every stage in the growing-up of all of us, but also that such transformations take place in the progress of civilisation and culture. Some such taming and transformation of the purely instinctual and animal in us is happening to us all the time and particularly at crucial or momentous times of our lives. The concrete act is transformed into the symbolic act or into the symbolic element of the cultural heritage.

These symbolic transformations are very rarely conscious at all stages in their achievement. Often these cultural elements, rituals, symbols, etc., are not consciously connected with the act being modified, inhibited, or transformed. Awareness can occur to any degree at any stage in these sublimations and transformations. Nevertheless the vital transformative elements are love or concern, a feeling of mattering, and hard work on the part of both parties to the transformation (in therapy, but no doubt in other relevant human situations as well).

Before these cultural achievements emerge as symbols, the therapy client behaves as if the state of affairs to be later represented in symbolic terms were literally true. The therapist is *really* a baddy and is attacked or avoided as such. The patient behaves *as if* he is a soldier, lion, magician, etc., and is not pretending, or at least in any way aware of pretending, to be the subpersonality in question. In other words he is "possessed" by the alien subpersonality just as in mediaeval times certain persons were held to be "possessed" by witches, devils, demons, and so on.

The concrete element is thus the actual acting-out of a part of oneself without awareness of being under the influence of the subpersonality, which only later enters awareness, for example, via a dream, or (still later) can be seen to be a part of oneself. It can then be treated as metaphorical rather than literal or, even more so, concrete or part of a mindless act.

In concrete or literal behaviour there is no "pretend" or "as if," no allowance for the metaphor or the symbol. In human groups symbolic and literal attitudes may compete and replace each other as the tide of battle dictates. If I lose my holy city, it may still remain a symbol of all I hold most dear. Then if I discern a chance of repossessing it, it may become a concrete necessity. The new Jerusalem may exist only symbolically in my heart, or it may be enacted concretely by an organized group of Zionists.

In neurosis, metaphors often become concrete necessities. I remember a clergyman, in the early days of my psychotherapeutic practice, who sought psychiatric help with a troublesome symptom. He complained of becoming sexually excited whenever he saw a "workman in dirty dungarees" (his words). *Dungarees* was the word at that time for what later were referred to as denims, later still as jeans. They were not so commonly worn in those days, fortunately for the clergyman.

Not only was the patient unhappily excited on these occasions, but his life was restricted by the fact that dirty dungarees were his only source of climactic sexual satisfaction. He contrived to become the secret owner of several pairs of such dirty jeans – how I do not recall – and whenever his needs overwhelmed his will, he would masturbate and ejaculate into the object of his desires, thus "dirtying" them all the more and increasing their desirability.

The clergyman came to therapy in order to be helped to rid himself of this compulsive behaviour. For him the behaviour was a vice and an almost constantly present temptation. If it was symbolic for him, it was symbolic of weakness and frailty. If he had been psychotic rather than neurotic, he might have had the idea that by his sexual act he became somehow identical to a workman, or that he lost his soul whenever he behaved in this way–in other words, the symbolic nature of the act would be felt as factual or concrete.

To the therapist, it seemed that his symptom was symbolic not of wickedness but rather of his best hope of health and manhood. He was pale, effeminate, and extremely pure, so that however he had come to find this satisfaction (and, of course, all neurotic symptoms have their history in the life of the individual), the workman in dirty dungarees represented for him the opposite of what he outwardly was and of how he had been brought up to be. The workman was what he (unknown to himself) wanted to be more like (and also did not want to be like). Therapy consisted of helping him find the healthy, strong, and "dirty" (sexy, nonprudish, generous) workman in himself. In other words, we were able to treat the neurotic symptom as an alienated but potentially valuable part of his total personality, at least in some symbolic sense. The concrete act was replaced by some sort of symbolic equivalent in his personality, now accepted rather than avoided, now generalized and metaphorical rather than concrete, fixed, and restricted. The workman subpersonality was no longer encapsulated in the personality as a for-eign body, diseased member, or sort of addiction.

Before coming into therapy the patient had acted in a very concrete way and might well have landed in serious trouble if he had continued thus. But his acts only make sense as compensatory, symbolic acts. The acts were somehow thrown up or chosen by some naughty, rebellious part of himself that was not being expressed in his normal life and his conscious ideals. There is undoubtedly a part of ourselves that seems to work in symbols and to attempt to compensate for biases and distortions in our conscious ideals or in the way we were brought up. The vital thing for us to remember here is that the unlived part of ourselves can somehow obtain expression in acts which are neither wanted nor willed nor in any way constructive except that they are nature's way (and usually a very clumsy way) of redressing an imbalance.

With this patient the imbalance was fairly obvious except perhaps to the patient. In other circumstances the patient might easily have become a persecutor of "workmen in dirty dungarees"–we see this happening in our patients and in social groups everywhere. Yet these behaviours are enacted and rationalized and are not regarded as symbolic acts or as ways of reaching repressed or neglected parts of the self. It is my contention that it is urgently necessary to recognise much of our unwilled and self-destructive behaviour (such as much of our intergroup and international behaviour is) as symbolic and compensatory, and potentially life-enhancing, but only if seen as such, in just the same way as this patient's fetishistic acts, when interpreted metaphorically, turned out to be his salvation.

Another reason I have chosen this clinical example of symbolic or compensatory self-destructive behaviour is that the clergyman's values are probably not shared by my reader, who may have a wider and less prudish approach to the lower half of the body. But the patient's acts would have seemed distressing and indicative of illness to the patient's mother, who was largely responsible for the values whose bias caused the patient's unconscious to step in and produce the self-destructive, compensatory acts. Many of our own self-destructive acts are distressing rather than obviously symbolic for the same reason – we are victims of the same outlook and the same narrowness of vision as the cultural background producing our self-destructive or perverse behaviour.

What is the nature of the imbalance that produces atom-bomb behaviour in the human race? I don't know what is most important and what not so important in the case of even one human being's acts, including people I have been seeing four or five times a week for years. So to make a diagnosis for the human race is merely an indulgence in self-exposure, a way of describing one's own self or one's own hang-ups perhaps. Nevertheless we should all attempt a diagnosis of the ills of humankind, and from what I have said about my patients' atom-bomb dreams, it looks as though the atom-bomb symbol turns up when there is a need to stop clinging to subjective peace, harmony, and contained aggressivity, and to face conflict, confrontation, or a complete disruption of one's subjective wholeness and feeling of order and goodness. If the ultimate ideal is goodness, peace, order, harmony, and unity, then an atom-bomb symbol has to appear when one needs to be shaken out of these rather static ideals and face existential insecurity and existential growth and change. This is certainly true with regard to what the explosive ending of the world represented for my patients – there is reason to suppose that this is one meaning of this potentially self-destructive behaviour of human beings at the present time. Whether it is an important meaning I cannot say. But only when we begin to stop enacting it will the fuller meaning of our self-destructive behaviour become clearer.

The Full Meaning of Behaviour Only Becomes Clear When It Is Forgone

It is only when we are able to inhibit our acts—usually for the sake of someone we love or are concerned for—that their full meaning can be experienced. The act is then replaced by the symbol, behaviour is replaced by the creative imagination and the cultural—religious, artistic, scientific, mythological—experience. This may be explained by another sort of example.

It was the habit of one of my patients to respond aggressively, with spiteful criticisms, when she felt she was being treated by me in an impersonal, unfeeling way. At first I was inclined to feel hurt, or to bristle defensively myself, when criticized in this way, but gradually we were able to discuss our feelings and work out that her spiteful behaviour was a reaction to some sort of impersonal, critical, coldly scientific attitude that she took to be mine at these times. At this point, she had a dream of a vicious, spiny, little fish swimming about in a glass fish tank. It was being kept as a pet, a prisoner completely under the control of its owner. She readily saw her spiteful behaviour at these times of feeling "looked at" as represented by her vicious little fish self. We both felt quite warm toward the nasty little creature, and the image of the fish became a symbol for her that helped her further modify her nasty spiteful behaviour. Instead of feeling helpless about it, she felt more in sympathy and accord with her spiny fish self and was able to choose whether to behave like that or not.

Although the image is a simple one, the physical characteristics of the fish, the fact that it is a fish, i.e., at home in water, the fact that it inhabits a glass tank, etc., all added content and meaning to the simple element of nasty vicious behaviour. It enabled us to make up a story that gave meaning to a piece of her behaviour of which she was becoming aware and which at the same time she was giving up for my sake, or the sake of the good parent, as it were. It is easy to see how children's stories, dreams, and games are being invented and used all the time as children both get in touch with and integrate their alienated subpersonalities.

In delineating this small but highly important change in my

patient, I am trying to point out a progression from the concrete to the metaphorical. In the earliest stages she simply behaves like the fish, without knowing why, when she sees a certain look in my eye or a certain tone in my voice. Not only does she not know why but neither do I. Gradually, as trust and confidence build up in taking an analytical, working attitude toward our feelings and reactions, we are able to form a hazy picture, a sort of hypothesis as it were, finally summed up in a statement such as, "When you look at me in that impersonal way, I feel and behave like a spiteful pet fish in a tank." The statement is not a mere figure of speech but a living reality, a statement about a living symbol, the fish symbol, a now acceptable and meaningful part of herself.

From there the work of analysis goes on and is not in any way concluded at this point. But this stage represents a huge cultural advance if it is projected onto the scale of history and sociological change. Supposing we could advance from the stage of doing nasty things to political neighbours to the stage of inhibiting our nasty behaviour and being able to say, "When you behave thus it is *as if* the situation were so-and-so and I feel *as if* I could blow you and the whole human race up in one cataclysm," instead of actually doing it. At present, when we do nasty things to our neighbours, we are quite sure it is because he is *actually* being nasty or threatening to us and *in fact*, because of our neighbour's unawareness, he probably *is* harming us. So the progression from the factual-concrete interaction to the evolution of continence, creation, and cooperation, and the birth of cultural experience is only achievable when the advance is progressive and two-sided. If analysis is anything to go by, both parties achieve the symbolic attitude concurrently as their relationship changes.

My object in writing this book is to describe some of the necessary conditions for the creation of working space between behaviour and mental experience. This space, the space between behaviour and mindfulness, is a very laborious and hard-won achievement, always a mutual achievement in some sense, if the experience of the helping professions is anything to go by. For example, the therapy of the violent, disturbed child usually involves many sessions of patient, nonretaliatory suffering coupled with hard thinking under difficult, emotionally taxing conditions, before the child can begin to reflect on his behaviour and impulses and take an "as if," metaphorical attitude toward them – i.e., "It is as if this violent part of me is killing this therapist-parent figure" rather than being possessed by the blind behaviour itself. Or (more likely), "This is a space gun and it's shrivelling you up." Usually it is the gradual buildup of concern for the therapist by the violent child which brings about this transformation from the behavioural to the "pretend" violence. The child learns from the therapist to reflect on his wishes and behaviour and contain his own violence, just as the therapist is finding ways of containing his own impulses to retaliate and to have similar emotions to those of the child, which is one's instinctive reaction.

Explosiveness as a Step in the Therapy of Depression

In the last chapter I described a patient, Henry, who suffered from self-destructive acts and depression, which after his atom-bomb dream were replaced for a time with murderous dreams and murderous feelings toward the mother-figure. He then recovered from his depression.

Irritability or aggressive feelings and outbursts may occur in the depressed patient who is undergoing psychotherapy and who is recovering from his depression (often at the expense, for the time being, of the people closest to him).

I have often noticed that patients who are depressed may have dreams of explosions, fireworks, etc., just before they begin to show signs of coming through the depression.

It is not flippant to speculate that the self-destructive atom-bomb behaviour of the human race is, in part, an abortive or clumsy and unconscious form of self-electroshock therapy – or that it would be if, like my patient's horrible accidents, it actually happened because we are at the concrete, behavioural stage. These destructive wishes must first reach into consciousness and be acknowledged. Then all that remained would be a need to distinguish between a wish and a need to fulfill that wish. Often we are afraid of knowing what we wish because we fear the fulfillment of our wish if it is acknowledged.

I need to pause at this point and state some facts about depression and depressed patients that are taken for granted by psychotherapists, but which are perhaps not so obvious to the lay reader.

(1) Self-destructive acts and bodily illness may take the place of, substitute psychologically for, depression or sad feelings. They are called "depressive equivalents" by many psychotherapists. For example, many bodily illnesses seem to "drain off" or "discharge" depressive emotion. A depressed person may become clinically less depressed

while he is suffering from a cold or some other bodily illness, or after he has had an accident or other misfortune.

(2) In the psychotherapy of depressed persons, there is usually a period when anger, first against the self, later perhaps against other people, usually in outbursts, is manifested either as angry behaviour or as angry emotion, or both. This behaviour or emotion is inevitably of a primitive sort because it represents emotions that are part of the more primitive and less developed part of the total personality, the part that was not recognized or was even actively disallowed by the parents or other powerful people during the childhood of the depressive person concerned.

(3) If he is to recover fully, the patient has to learn how to experience and express these positive, aggressive, feelings in a creative way. They may be adequately discharged in the form of work, thinking activities, and constructive separations and distinctions, as well as expressive actions of forthrightness and normal self-assertiveness and standing up for what is felt to be right. But just as a child has to learn sophisticated ways of asserting itself, the grown-up depressive person has to learn adult ways of expressing anger or outgoing positive feelings, usually for the first time.

(4) In other words, depressive feelings, self-destructive or murderously aggressive feelings and actions, anxiety, creativeness, self-assertion, love, and sex do not exist in separate packages which cannot be exchanged or substituted for each other, but the laws governing their interchange are complex and are to be teased out of the accumulated wisdom of mankind.

We may have differing views and theories to account for the facts I have just enumerated, but facts they remain, to the best of my knowledge.

The period of violent dreams in Henry's therapy following the atom-bomb dream, during which his angry feelings were discussed and during which his depression improved, can therefore be taken as a general phenomenon in the therapy of depression. Parallels with this sequence of happenings could be drawn for depressed communities and historical sequences of many sorts. They should not be advanced over-confidently, of course, but they are worth making nevertheless.

In order to emerge from our collective depression, it may be necessary to realise that part of us wants to blow the other fellow to bits, or to blow up the world. To have fantasies, plans, or war games elaborating our fantasy images and wishes may even be an essential stage. It is from these impulses, when acknowledged and forgone, that creative solutions will emerge, not from their denial, for denial is more likely to lead to concrete enactment of the atom-bomb part of ourselves, a potentially healthy part of our makeup, and, of course, only healthy if not enacted concretely.

CHAPTER 4

The Interdependence of Our Outer and Inner Worlds

If I were taking an anthropological look at a community or tribe, I would be looking at the real environment in which they live and which they also make for themselves. I would be looking at their social structure and division of labour, at their standards of behaviour, their ideals and aspirations, and their ways of bringing up their children and young people. I would be expecting all these aspects of their lives to be related to each other in a meaningful way. I should expect to be able to make some sort of meaningful whole and see some sort of internal consistency between these different aspects. Studying their language, their mythology, their dreams, and their ways of explaining themselves to themselves, I should expect these aspects of their "inner" lives to be to some extent consistent with their "outer," behavioural and environmental lives, to provide meaning to the latter, both to them and to me, the anthropologist.

In other words, the stories we dream up and tell each other are the stories of our lives and our possible and improbable lives. They are affected by outer reality, and they enrich and change our outer reality.

I have tried to argue that our behaviour, meaning our habitual ways of relating to each other and to things, or at least that part of our behaviour we take for granted, is our unconscious, out of which our creations and cultural achievements are born.

Looked at in this way, it follows that my inner world and my outer world are closely interdependent. To some it would be a banality to say that the ways we order our outer worlds are reflections of our inner worlds or souls. Nevertheless I have thought it worthwhile to deal with this truism in more detail. Explosions are an integral part of our inner *and* our outer lives. We are all using bombs, bombshells, and explosions for personal and political ends – this is not at all confined to our terrorist brothers. Centuries ago, we started dreaming up bombs, and now we have dreamt up several ways of destroying the world. What is the element of our inner world that is a bomb in the important sense of providing the emotional energetic basis for world destruction?

My opinion is that the underlying fear, which at another level is a wish or a need, is for the shattering of the integrity of the "I, me, mine" part of the personality, which we might, in shorthand, call the self – the self which has to do with feelings of security, the self which our 'complexes' and 'defences' self-defeatingly seek to preserve and defend. This self is a structure within the larger whole of the personality, or even the totality of one's world, which, comprising both "self" and "not-self," has nevertheless been seen or experienced by some as a kind of greater Self. I shall distinguish this greater Self, from the more personal, everyday self of "I, me, mine" by the use of the capital S. We are therefore talking about a fear, and an underlying wish, for the smaller self or "I" to be shattered by the "not-I" part of the Self. Some people might say that there is a fear, and a need, for one's ego to be shattered or humbled by God; others might use the word *Unconscious* instead of God.

I, Not-I, Self

As I sit at my desk writing, I am aware of myself with my sense of struggle and of my body and of my hand in front of me. Then I am aware of the room in which I write, and that is not myself. I look through the windows at the back of the house in the next street, and that is still less myself than the room in which I work and the pen with which I am writing. But if I think of the houses in the next village, they are even less myself than the houses in the next street, which now in contrast seem to pertain to myself after all.

Normally my hand would be felt as part of myself, but even this varies. It can become the object of my attention and be felt to be distinct from the I who is attending to it. My hand, or my intestines, may be experienced as distinct from myself, especially when they are in pain or "playing up" (misbehaving themselves).

So we must conclude that "I, me, mine" is a somewhat relative affair. The intensity of the feeling (if we can call it a feeling) and also the boundaries of "I, me, mine" are subject to much movement.

In other words, one's body, one's dear ones and one's possessions, and the real and not-so-real world beyond can be imbued with smaller or greater amounts of I-feeling. We use the term *alienation* for the unwanted absence of I-feeling. The house in the next street, and even the house of a stranger in a distant country, is not normally experienced as alien: only when an element of rejection or repression is involved does this tend to be the case.

I have said, and I keep saying, that the dynamic source of the unconscious is, in practice, affective behaviour that is separated from the feeling of I. Where dissociation and repression are concerned, the relationship between I and my behaviour is one of not wanting to know. For example, not long ago I dreamt of a threatening young man, dressed in black, practising martial arts and, as one of a small gang of similarly dressed, masked, and anonymous young men, terrorizing me and my childhood family in the home of my childhood. In the days after the dream, when I got into a bullying, boorish mood with my wife, I realised that in a very important and meaningful sense the young man was an unacknowledged part of myself and my behaviour, with an understandable history rooted in my childhood. The young man was very much not-I in my sense of myself and of the way I liked to think of myself and my behaviour. But now knowing myself better, I realise he is very much part of my total personality (showing himself when I am tired, etc.) and has been for well over sixty years. This subpersonality can be said to "possess" me from time to time. Here I am using the word *possession* in the same sense as the New Testament expression of possession by devils, demons, etc.

That previously repudiated, alien, gangster subpersonality was clearly part of my total personality, although not a part which I previously experienced as myself. As I feel my way into him, he is gradually becoming part of my conscious self.

Psychotherapists recognize that the conscious I is only the tip of the iceberg of the total personality. To become aware that there is a total personality, to develop a working relationship, even a kind of trust in it, although it is mostly unconscious, seems to me a worthwhile experience of psychotherapy, but an experience by no means confined to those who have had successful psychotherapy. It was Jung's great contribution to draw attention to the organizing centre of the personality which is more not-I than I in quality. He called it the Self and pointed out that it can be experienced in symbolic form, the god-image being one such form.

Sometimes he wrote of the Self as the not-I centre, sometimes as the totality of the personality.

It follows from all this that it is not at all possible to make a permanent and stable boundary between inner and outer, any more than between I and not-I. The gangster is part of me, and, as a dream figure, he is part of my inner world; yet I experienced him as an alien character and kept him outside my self, and I had to make an effort to get into him. There may be every point in learning to make the distinction between inner and outer in the first place and to use this distinction as circumstances indicate, press, or dictate. For example, when I was about three years old, I dreamt that a toy I had broken the previous day was repaired. I rushed downstairs the next morning half expecting the toy to be repaired. I was only beginning to learn to distinguish between inner and outer reality, or between dreams and "reality." At the same time, I was learning that the ghosts and nightmare creatures of my anxiety dreams were "only dreams." So it worked both ways. It is simple to learn to make these distinctions, but not so simple to learn how inner and outer are connected or related. Furthermore, our most magical, mystical, and thrilling experiences have to do with the breach, penetration, or dissolution of these boundaries, for example, that between I and not-I. Once having grasped and experienced such feelings of union or unity, we are tempted to cling to generalizations such as "inner and outer are really One" or "the Will of the Great Not-I must always prevail over my own petty will (or wishes)." These are the sort of lazy, blanket, all-or-nothing pronouncements we all indulge in, if only for teaching purposes, but they ensnare, seduce, and control us if we succumb to their regressive temptation. The mystical experience of union of the I with, or penetration by, the not-I can take the form of a life-enhancing flow into the subjective body-self, an experience of being engulfed or taken over (in a positive sense, of course), or it may be experienced as a more sudden, implosive (as opposed to explosive) incursion of the not-I into the I. Here we are dealing with the imperceptible gradation between the mystical experience and the shock or bombshell type of revelation, which can be experienced as implosive or explosive.

If I am relating to another person, or to a thing, with a frontal posture, it tends to partake of thou-ness. To a certain degree he, she, or it becomes a thou or you, even if it is only a nail we are vainly trying to hit with a hammer. The thou partakes of some qualities of the I feeling, but these are regulated by love/hate, thing/person, approaching/distancing feelings, etc., so as to keep comfort and well-being at a maximum. We can tell from a person's mouth and eyes what feelings he or she is having toward us, and in the case of a loved person, this determines to a large degree how we feel about ourselves. It is feelings of this sort which determine optimal distance. When we speak of inner reality and outer reality, to what entity do the words *inner* and *outer* refer? If I speak of *my* inner reality and *my* outer reality, I am clearly inferring that there is an I with an inside and an outside. And that is how it feels, by and large. I feel as though I am roughly coincident with my body. As far outwards as my skin there is an I, especially if I am supplied with sensations from the part of my body concerned. There are circumstances when part of my body feels like not-I, and there are out-of-body experiences when I experience myself as outside my body – for example, in dreams and near-death states. Furthermore, my I is continuous in time back to my earliest memories and forward into the future as far as my bodily death or beyond.

What is this I which is the subject of our experience who can also be the object of our love, hate, respect, and other attitudes? This I can experience well-being, or its opposite, and all the other feelings corresponding with bodily states and attitudes. It is necessary to describe and characterize this I, since it is the entity or feeling which we defend with such immense energy, the energy of the bomb, as it were. This is the I we are destroying the world to try to preserve. Yet it is this I whose sacrifice, loss, or modification is constantly necessary for our spiritual and psychological renewal. The psychotherapist has an important contribution to make to this classification, because it is this I, its boundaries, rigid defences, and the complexes associated with it, which are the focus of his work. Practically alone, the psychotherapist is learning to dispense with exhortative and judgmental terms that interfere with the liberating work of healing, and the new knowledge we have been acquiring about the I part and the not-I part of the total personality or total Self has helped the psychotherapist more than anything in advancing his skills, which in their modern form were pioneered by Freud and Jung.

The Subpersonalities

I should like to supply a pocket guide to the structure of the personality as conceptualized by the modern therapist, without involving myself in too much partisanship for any one of the differing schools of psychotherapy. Yet I have to declare that I was apprenticed, psychotherapeutically speaking, in the Jungian tradition.

First I must emphasize how fluid and interchangeable the various structures or units of the mind are, both in everyday life and in the vicissitudes of day-to-day therapeutic practice. In particular, the categories of inner and outer elements are themselves interchanging constantly. Second, it must be understood that the concepts used by the psychotherapist are like the tools used by craftsmen, or like the maps used by the walker, the motorist, the administrator, or the geologist to enable him to orientate himself in relation to the particular task in hand. Different tasks call for different kinds of maps. There is no such thing as a mind. The concept, like the tool we choose, depends on the purpose at hand.

Concerning the fluidity and interchangeability of I and not-I, let us take a person with a complex (or hang-up). In a complex there are usually two or more persons or one person and a thing in relation to one another. For example, if I have an antifather or antiauthority bias or complex, I may have frequent dreams involving a child-figure and a father-figure. The relationships or transactions between the two figures will be of a hostile or rejecting nature for the most part, at least during the early stages of therapy. Later in therapy, if the therapy is successful, more positive or good-and-bad elements will occur in dreams and then in the outer relationships. For example, I may have recurrent dreams in which an oppressive and cruel governmental authority is ordering the shooting or torturing of the unfortunate people under its control. In my waking life, I experience authority figures as rigid or oppressive, I complain of rigidity and red tape, and I have frequent outbursts of indignation on behalf of the victims I discern all around me. In this case the psychological situation is that my I is somewhat under the control of the child-victim figure of the complex. That is, I normally feel myself to be the victim of the negative father-figure. I see hostile father-figures all around. The therapist often uses the term *projection* for this. I project the negative father part of my antifather complex onto people and circumstances who are at all susceptible to this projection.

But having such a complex, what sort of a father or boss am I going to be? It can be imagined that I might avoid such a role where possible. I might, for instance, prefer to work on my own rather than have a boss or be a boss. Or I might be a very gentle or conciliatory sort of boss or employer, leaning over backwards to avoid being the kind of father-figure I detest. I might marry and be perfectly happy relating to my wife as equal or even as daughter or mother, but when sons come along I will tend to project the hating son onto them. This will have one of two outcomes, or some mixture of the two. Either I shall become depressed and a weak father, projecting the imagined hatred of my sons onto myself, or I shall be trying to compensate in various ways and to remedy or repair the negative father-son relationship of my own childhood and my own complex. If I try to be a kind father, it will be a strain, and I shall be subject to outbursts of irritation or even episodes of surprising cruelty toward my children or employees. In these states of not-being-myself, I am possessed or controlled by the hated, normally alien, oppressive father-figure.

In other words, my childhood experience of my father and other father-figures will determine the child image and the father image I carry throughout life, and through this it will determine the behaviour I exhibit both in the child or subordinate role and in the parental role. If I am in the son role, I shall be projecting the negative father role onto someone else, and if I am in the father role, I shall be projecting the negative child role onto someone else. My I and my not-I will have switched subpersonalities.

The I and the not-I are not fixed in any one of the many such figures or, as I call them, subpersonalities, comprising our total selves. The I and the not-I are reversible, with infinite variations of the sort I have mentioned in this example. The I is a very migratory, a very nomadic "person" in the universe of our total personality.

Now suppose that I have had a good and loving relationship with my father. I may grow up to have a flexible and mostly positive relationship with superiors and subordinates, and I may become a relaxed and loving father myself. But the same kind of projective phenomena apply, by and large, as in the negative father-son case. Blessed with a positive father-son bias owing to my own experience, I shall tend to project positive father or son subpersonalities out of myself onto other people, seeing them in the positive light of my own experience and bias.

My own experience of my father depends partly on my innate temperament and health, and partly on the sort of person my father is. The interaction will determine how we relate to each other, how we experience the other.

Although as a human being I am innately capable of a loved-child feeling and of loved-child behaviour, and also capable of rejected-child feelings and behaviour, how much of each kind of behaviour becomes habitual in me will obviously depend on my actual experiences with my father. If I have no father, owing, for example, to early bereavement, I still have the capability of loving-father experiences (probably of a relatively undifferentiated, daydream, or yearning sort, for example) owing to my innate instinctual predispositions.

Subpersonalities as the Basic Units of the Personality

Of the two great therapy pioneers, Freud stressed the importance of actual life experience as determining feeling-tone of the father image in a person, while Jung drew attention to the role of innate patterns and dispositions in determining our expectations, our behavioural predispositions, and the figures we see and imagine in our lives and in our dreams. These basic, commonly occurring patterns of behaviour and expectation Jung calls the archetypes. Experienced subjectively as images, the archetypes are observed objectively as behaviour patterns or instincts. Thus the good-father image will correspond with loved-child feelings and behaviour in the positive father complex I have just described, and the bad or frightening father image will correspond with the rejected-child or the rebellious-child feelings and behaviour. Both the good and the bad father-figures and the corresponding behaviour patterns are part of our total personalities or instinctual makeup. In my terminology, the positive and the negative child and the positive and the negative father-figures are important subpersonalities of our total personality, and they can all take possession of the I and of our behaviour, under differing circumstances.

In practice, just as the real J. Redfearn comprises many subpersonalities, so my actual father was many people. He himself, of course, had a loving child and a hurt child, a soft and a hard parent, a playboy and a prude, to mention only a few of his subpersonalities. All of these I came to know and take in and accept and reject to varying degrees, in differing circumstances, in different ways. All these things are true of other important people in my life, particularly of my mother, of course, and of my siblings.

The psychotherapist's concern is usually to help his client live life more fully, and this entails both becoming aware of, and becoming able to deploy or not deploy, at will, the different parts of himself or herself. The structural units of the personality, from the therapeutic point of view, are the units commonly met in the therapeutic work, especially in dreams, imaginative activity, and in the interaction between client and therapist. Freud used the terms *ego, id,* and *superego* for the basic structural working units of personality; Jung used the terms *archetypes* and *complexes* for those various selves within ourselves. I use the term *subpersonality* for the structural unit of the personality because it begs no theoretical questions and it is not only an empirical finding of everyday life – we all readily recognize and describe each others' main subpersonalities – but also the main working unit of analysis and psychotherapy. Its occurrence in dreams and in the client-therapist interactions is easily demonstrable. If a client dreams of a crocodile, it is usually easy to demonstrate the crocodile in him or her, especially in his or her projections, whereas it is often fruitless and unjustifiably partisan to try to clarify the crocodile bit of the client as ego, id, superego, archetype, or complex. The crocodile is a real subpersonality and is or can be all those things.

Although the subpersonalities are not complete human beings, they behave like persons in so far as they behave like characters in a story or on the stage, or like mythological or religious characters, or embodiments (personifications) of virtues, vices, instincts, etc. They may occur in dreams as things or institutions. For example, a rigid, controlling part of oneself may occur in a dream or a projection as a prison. Subpersonalities may change readily from "persons" to "things." The distinction between "person" and "thing," as far as the unconscious is concerned, is a quite superficial one. Basically we are all animists who inhabit a world of persons rather than things.

I must permit myself once again to stress that subpersonalities are units of behaviour as well as of the personality as experienced subjectively by the conscious I. They are indeed primarily units of the observed behaviour of the person, enacting themselves smoothly and unconsciously as behaviour in the normal state of affairs, only reaching awareness when blocked or in conflict with other predispositions in oneself. For example, I behave like a father in surprising degrees of complexity when with one of my children and for long periods of time, without being aware of any image of a father or a child, apart from the actual child who is engaged in his or her side of the behaviours concerned. Some of the unresolved or conflictual bits of the day's events may occur in some form in my dreams, of course. But in the main, our subpersonalities behave as themselves in the complex to-ing and fro-ing of everyday life, as I and all people of all kinds live it and are accustomed to living it.

Subpersonalities that are part of complexes due to traumatic experiences are, of course, more likely to obtrude into awareness than those which are part of our ordinary, taken-for-granted selves. These subpersonalities are the ones which receive most attention in dreams and in much therapeutic work. They attract other mental contents to themselves and form a nucleus of emotion which interferes with ordinary living. Furthermore, the subpersonality which is part of a traumatic complex is the one likely to be noticed and described by other people whose everyday, ordinary behaviour in relation to that person has been blocked or conflicted or otherwise brought to unexpected attention because of the emotions, inconvenience, etc., concerned in the interaction. An anxiety, a rigidity, a meanness, an undue sensitivity, an unexpected generosity or benevolence, all these things are noticed more than expected everyday relating is noticed.

In therapy, too, it is the emotionally toned complex that is the subject of attention more than anything else. Take a person with a hurt-child/implacable-authority complex. Sometimes he behaves or feels like the former, sometimes the latter. The therapist may become bullying or dogmatic on occasion as a reaction from always being the crushed and browbeaten one. The ramifications of the complex are unbelievable and form a dominant subject in the therapy sessions in one way or another.

The I as a Special Subpersonality

Some of my subpersonalities I recognize as aspects of myself, some I tend not to. For example, I might acknowledge the kind father in myself, but not the frightening tyrant. Yet there may undoubtedly be times when the frightening tyrant possesses me or my behaviour; this is when I am projecting a stupid, incompetent part of myself onto someone, usually a subordinate or junior person.

My mother, too, like everyone else, was in one sense many people (subpersonalities), yet I have an overall concept of her which includes many memories and many different aspects of her as I experienced her at different ages in myself and her. There is a sort of category of attributes, experiences, feelings which pertain to my mother. I have a predominant feeling-tone in relation to her of love which is a kind of composite or meld of all the different feelings I have had about her.

Roughly the same applies to myself. As an overall concept, as a boundary containing some things and excluding others, as a continuing object covering many experiences good and bad and many different times as far back as I remember, I am an object or person in the same sense as my mother in my own mind. Yet I have sensory experiences from my external senses and from my internal bodily parts that are unique to me and to no one else in my world.

My overall feeling about myself – my self-regard or otherwise – is likewise composed or computed from many experiences where I am an object of someone else's feelings about me as reflected in their looks of love, hate, approval, etc., as well as experiences when I am an object of my own attitudes.

The conclusion we draw from our therapeutic work is that one's concept and view of oneself in general is laid down in the early years of life and is shaped by the feelings and assumptions playing on oneself in the family environment – mother, father, and siblings all having tremendous importance in their interactions and in the roles into which one is obliged or encouraged to fit. How I feel about and see myself is laid down in childhood according to how I saw myself in my mother's eyes and feelings toward me. Father and others are not excluded in this context of the experience of myself as a relatively distinct person. Before I am a distinct person in the family, my whole world, the world in which on the whole I shall live, is determined by the general level of animation and happiness in the family, mediated, of course, predominantly by my mother's looks, smiles, movements, cuddling, holding, the music of her voice, the conversations with me from the first weeks on – long before I can formally talk. Those things will determine whether my subsequent world will be a desert or a living, animated place or throng. My subsequent world may be a bloody, gruesomely sadistic menagerie of horror, and if I experience this sort of world as the more real, more truly mine, I shall undoubtedly act in such a way as to bring about this outward manifestation of my inner state. The early emotional environment seems to determine the predominant feeling-tone of I and my world. Therapeutic work with patients in regressed states can to some extent change this for the better.

The Body-Image, the Self-Image and the World-Image

The body, its surface and its insides, in the sense of its general topographical arrangement, is represented at all levels of the nervous system, including the cerebral cortex. This is true in a unique way which is nothing like true of the external world's representation in the human brain.

Before we make any distinction between I and not-I in our early years, we are therefore assembling our images of other people and of the world in general as projections of the topographical relationships between the various parts of our bodies.

When we are in the womb and ever afterwards, we are receiving sensations from the insides and outsides of our bodies. These sensations are arranged and routed, roughly speaking, according to the position in space of the part of the body concerned. There is not much criss-crossing of nerve pathways at various levels of the nervous system, no system of scrambling followed by reconstituting or repositioning relative to each other of the various parts of the body. This is true at all levels of the spinal cord and brain. For example, in the sensory area of the cerebral cortex, our body is represented as a map or personlike area distorted so that important areas of the body have more emphasis than unimportant ones.

In short, our neuroanatomy presents us with a primitive body schema or body representation, and it is to be expected that our notion of the universe or total sphere of experience would at a primitive level be based on or derived from this basic bodily topography. Not only the universe at large, but venerated and familiar things within it, tend to be seen or pictured in our own image. The universe, the earth and sky and sea, the mountains, hills, valleys and the rivers and streams, the animals and the insects and plants are, primitively, felt to be persons with similar bodies and instincts to ourselves. By primitively I mean historically, in our feelings, and in our myths and dreams and stories, as well as in many of our intoxicated states.

Furthermore, and of crucial importance to my argument, is the fact that we hallucinate, imagine, and create artifacts which project and reflect the existential, i.e., circumstantial and affective, state of our body or body–world image. If the body-image of our feelings and psychosomatic state is tortured and distorted, we shall produce tortured-looking artifacts. If we are afraid of ourselves and of what we are making of the world, we may reverse or in some other way deny the psychic reality and produce inferior art.

So we both perceive and create a world and a culture that expresses ourselves at a primitive feeling level.

The relationships between the body and the world-image of feeling are illustrated in the phenomena of psychosomatic medicine. If I am held up in a traffic jam and late for an appointment, I may have an attack of diarrhoea or a fit of temper when the emergency is over. The impulse to overcome the obstruction or speed up the flow is reflected in the behaviour of the internal organs. If I feel rejected by someone or some institution, I may vomit. If I am afflicted by nausea or vomiting, I may dream of being thrown out of some group or building, or otherwise rejected. One's actual body is behaving as the not-self with respect to the I, which tends to be identified with the object of the bodily action, in this case, intestinal contents. Many images pertaining to containers or to the contained and to flow, discharge, and explosion reflect the feeling-state of the body and body–world image in this way.

A complication of the above formulation arises from the undoubted fact that we not only seek to express ourselves by means of our environment, but we also seek to compensate for the distortions in ourselves and the wounds in ourselves by seeking or creating a healing environment. Usually this produces distortions of an opposite or reversed kind in the environment.

In our survey of the correspondence between one's body-image and one's world-image, we have to give due weight to the enormous need for empathy and for imitation in each one of us as social beings. At the age of a few weeks, we smile and perhaps coo or gurgle with apparent pleasure, as well as giving much pleasure, when our mother smiles and voices her love for us. The mysterious connection between what we see, how we feel, and what we instinctively do works in both directions. How I feel will determine what I visualize, especially in dreams. For example, this connection between feelings and visual imagery results in the invention (and repeated reinvention) of the wheel and the ball. The same is true of gentle curves or sharp angles – the connection is obvious and works in both directions.

We tend to assume an identity of feeling and meaning in the other person unless proved wrong. The six-week-old smiling baby is only the first such case of sharing (strictly, imagined sharing, as baby and mother are having nothing like identical feelings). We keep on teaching our children words and behaviour until we are satisfied that meanings and motives are being accurately shared. The use of a common language means that the assumption of a shared meaning is good enough for practical purposes. Much of the apparent sharing of words and symbols is illusory, but the social cementing is of chief importance. A person who denies the separateness of other people and who automatically tries to impose his or her view of things on the other person is someone who has not learned sufficiently to give up or modify this primitive assumption of identity with the other person.

The harmonizing of inner and outer experience seems to occur through the medium of feeling or affect rather than through the appreciation of the "real" world of space–time or the need to find one's way within it. The same harmonizing occurs between the various sensory modalities and their imagery and is known as synaesthesia. We can equate musical, visual (colour and form), and social interaction in an accurate way – how else could we have a ballet or an opera? The equating is done because of the feeling-equivalence of the various modalities, and the common element is what reaches down to our ultimate depths, beyond images and words to bodily states and that which is prior to body-mind separation.

Prior to the separation of self and not-self, bodily states are experienced as world events, or so it seems from our knowledge of infancy, dreams, psychotic states, and cosmological myths.

Not only is the body equated with the world, but bodily states are imaged as cosmic events such as floods, hurricanes, earthquakes, paradise, beautiful landscapes, waterfalls, mergings, and separations. Different kinds of infantile rage are expressed or experienced as different kinds of catastrophe, a particularly important one being the complete breakup of the world (self-world-mother) into bits, and another one being the arctic or the hot desert or wasteland. The wasteland experience predates matricidal rage because it is prior to the stage when self, mother, and world are separated effectively from each other. The impulses to destroy the other person by flood, death-ray, or the huffing and puffing of the wind are very primitive ones and are present even before self and other person are separated. They are then represented by cosmic and divine imagery. A Kleinian analyst might, when appropriate, interpret a flood dream as a wish to destroy the mother-analyst with his angry urine, the appropriate reconstructions being based on whatever was known or felt about the early experiences of this sort of anger, how this anger is experienced by the analyst, and so on. Psychotherapists of many persuasions are confident of the connection between states of feeling, imagery of this sort, and infantile experience. If you are the whole world to me, a rupture between us will be experienced and probably dreamt of by me as a world rupture of some sort. Your poisonous moods will be represented in my dreams as world-poisoning gas or contamination, your generous gestures will be rivers of milk and honey to me.

The Separation of I and Not-I

The mother-world-Self, developmentally, becomes eventually the world-other in relation to the I which is struggling to survive in relation to the loving or the hostile mother-environment.

Is there any need for this sort of I, this sort of individual self, or this sort of security? The answer to this depends on my affective state. In a state of love, I would give all to lose my individual self and merge with my beloved. In a state of hate or fear, I would give all to preserve it from contamination, invasion, engulfment, or injury.

In other words, the I–not-I boundary is essentially a defensive one, and it seems to have its basis in the bodily defence mechanisms of closing up, tightening up, spitting out, eliminating, forming immune reactions, rage reactions, avoidance, attack, and so on. The reactions that dissolve the boundary between I and not-I are to do with love, eating, approach, and so on (i.e., parasympathetic nervous system activity as opposed to the sympathetic activity of fight and flight – unfortunate physiological terms).

An organism needs to defend itself against poisonous substances and dangerous objects, animals, and persons. Mammalian animals need to struggle for mates and protect themselves and other members of the group. This is what our nervous systems and our instinctive behaviour equip us to do. The I–not-I boundary is based on this primitive need for security and uses the energies from these basic self-preservative instincts for its maintenance.

Yet, love demands the dissolution of this boundary. If love and lovedness are not experienced habitually as part of one's self-feeling, then selfishness, forcing tendencies, power-motivation, pedantry or rigidity, and legalistic thinking are used as substitutes for the missing lovedness. All these are defensive in purpose, yet, paradoxically, they are the defences that prevent our reaching what in this unenlightened state is felt as life's goal or purpose.

These primitive defences separating I from not-I are essentially paranoid in that the good is felt as what is inside the defensive boundary and the bad is felt as what has to be attacked or kept out. Rage and the total mobilisation of aggressive and destructive feeling are part of the instinctual repertory at the disposal of this boundary, as are avoidance, denial, and other forms of flight. But how does this boundary prevent me from reaching my life's goal, my heart's desire?

It is easy to see that a strong fixed defence of this kind can function as a prison. If I am paranoid, vulnerable, suspicious, experiencing others as threatening, overpowering, or possessive, I am not able to let in other people in loving interchange. But who is this enemy I am trying to keep out? It is none other than myself – my greedy, needy, excluded, deprived subpersonality who is trying to get into the citadel of my own defences, to the treasures forever beyond my reach, guarded as they are by my vulnerable, paranoid defensive wall.

All our defence mechanisms are of this nature, comprising as they do fixed behaviours or subpersonalities opposing each other on either side of the defence in question. We need all our defensive instincts and equipment, but we need them to be flexible and mobile, not fixed and unconscious and used by subpersonalities unknown to ourselves.

Let me explain in more detail how these defensive barriers are set up and how the I can feel himself or herself to be either inside the defence and hence threatened or kept outside by the barrier and hence deprived and frustrated. A simple example may help. Suppose my mother is possessive and invasive (because of her own feelings of deprivation and of being excluded, which are no fault of her own). Then I need to strengthen those defences which keep her out and which enable me to have my own identity, integrity, and security. I experience my mother as a person who is out to take me over or rob me of everything inside me which is precious. My life is devoted to strengthening my defences and becoming secure and invulnerable. Yet I never achieve that goal except perhaps momentarily. I spend my life amassing money and property in order to keep away poverty and ruin. I am hypochondriacal because of the same fears for my body. I am cold and selfish because I cannot afford to be generous. The invading robber is always there threatening me. You, and other people, are always felt to be that invasive robber who my mother originally behaved as.

But the important truth here is that besides feeling vulnerable, with a tendency to project the invasive robbing mother onto all and sundry, I also have a strong tendency to become possessed by that invasive mother figure. When my I is possessed by that particular subpersonality, the other member of the threatened-child/invasive-mother complex, then I feel kept out, excluded, and deprived of my rights. I feel like crashing down the unjust barriers that separate me from happiness, love, and wealth, etc., which are after all my life's dues as they perhaps are for everyone. Now you, as well as other people, are always the lucky one with the happiness and the wealth, and I keep trying to invade you or lay siege to you, encamped as you are behind your hateful, exclusive, defence.

So the defensive complex acts between the two main subpersonalities of the complex, the vulnerable child and the invasive parent (who is, in fact, a needy, deprived child in the present context).

Fortunately, my internal mother is not always invasive and possessive. When she is unthreatening, ordinary, or loving and generous, I do not close up and have to keep her out. The defensive barrier does not exist between the loved-child and the loving-parent subpersonalities. When my I is possessed by one of these, the vulnerability, the barrier, and the unattainability of the goal are not the point. When my I is feeling loved, you and other people are welcomed and nonthreatening. Of course, it helps if you are, in reality, behaving in a loving, nonthreatening way yourself, but that is another matter.

One important, bomb-producing subpersonality, the omnipotent, apocalyptic God subpersonality, is a product of repeated threats and invasions, causing the buildup of very rigid walls and correspondingly violent forces both within (wanting freedom) and without (wanting satisfaction). It is these forces that may be attributed to the God of the Apocalypse. Our ways of bringing up children determine the nature of these defences and particularly those rigid, paranoid ones that are the important ones separating inside from outside in the present context.

The scenario comprising a vulnerable person with treasure-defensive barrier-deprived invader is, according to this view, a picture of a fixed defence or complex produced in childhood. When not too fixed, it is part of normal behaviour and needful defences. The scenario can be acted out at a personal, group, or national level. It could have been the main factor producing walled cities and the corresponding marauding armies. The development of separate individuality (separation from the mother, the parents, the family, the social group rather than a group identity) and the idea of the walled city (and of invading walled cities) would therefore develop in human historical process. It is in this sense that I write of inner and outer reality being interdependent. If I feel basically threatened and my defences are all too readily mobilised, then I am going to try to increase my sense of security by every possible means and in all the spheres of my life – money, home, and territory, national security, the preservation of group identity, customs, religion, etc. Feeling loved (by other people, God, oneself, etc.) naturally diminishes these defensive barriers. The cultivation of loved feelings by adults is an interesting possibility and seems to be a practicable aim in psychotherapy and in some religions. The capacity to love and be loved is, of course, part of our instinctual makeup and as such can be blocked but not, apparently, destroyed.

The Bomb Image: An Image of the Dark Side of self or Self?

The bomb image in dreams comes in all sizes, from handheld bombs to world-destroying, gigantically powerful ones. Actual bombs, too, are now available in all sizes.

The self-image and the feeling of oneself vary commensurately, from tiny to world-containing (in the latter case, we speak of an inflated self-image, an inflated ego). Such images are more appropriately experienced, at least in the everyday life which must go on, as God or Self images, i.e., as outside the normal, everyday self and as much vaster than the self. But the Self or God image can itself be experienced as tiny or man-size, albeit in a paradoxical way, in many theologies. Smaller than small and greater than great, the God image may finally encompass the whole of one's universe, or be commensurate with it.

The bomb image represents the explosive self (I-me-myself-mine) and also the explosive Self (the same underlying psychic structure projected outside the self and imagined in apocalyptic dimensions).

The essential feature of the bomb consists of opposing or conflicting drives or attitudes generating intense energy which is hopefully contained within a rigidly inhibitory boundary or container. If the contained or frustrated contents possess the I, one experiences oneself as inhibited or imprisoned, and one wants to burst free. If the I is possessed by the container or shell, for example, if one identifies with the containing elements, the explosive contents may be experienced as revolutionary elements, as dangerous internal bodily processes, as unruly children, or as impending insanity.

The subjective size of the bomb or explosion depends on the confidence of the ego to cope with the conflict or clash. An infant witnessing intercourse or quarrels between parents would feel very small and powerless, so that the explosion or war would be experienced in titanic dimensions. With greater confidence in handling the conflict, the subjective size of the warfare tends to diminish until the explosion or conflict can be successfully contained and the liberated energy harnessed.

As to whether the bomb image has to do with defences of the ego, of the self, or whether it is the dark side of God, I can only say that the bomb image and explosive behaviour result from a subpersonality reflecting a negative relationship between interaction and its containment. Interaction (the clashing or meeting of opposites) is experienced as dangerous and is counteracted by rigidity (the basic defence against the felt danger). This subpersonality can be experienced as part of the I, as a conflict between unconscious and I, or as an attribute of the outside world or cosmos. Probably, being a subpersonality, it will enter into all these parts of one's entire world.

The Ultimate Horror as the Gateway to Heaven

The myth of death and resurrection is a hope, an actual psychological experience, and an example of an even wider experiential phenomenon which is a fundamental property of the human mind.

From our own experience, and from observation of young people falling in and out of love, we know that the fairy tale of Beauty and the Beast transformed by love is an almost commonplace phenomenon. Everyone knows that hate is close to love, even that "the stone that the builders rejected shall become the headstone of the corner." And we are all aware, preferably second-hand, of the glory of self-sacrifice.

Freud pointed out the connection between fears and wishes. The feared object is in some way an aspect of the longed-for object in which the object or the feelings about it have been reversed or negated in some way. In a similar way, in countless examples, the psychotherapist finds that one's highest hopes and ideals, and one's deepest regressions, even one's ultimate horrors and fears, have a mysterious connection, a kind of paradoxical identity even.

An example of this occurred in my early days of psychotherapy. I was regularly talking to a woman who for many years had lived in a nightmare world in which everything and everybody felt unreal and impersonal. She said that it was like living at the bottom of a pit, tormented by insects and other horrors. Sometimes these horrors achieved hallucinatory intensity, and often they inhabited her dreams and nightmares. One day she arrived in a happily transformed state of mind, saying that she had fallen in love with me. It was in some ways like falling into the pit of her previous state, but wholly blissful and positive. The horrors of the pit were now transformed into imagined kisses and beautiful flowers, etc. Her depersonalized state, which had tortured her for so long, had been "cured" overnight! The work of psychotherapy had only just begun, of course, but the relationship between ultimate horror and deepest wish had been firmly imprinted on both our minds. Psychotherapists, even the least experienced, cannot regard this sort of reversal of feeling as a completion of the work, but at least it indicates movement in a previously intractable condition.

Whether as individuals or groups, we all have our ultimate horrors, nightmare images or situations that we cannot possibly face. But when courage, love, or support help us to face them, they may turn out to be blessings in disguise, gateways to happiness, salvation, a fuller life. The facing of the fear does not necessarily involve undergoing an actual external event, an actual death, torture, unthinkable eventuality, etc. The feared (internal) thing is, in a sense, the threat to the self, or rather to the ego or self-image in the everyday sense of these words. Nevertheless what one is avoiding cannot be psychologized away. The moral, emotional facing has to happen, and this may well include facing something previously unfaced in the actual world. Ideally the unfaceable has to be faced at the point of maximum psychic reality, and often this involves the facing of some real external fact or possibility. In the case of my patients, this was *in fact* facing marriage, facing a confrontation with a real person, facing a wish to murder the mother, and so on. How absurd this sounds! One's *real* fears are subjective ones and are not necessarily real to others or even to our conscious selves. Yet going with the feeling of fear is the way through the needle's eye. The feared thing is the blessing in disguise.

Contrary to popular fiction, the facing of these unfaceable fears is not usually a once-and-for-all event and is not a dramatic victory, especially when it is really therapeutic and permanent. When therapeutic, it is often tinged with defeat, has its negative aspects and its sorrows, and concerns matter-of-fact everyday living and real, important people. Dramatic abreactions, conversions, heroic feats, victories of conscience or victories over temptation obviously may be important but are only the first step toward wholeness. Another sobering fact is that what feels like a heroic victory subjectively may seem a very ordinary achievement to another person, something already achieved and forgotten.

The ability to preserve an intact self seems, in my therapy experience, to be associated with the ability to keep one's loved one intact within oneself even when the loved one has gone away (perhaps for good) or however much the actual or internal loved one is being rejecting or in some other way hateful. The destruction of the ego and the inability to preserve love go hand in hand. But this is the sort of existential shattering (of love, self-respect, integrity, and so on) that is part of the cycle of life and part of the necessary loss of moral virginity. An ego which is not defended against minor and some major shatterings is synonymous with an open heart and lively mind.

If the bomb image represents a subjective threat from within and a corresponding wish to burst out of a rigid container, there is an equally important image belonging to the early stages of individual and social development, and this is the image of the threat from without to the self or its precious contents. What is good is incorporated, what is bad is expelled from the early self and constitutes the threat. Strangely, and paradoxically, if what is bad threatens to be perceived as good, an internal conflict of bomblike intensity may also be produced. This is simply an example of the conflict of opposing feelings.

In the outside world, the early paranoid personality structure of individual differentiation from the group/mother might take the form of the house, the barricade, and finally the walled city, with its modern counterparts. The walled city is the early self or ego with its defences and its need for integrity and security; the invader or destroyer is the envious, deprived, excluded part of the self projected outside the defensive walls.

If I refer with some confidence to the early stages of the development of the personality, it is because of the phenomenon of regression, as seen not only in the protective environment provided by psychotherapy but in the unguarded behaviour of oneself and other people in times of illness, stress, or in crowds, etc. Stages of regression do not accurately repeat historical development either in individual or social history, but recapitulation and reconstruction of the past play such an important part in psychotherapy that the psychotherapist's observations of individuals and of babies and infants are vastly enriched.

It is not difficult to distinguish various degrees (or depths) of regression, but it is not always easy to distinguish between regression in time to an *earlier* pattern and regression in mental function to a *simpler* or more primitive or basic pattern. This makes it difficult to develop a temporal account of psychological development that is clearly differentiated from the clinical phenomena of regression encountered in normal and abnormal adult human beings. In an analysis, we encounter deeper and deeper layers of the psyche, and it is easy to confuse "deeper" with "earlier," and to confuse what is defended against most strongly with the earliest developmental features. Furthermore, one finds that the most profound (and paradoxically the highest) truths are also found at the levels of deepest regression. This complicates, if it does not make nonsense of, the idea that we have evolved in a bottom-up dimension either individually or collectively.

For the sake of completeness, it is necessary to say that the idea of "regression to more archaic functioning" is a gross oversimplification in that it implies movement along one dimension, whereas the truth is multidimensional. For example, alcohol and hallucinogens both bring about regression to more archaic functioning, but the disinhibitive effect of alcohol is quite different from the psychologenic, "mind-expanding" effect of hallucinogens. Regressions without drugs may also differ in being more in the nature of disinhibitions or else of hallucinogenesis.

When psychotherapists and analysts speak of "the early ego," they are referring to inferences about individual psychic development, partly drawn from the observation of babies and their mothers, but mostly, as I said, from observations of regressed patients, especially psychotic patients. It is not easy to match up these two sources of material. A baby's mind, as far as we can tell, does not work in the same way as that of a dreaming, psychotic, or neurotic adult person, although all these have something in common. Nor does it work in the same way as the adult mind of a person in a Stone Age-type culture. All these studies throw light on each other, nevertheless.

With these qualifications, I still think there is much validity in the idea that, to a certain extent, the country, state, city, or group with which one identifies is a representation of one's self in one's mind; also, that social structures represent different parts of one's self, different parts of one's personality. I am also arguing that the evolution of social groups and of civilisation itself must have been accompanied to some extent by the evolution of the human personality because of the mutual interaction between social structure and intrapsychic structure. If one thinks about it, social structure and personality structure must develop hand in hand.

More about Self-Representations

Ask a person to describe what he "sees" in an ink blot, or in the embers of a hearth fire, or in the shapes of clouds, and he will be telling you about himself, to a psychologically usable extent. The Rorschach test is a clinically useful tool which has developed this principle in a methodical way. Ask a person to draw a tree, or a house, or a human being, and what he draws and the way he draws it will be himself or reflect himself to an extent that can be of use to psychotherapists or others. Thus the subject of the drawing can be or can be used as a self-representation.

Naturally, the drawing or painting is simpler to interpret when the person concerned is not aware that his drawing is revealing himself in some way. Otherwise he may try to draw more how he wants to appear and less what he unself-consciously is.

In psychotherapy, once an attitude of trust between patient and therapist is established, drawings can be used as tools for self-revelation which, like dreams and other creative products, may take part in a dialogue between the unconscious and consciousness.

If a child patient draws a house, we should no doubt want to look at it from several points of view. We should try to understand it as a representation of himself (or herself), as a representation of how he (or she) perceives his (or her) own body. We should look at it as a representation of the family perhaps, or of what holds or contains the family, and we should want to look at it, no doubt, as a symbol for, or representation of, the mother's personality or her body as a container, both metaphorical and literal. We do not say "the house is a symbol for the mother's body or the patient's body" (although this is always partially true and sometimes the main relevant truth), and we do not say a certain painting "means" this or that. We look at all the meanings or all that occur to us, knowing that the products of human creativity are very richly and multifariously determined, and knowing that which meaning it seems fruitful to explore further will be determined by operational factors (therapeutic considerations and so on).

A patient's drawing of the human body, its outline, its parts, and its surfaces will depict much of what he feels about his own self and about his own parts and boundaries (e.g., strength or weakness of parts and boundaries) in a metaphorical as well as in a literal or physical sense. A felt weakness of his body or his personality may appear clearly in the drawing, as might an attempt to compensate for or deny this weakness. Physical defects, from protruding ears to fatal disease, are very often poignantly reflected, denied, or overcompensated in patients' drawings of humans and also of houses, towers, animals, ships, and all the other common symbols for and representations of the self. (They are representations of the self from the point of view of the therapist and the unconscious of the patient, rather than from the patient's conscious point of view.) It is usually sensitive or painful aspects of self which are featured. The drawing is thus a means of communicating or not communicating these sensitivities.

Self-representations tend to depict a wished-for aspect of the self in healthy optimistic persons. For example, the fiercely potent warships, guns, and aeroplanes of the young boy may help him develop his phallic potency and indirectly boast about it—an essential part of developing his masculine self-confidence. They help him feel good about his phallic and aggressive parts. A child who is very depressed about his/her potency would not be able to produce potent self-representations to this degree of wishfulness and hopefulness.

Large, fierce, gentle, disgusting, small, curious, tender, or appealing animals similarly express and represent corresponding aspects of the self, usually unconscious, and usually aspects that the patient needs to communicate to us, test the therapist with, or retrieve into consciousness. In other words, they represent lost bits of the self, alienated from the conscious ego because of parental disapproval or the disapproval of society in a wider sense, perhaps.

The self, or aspects of the self, that are wishing to express themselves appear in the dreams, wishes, fantasies, fairy tales, myths, religions, cultural and political activities, and aspirations of people in the same way as in drawings or paintings or any other creative activity. From the present point of view, we are particularly interested in the state or motherland or social group seen as a self-representation, because inter-state relations are important for our separate and collective survival at the present time.

The Group as a Self-Representation

In group therapy, where we have a therapist and about eight participants, we usually find that each individual has a tendency to take up a particular role within the group, and the group has a corresponding tendency to cast individuals in those roles. One person may tend to function within the group as the good mother, another as good father, another as bad parent or enfant terrible, another as good boy, another as good or bad girl, another as the baby; or we may have the thinker, the person who is strong on feelings, the down-to-earth person, the scapegoat, the artist, and so on. Now all these roles are part of the potential in each of us. We are all, to an extent, all these "people." Our total personalities, in other words, contain all these roles, instincts, part-selves. The group, which spontaneously tends to develop these "divisions of labour," comes to represent more of a whole self for the individuals than he, in his limited function within the group, comes to represent for himself.

The larger group, whether community or state, divides itself up in a similar manner into leaders, parental figures, scapegoats, criminals, good subjects, thinkers, artists, and so on. The picture is complicated by the fact that we may have one role in one group and another (even an opposite) role in another group. Nevertheless the large group image comes to represent the human totality or Self with a wider, even divine or semidivine connotation. It may come to be the focus of the highest ideals and aspirations for the component individuals. In that case, it does not represent the whole Self, being devoid of negative parts.

The Paradoxical Equivalence of Highest Ideal and Deepest Regression

High ideals, and the tendency of a person to idealize certain people, qualities, institutions, social groups, receive a lot of attention in psychotherapy. The issue is very complicated.

Psychotherapists tend to be sceptical about idealizations. They recognize the envy, the destructive comparing and contrasting, the specious and overprotective sentimentalization underlying many of the idealizations that patients show in therapy. I do not intend to discuss these kinds of idealization here; most people would recognize them as pathological, too good to be true, syrupy, wishful, and unrealistic. However, in describing the paradoxical nature of the core of the self, it is necessary to refer to "high" principles, "high" ideals and aspirations, "higher" pursuits, as opposed to low values, low standards, and so on.

The fact that one's highest aims and ideals, one's sources of inspiration and motivation, are paradoxically coupled in the unconscious with one's most archaic regressions may cause surprise and even revulsion to some. But as we grow older and wiser, we become more and more aware of paradoxes of this kind, even in the moral and theological field. Suppose (as is often the case) that in therapy a patient dreams of trying to gain admittance to a place of religion or learning and finds, either in the dream itself or in his mental associations with it, that the most desired goal has unequivocal allusions to a womb, or to the procreative activities of persons or animals, or to incest, or to "lower" parts of the body. One has, however regretfully, to admit that that is life, how things are, how the mind works. "Highest" and "lowest" are manifestations of the core of the self and Self. The realization of the paradoxical nature of values gives depth, wisdom, and humour to a person. It does not destroy value, but it adds body and reality to values and valuations.

The Paranoid Core of the Self-Concept

The person in therapy who is seeking the truth about himself, seeking his true self, finds deeper levels within himself as therapy proceeds. Toward the core of the personality, beyond the level of concern for others, of tolerance, self-sacrifice, and of practical realism, we come to a part of ourselves which embraces "the good" and rejects "evil," eating or taking in the good, loved thing or person and turning away from or rejecting the bad, hated thing or person. Good and evil, and those corresponding primitive bodily responses (literal or metaphorical) of acceptance and rejection, occur together so that we cannot say that one comes before the other or is primary compared with the other. Myself, as I come to experience myself, accumulates good feelings, and what is not myself is what is rejected and bad. It is probably necessary for my bodily survival in infancy that these bodily protective reflexes and what come to be their psychological equivalents constitute core feelings of the self-concept.

"Knowing" what is good or bad, right and wrong, is a feeling that comes before, or exists at a deeper level of the personality, than tolerance, concern, or commonsense expediency. It is at the same level as self-preservation and maintaining one's sanity and integrity. This being so, it is extremely powerful, and dangerous when impinged upon. The person's self, his subjective existence as a whole person, is threatened and will defend itself with the full resources of fight or flight at its command. The screaming anger of a paranoid patient when his delusions are questioned by a person of whom he is not too frightened is a memorable experience for the psychiatrist. It gives one a vivid experience of the energy available to the self for its defence.

Love and hate, good and bad, are not simple, single, feeling entities. The anger or anxiety that occurs in the infant when the mother is pushing too hard or coming on too strong is not the same as the hatred toward the normally adored mother or nipple that is withdrawing in an unwished-for way. The former experience corresponds more to fear of invasion and persecuted feelings, whereas the latter corresponds more to murderous feelings, or feelings that the other person is a murderer or a witch.

What is true of the overall boundaries and defences of the city or other grouping is also true of the other cultural and social contents of the community, which also are based on, and help to form, the personalities of the members of the community. They affect each other through the upbringing and conditioning of the members, which depend on and mould the social and cultural patterns of the group. Thus the physical and material aspects of social life are a part, but only a part, of the inner life.

The Self-Fulfilling Self-Image

The paranoid model of the self (walled city) experiences the bad, the enemy, as not-self. It perceives and (for "health" reasons) needs to experience the bad as not-self. There is a real need for an enemy. It therefore creates an enemy. A vicious circle is set up.

This state of affairs precedes concern and reason. The power and reality of the paranoid self is, however, only too obvious, not so much in our personal lives as in our vicarious political and social lives.

Both our instincts and our complexes or personal biases due to distortions in our upbringing need to mould outer reality so as to bring about their own fulfillment. A boy who was bullied by his father will tend to have a timid attitude which brings about bullying by all around him. Occasionally he may succeed in reversing the situation, only to find that he has become a bully himself. He is trapped in the bullied-bullying mode of living and seeing the world. It is the same with all our complexes, which interact with each other and with our basic instincts to produce the complex patterns we call our life stories or personal fates.

CHAPTER 5

The Explosive Self and the Maternal Container

A strictly brought up young man felt trapped in his marriage. He felt his wife to be commendable and intelligent but unimaginative. For years he struggled to contain his wishes to be free. He dreamt that a terrorist placed a bomb in a stuffy bourgeois hotel and blew it up.

A few months later he fell in love with a woman and experienced the exciting intellectual stimulation and physical passion he had missed in his marriage. For a time there was no actual affair, but after some months more, they met secretly and went to bed together.

Until then he had had no important secrets from his wife. But now he decided not to tell his wife of this momentous event.

That night he dreamt of himself as a Lazarus-like figure coming to life and bursting out of bandages like those used to enwrap mummified bodies in Egypt. His reaction to the dream was a feeling of liberation and of being reborn.

The new relationship continued and led to successful remarriages for both husband and ex-wife. Unusually, the two couples remain good friends after twenty years.

The man was a calm and considerate man. He was very much not an explosive sort of person. Yet the events I describe were clearly an acting out of the dream of blowing up the stuffy hotel.

The exploding contents of the bomb represented the passions or the growing infant part of him which could not be contained by him or his life situation. Or you could say they represented his newborn self bursting out of the imprisoning maternal womb-container that his first marriage had come to mean to him.

His first marriage was at first a womb, a refuge. The security allowed the arousal of his feelings and energies which turned the haven into a boring prison. Thus, his first marriage can be seen as good and necessary for his development at that stage of his life.

The outer imprisoning container (i.e., the casing of the bomb, or the stuffy hotel) represented not just the outer environment of marriage and convention, but also his own rigidity (rigid attitudes, rigid muscular tensions, both voluntary and involuntary muscles taking part in the armouring and closing off of dangerous contents). These attitudes were taken in from the young man's mother.

The bomb image here consists of two fairly distinct, relating sub-personalities, the container and the exploding contents. The I can be located in either. I can feel like the imprisoned infant needing freedom, or I can feel like the container trying to contain my mounting passions. So clearly the I can be located in either the one who wishes to explode or the one who wishes to contain and can even be located in both container and contained at the same time.

In infancy, the fragmenting or exploding early self is contained or held by the mother's physical and emotional holding. No doubt holding and containing behaviour is part of our maternal instinctual endowment, but in practice and to a very significant measure, it is learned from and refined by our mothers. This is not so much a theoretical as an empirical finding derived from psychotherapeutic experience. Briefly, one finds that the characteristics of the mother's containing or holding functions, good and bad, present and absent, are repeated in the feelings between patient and therapist. Furthermore, new containing and self-liberating functions can be learned from the therapist or from others.

Construction and Mechanism of the Fantastical Bomb

From the age of about eight to eleven or twelve, I spent a good deal of my spare time during winter evenings working in my chemical laboratory. (Adults might patronizingly refer to this activity as "playing with his chemistry set.") When my chemistry education proper started at secondary school, my amateur researches on the kitchen table waned, but not before I had burnt a large hole in it while preparing and testing a kind of ornamental gunpowder for use in fireworks.

What were my motives for this work? Clearly not the accumulation of actual chemical knowledge, except possibly as a means to the end of the work. While no one overriding purpose obsessed me, I can recall the half-dozen kinds of projects in which I became absorbed. One consisted of transforming everyday objects, especially bronze coins, by various "silvering" and electroplating techniques. Another was growing beautiful coloured crystalline "chemical gardens" from supersaturated solutions of salts. Another was the electrolytic decomposition of water into its elements. The manufacture of hydrogen, hydrogen sulphide, and noxious brown nitrogen peroxide by nonelectrolytic methods occupied a fair amount of time. When permitted, I made fireworks both for the beauty and for the bangs. And finally, distillation was a fascination, mainly because of the beauty of the glass chemical retort, one of my most treasured objects, and the fascination of purification and the mysterious translation of substances.

In other words, my all-absorbing interest was completely prescientific and fantastical, although I was quite ready to use what intellect and scientific knowledge I then possessed. Jung has convincingly demonstrated a similar sort of symbolic, self-transformative motivation in the work of the alchemists of the Middle Ages and later. He stressed the psychological truths underlying their work, in the quest for transformation and redemption. We cannot doubt that the motives of individual alchemists differed widely, and that whatever complexes or unresolved unconscious problems they had would be clearly discernible to us in the symbolic content of their experiments. For my present purposes, I shall oversimplify the alchemist's *opus*, which we shall then understand as a symbol of a deep psychological goal for which the reader will be left to find his own name, be it God, the Philosopher's Stone, the Elixir of Life, the New Man, the Anthropos, the divine child, or some other name for the reader's own personal life's goal.

The caricature of the alchemist at this work, then, which I have distilled for the purposes of this book, consists of the alchemist and his mystical sister striving together to perform and understand meaningful alchemical transmutations. There is a retort or rather a well-sealed vessel (i.e., a vessel of perfect containment) to which external heat is applied when necessary. Inside the vessel we have two opposite substances, creatures, or divinities. They may be referred to symbolically as sun and moon (personified), brother and sister, king and queen. These opposites combine and, it is hoped, after various stages, additions, and chemical manipulations, the goal of the mystery is attained.[1] This union of opposites is understood symbolically as a divine incestuous intercourse with a monstrous and finally divine outcome.

"But wait," I can hear you saying, "is this not the symbolical model for the atom bomb which you described – the meeting of opposites within the sealed container which results in the explosion?" "But precisely," I reply, "the bomb *is* the Philosopher's Stone in its negative aspect. It symbolizes infinite destruction as opposed to infinite creation."

So the blueprint for the symbolic construction of the omnipotently destructive exploding self is, at first sight, indistinguishable from that of the omnipotently creative self. Of course, both are "fantasies," but they both contrive to get themselves realized concretely in all of us at times.

In the short case studies I presented in Chapter Two, the opposites which were the ingredients for the explosive mixture were of a deep-rooted psychological nature. Conflicting feelings about the primal scene as well as the intrinsic opposition in the two protagonists of the primal scene itself, conflicting feelings of love and hate for the mother, the father, the lover, the self – all these opposites are more or less basic to human nature, and certainly they are basic to the human predicament as we know human life to be lived.

The potentially "world"-destructive, omnipotently creative nature of the meeting of primal, fundamental opposites of human nature is an existential phenomenon – some would say a truth – known to many of the religions, mythologies, and philosophies of civilised and self-aware mankind for several thousands of years. Yin and yang, light and darkness, good and evil, Christ crucified and Christ in glory, love and hate are all opposites whose conflict and paradoxical closeness or identity gives rise to immense energy in the human being. Modern statements to the same effect, apart from the mysterious communications of the alchemists, would include the opposition between Freud's life and death instincts (love versus destructiveness) which when successfully contained leads to the fusion of instincts necessary to normal mental functioning. Pavlovian excitation and inhibition are a physiological-behavioural conception of the opposites in question (see Chapter

---

[1] For a more complete account, see volumes 12, 13, 14, and 16 of Jung's collected works.

Eleven). In the right conditions, a creative personal and cultural outcome occurs, as we shall see. But explosion is, of course, another possible outcome, and explosions are often destructive.

Ideally, or rather in the most favourable of situations, the fusion of the two opposites can be of a nonexplosive, nonexpanding sort. The maternal container is then not necessary. The need for the maternal container could indeed be said to be an indication of imperfect fusion or synthesis. It indicates some destructiveness in the reaction between the opposites, which is not always the case. The container itself may be constraining and rigid and, if strong enough, may produce some sort of forced fusion, with the danger of lovelessness. For example, a husband and wife may work harder at making a success of their marriage if children, marriage laws, public opinion, or material considerations exert pressure on them to keep working at the marriage. But as loving parents or as therapists, we know that forceful constraint, even when disguised, is neither a desirable nor a particularly successful form of parental holding. A mother tries to understand her child's narcissistic needs (for self-confidence and self-respect) and the child's need for magical, omnipotent experience just as well as she understands the demands of reality and social adjustment. If she does not actively adapt to these omnipotent needs, a compliant, false person will result, as Donald Winnicott has demonstrated (Winnicott 1958, p. 225). Just as meeting a person's anger is easier if one is empathically aware of the hurt love underlying it, meeting a person's omnipotent destructiveness is easier if one is empathically aware of the impotent creativity underneath. This applies to one's own anger, omnipotence, and narcissism just as much as to those of other persons.

The Exploding Jewel—The Focusing, Reversal, and Depersonalization of Omnipotent Rage

The goal of alchemy was sometimes imagined as a jewel or concentrated substance of great power, luminosity, or value. Sometimes this was resolved into a sort of human or divine mating of male and female, virtually of persons. The same sort of resolution occurs in therapy. We can imagine that during the latency period of childhood a hated or envied person or part of oneself is transformed by the energy of one's hatred. A person or pair of persons can become a thing; a hated and devalued person may sometimes be transformed into a thing of immense value – a jewel. The hardness reflects the hardness of the feelings resulting from all this. We know this can occur because, during therapy, in the warmth and humanity of recovered feelings, the reverse processes seem to occur – jewels and other precious objects turn into people, hated and loved and above all envied. The jewel image may explode into a liberation of energy or a Garden of Eden theme. The body comes to life, sometimes painfully at first. Abstraction and depersonalization are reversed, reverting to the more botanical, the more zoological, and eventually the more human, the more "ordinary." Hardness, however idealized, is softened. The jewel changes into the plant, the animal, finally to the human.

The rage and envy may take the form of a cancer or other dangerous subpersonality (for example, a robber or rapist or invading army). Again, the cancer image may change into a jewel before exploding into humanity of feeling. In short, all these images represent feelings that can transmute in the course of life and of therapy.

The Containing of Projected Subpersonalities

One of the chief tasks of the parent, the family, the group, and sometimes the therapist may be to contain negatively toned subpersonalities (i.e., negative in relation to the I, hence denied and projected or subject to the various schizoid and other defences) which are being projected onto the containing person or group. Often great physical and mental stress is experienced by one or both parties (e.g., patient and therapist), and this may attain explosive intensity.

The therapist has to learn to contain projections, reflect upon what is going on, understand it, and react in some way which helps the patient relate to the subpersonality he is projecting onto the therapist in a more positive way.

Explosions as Uncontained Projections

I hope to say more of the therapist's role, but first I should like to comment on the curiously physical character of the energy involved in the process of projection. An incident which occurred at a meeting between Jung and Freud in 1909, recorded in the chapter on Sigmund Freud in Jung's autobiography, *Memories, Dreams, Reflections*, will serve as an example.

According to Jung's version, he asked Freud's opinion of parapsychological matters, including precognition. Freud replied in such a shallow, dismissive way that a sharp retort sprang to Jung's lips, which he naturally suppressed. But at that moment a burning sensation commenced in Jung's diaphragm, only relieved when a loud bang occurred in the bookcase next to them both. Jung was convinced that he had proved his point, and when Freud persisted in his opinion that it was all nonsense, Jung predicted another bang from the bookcase, which sure enough occurred immediately. Freud was aghast, but managed to maintain his materialistic opinions and his assertion that it was all coincidence. However, the incident increased Freud's mistrust of Jung, and the rift widened disastrously from then on.

We can understand the psychology, if not the physics, of the "explosion," better if we realize that it took place at the very meeting when Freud was attempting to adopt Jung as "an eldest son, anointing you as my successor and crown prince" (Jung 1963, p. 333). Jung's heresy did not accord with such sentiments, while Freud's dismissal of his cherished ideas and interests was deeply hurtful to him. Jung certainly had a negative father complex. The mutual projections could hardly be contained, but although both behaved acceptably, the explosion, we may possibly assume, occurred not in the form of a physical illness in Jung but in the form of the bang in the bookcase! The reader is permitted to treat this as fanciful nonsense, but the therapist faced with poltergeist and other paranormal phenomena has to deal with them as split-off subpersonalities – bits of the self, in the same way as dreams and unconscious behaviour can be understood and dealt with. Scepticism is understandable if one realizes that acceptance of such findings suggests that, far from mind being an epiphenomenon of matter, matter would have to be understood as in some sense an epiphenomenon of mind.

Whether or not we permit ourselves to speculate along such lines, we have to admit that our bodily and mental survival sometimes seem to depend on forcible, explosive expulsion or projection of a subpersonality from ourselves. More often than not the process is not voluntary in the ordinary sense – in fact, the will may often be antagonistic to the projection and will try to help in the bottling-up of the parts that are wanting to burst out.

As a screaming baby, I am threatened with this invasive monster which is threatening to overpower me. I have to scream it away, keep it out. My survival as an I depends on it. My mother, the monster, is able to contain this projection without feeling too upset, knowing that I am "just overtired."

As a frightened employee, I have to contain my screaming boss's projection into me of a stupid turd subpersonality. I behave with suitable dignity, yet self-apology. My containment may only survive until I get home, when some mistake of wife or child will release the introjected subpersonality into the source of irritation, and I shall be releasing a stream of vituperative accusation at the unfortunate member of my family, perhaps the dog.

In the case of Freud and Jung, we have an example of failure to contain projections on both sides resulting in an explosion. Roughly speaking, it is one's narcissistic needs – the need of the insecure or endangered I to preserve itself – that prevent one from containing projections. As a therapist, one is often struggling with the task of containing the client's projections, just as the client has to struggle to some extent to contain those of the therapist. Some patients suffer very much from the fact that they provoke explosive anger in others – for example, they may be overbearing people, know-it-alls, authoritarian pedants, helpless inadequate people who make others want to shake them or tell them to smarten up, etc. At the beginning of therapy, explosive impulses are felt by the therapist, just as by others when the client behaves in his customary provocative manner, but the therapist tries to use his natural impulse to explode in the service of the client. He will try to observe his own bodily impulses, emotions, and particularly his images of the client and understand the subpersonality that is being projected by the client — there will be plenty of biographical material, dream material, behavioural observations and introspective material from the client to enable the therapist to do this and help the client integrate the subpersonality in question. In the early stages of therapy, however, the therapist will be suffering a good deal in his own pain and in his efforts not to react spontaneously and irritably or explosively.

The explosive response to such provocative people is usually due to one's spontaneous violent rejection of the subpersonality being forced into oneself by the patient concerned. This is often a hurt, crushed, weak, or dead subpersonality which it is too painful to admit to being, unless love or skill or practice helps one to do so.

The psychotherapy literature is so very much concerned with holding situations and holding skills that it is unnecessary to overload the present volume with clinical examples. Although examples of disastrous explosive failures in the holding functions of the therapist are not so easy to come by, as it would be poor public relations to advertise one's disasters, it is nevertheless important to explain in greater detail the interconnections between explosive or schismatic behaviour due to one's narcissistic defences on the one hand, and on the other hand the holding and interpretive work of the mother, therapist, partner, opponent, fellow negotiator, or whoever is saddled with the containing task.

"Something Has Got to Be Done"

A situation that is subjectively reaching the unbearable usually means that a subpersonality is about to be violently projected. Explosive behaviour in therapy almost always means an abrupt termination of the treatment or of some other relationship. Such schismatic or severance behaviour is much more common than violence, murder, suicide, or physically destructive behaviour. Recently I spoke to a young woman, now divorced, who said, "I suddenly realised that we had to part when I found myself rushing upstairs with a knife to stab him." This was after several days of rows and discussions with her husband with no rational solution apparently possible for their marriage difficulties.

Suddenly having an affair, suddenly getting a job in a distant place, suddenly finding oneself too poor, suddenly not having the time, and above all suddenly finding oneself without problems are all ways in which the therapeutic relationship that is not proving adequate as a container can be terminated. All the cases in Chapter Two could have come to this. The atom-bomb dream is a signal that containment of a fundamental conflict is going to be possible, but will need working on.

Seeking treatment by physical therapy, exercises, pastimes, or by psychotherapy are other ways in which negatively toned subpersonalities can be evacuated (i.e., in which feelings can be relieved). The analogy with bodily continence and incontinence is profoundly true. Often in therapy when feelings, good or bad, are becoming overwhelming, relief is obtained by needing to go to the lavatory. Sometimes, too, mounting anger or sexual excitement can also mount or ascend physically in the body until it reaches the chest, voice, or head, when the patient suddenly "blows his top" (explodes, regresses, acts out).

Not Wanting to Know the Truth

The truth, if accepted, can be explosively shattering, but it is more often denied by means of explosive behaviour. The truth is hardly ever *wholly* on one's side. It is almost never wholly in favour of one action as opposed to another. If we have to act or decide, we have to suppress a partial impulse to act in an opposite way or at least in some other, incompatible way. If we are to be efficient, wholehearted, and successful in an act or attitude, we need to suppress conflicting feelings, facts, or facts about feelings to some extent.

Let me invent an everyday example of minor explosions or failures in containment in which the result is an almost spoiled evening out for a married couple who have booked tickets for the opera. The husband is late home from work, late enough to annoy the wife but not late enough to make it at all difficult to get to the opera in good time.

Wife (bristling slightly): "You're late; the soup's been ready for a quarter of an hour." Here the wife opens up an attack on the basis of downtrodden housewife and inconsiderate male.

Husband (stiff and defensive): "Sorry. Smith brought up a point just as I was leaving."

Wife (unmollified, because this explanation is a rationalisation and she wants to expose it): "But you are never late from work on a Wednesday." Here the wife fails to contain the husband's need to avoid the truth and uses her superior psychological insight to begin to penetrate the husband's defences. The wife's persistence, however, strengthens the husband's defensiveness.

Husband: "Smith is new to the job and needed help. That's the only reason it's happened on this particular Wednesday." This is true and the husband genuinely feels quite sure that this is the real reason for his delay. But the husband's "blindness" and lack of contrition annoy the wife and in any case she would be too hurt and humiliated if she let the matter drop.

Wife: "You know it's because you don't like the opera and resent going because I'm so keen on it." This is getting near the heart of the matter. The husband is bored by the opera. He resents the expense, he tends to doze during performances and has even been known to snore, much to the wife's chagrin. He considers the opera pretentious and effeminate. All this is hurtful and offensive to the wife, who loves everything about the opera and defends it as she would defend one of her children. Her direct attack here almost amounts to an explosion. But you have to say that the attack is also a defense of her beloved opera. Her father loved the opera, and she and her father spent many precious evenings there before he died. However, this outburst opens up a whole can of worms – painful unresolved issues between husband and wife which the husband is simply not ready to face.

Husband: "For Christ's sake, don't you psychoanalyze me. I was quite looking forward to this evening. I always enjoy our evenings together. You seem quite determined to spoil everything." It is true that the husband has consciously been looking forward to the evening together. He is aware of his problem with opera, and he has made an effort to suppress his negative feelings and enjoy the evening for his wife's sake as well as his own. But this has left the balance of his defences somewhat precarious. Hence his outburst, which just about qualifies as an explosion. The accusation about the wife "spoiling everything" meant that the wife's reference to the negative side of his feelings is bringing out a flood of negative feelings toward the opera and toward her and so on, which threatens to destroy her as a beloved person in his mind for the duration of the evening.

Wife: "I only want you to admit the truth." This is slightly conciliatory and also excuses her failure to help contain the husband's negative feelings toward her and the opera.

Husband: "Okay. So I don't like the opera. I was making the effort for your sake. So I don't really want to go to the opera. So you can damn well go yourself or take someone else if you can arrange it." This is said with a furious anger that frightens them both into silence. I think all would agree that it is an explosion. It is felt by him to destroy all good feelings about the evening which he has made a genuine effort to build up and defend. He knows that he is reacting childishly and that he does not have any serious intention of not going to the opera with his wife, but no other way of expressing his anger occurs to him.

There are some minutes of silence after that, with both persons trying to think of ways of restoring the situation. The couple end up by dropping the subject, having their meal and simply going off together and enjoying the evening, without apparently noticing what they are doing and without either having to climb down or apologise.

The husband's explosion and the wife's failures to contain the husband's negative feelings about the opera occur because the feelings have not yet been worked through sufficiently for a relatively stable and secure defence to have been established. The husband is having to make an effort to enjoy the opera, and the wife is still slightly resentful of the husband's still having to make that effort. Underlying this are the husband's fear of effeminacy and the wife's fixation on her father, factors making it difficult for them to work together on the opera issue without opening each other up in a dangerous way. Exploding so violently as to prevent their going to the opera together would be antitherapeutic as regards the deeper defences. Loving each other enough to ensure they still go together and enjoy it is a tiny therapeutic advance in the deeper issues.

Going their separate ways in order to avoid upsets of this kind or worse explosions would be the typical normal schismatic behaviour which we all use to make life more peaceful. "Agreeing to differ" avoids explosions, but the healing of differences, which would entail subjective explosions or overt upsets, is necessary if a deeper or richer interaction is to be attempted.

The explosive formula here would be the clashing of unworked-through opposing feelings (dislike of opera, love of wife, etc.) in the husband, a clash which, for her own good reasons, the wife is provoking and exposing. The explosion is contained in the context of practical considerations and of the secure marriage.

A strong and secure self or a strong and secure relationship enables a person to face and experience the physical or narcissistic pain, and the grief of loss or of not having, entailed in healing splits and bringing together subpersonalities who cannot bear to know each other. My loving-husband subpersonality does not wish to know about my hating-husband subpersonality. I do not want to know that my enemy is generous or honest. It is easier to maintain splits, compartments, and categories – black-and-white feelings. It is easier to swallow things and people whole or else reject them as wholes than to chew them, separate their good bits and bad bits, and thus assimilate them as real things or human beings.

In the therapy of patients who have such problems of splitting the self or of splitting up people into good and bad, etc., the task of containing potential explosions and avoiding explosive schisms is very demanding of the skills, the sensitivity, and the heart of the therapist.

A schizophrenic patient of a therapist in supervision with me told her therapist that she could not bear her colleagues at work getting into huddles and talking about her. If they kept on doing that, she would explode. Asked what the delusory accusers were saying, the patient said they were accusing her of being greedy, fat, and selfish. The therapist himself knew her to be greedy, fat, and selfish, so it was perfectly obvious that the accusations came from her own knowledge of what she was like, her own knowledge couched in the worst and most hating of terms, language, and feelings about herself, quite the opposite of therapeutic. The patient had no way of bearing the knowledge that she was greedy, fat, and selfish. The therapist had to help her bear this and also the resulting painful and hurt feelings, the avoidance of which made her behave in a greedy and selfish way, so that she was overly self-indulgent and fat. The words of an interpretation that could include all these considerations were easy enough to work out, once the therapist could feel the pain that made her so and the pain that made her accusatory self so judgmental. Of course, no one could actually feel her pain all that accurately – the therapist will have to learn it gradually, and the patient will have to learn gradually how to teach him, and that will be a longish process. But it is easy to see how an explosion could occur, either in the form of physical violence with her work colleagues, a disastrous quitting from the work scene, rows and accusations about accusations, or, if the therapist was too "honest" or too protective, the rapid termination of therapy. The task of therapy is to bring creatively together the part of her which is lonely, greedy, and selfish and the part of her which hates herself for being so. The explosion occurs when the two parts are pushed too much together or too suddenly together or too cruelly together. The therapist learns quickly enough that none of us can bear too much of the truth about ourselves all at once. The truth can only be borne indirectly, and in relatively small doses at a time.

What therapeutic containment involves in practice with patients whose splitting off and projection of parts of themselves attains explosive intensity is beautifully described by Herbert Rosenfeld in his book, *Impasse and Interpretation* (1987). In the chapter devoted to projective identification and the problem of containment, Rosenfeld tells the story of the sufferings of a woman, her husband, and her therapist as they struggle to cope with a dead-baby subpersonality with whom both patient and husband strongly identify and also strongly project. The sensitive but somewhat inexperienced therapist suffered physical pain and mental anguish in trying to help the patient and eventually did succeed, but only after a tragic explosion when the patient ejected the husband, and the husband committed suicide. Explosions are often brought about in therapy when two opposing subpersonalities are being activated and brought closer together in a situation that cannot be contained. The experienced analyst is much more able to keep his head when violent feelings are being projected into him by the patient, and this is immensely helpful to the patient.

The creative alchemy whereby the opposites are successfully contained and combined is a phenomenon known to Freud and the psychoanalysts who followed him as "the fusion of instincts." The opposing instincts referred to were love and hate, love and death, love and destructiveness, Eros and Thanatos, in fact. Upon the successful fusion of these opposites the structure and organization of a well-functioning mind depend. The undoing of this fusion may occur explosively in the ways I have described, but anger and hatred may, of course, be activated without an actual explosion occurring.

The fusion of instincts may be compared to a successful marriage achieved on the basis of, and following, a tumultuous and passionate love affair. Defusion might well in fact occur if one of the partners came home and found his beloved in bed with another. Murderous explosiveness is to be expected, although the explosion may at first be apparently contained. Regressive defusion is also to be expected following the withdrawal of love by one of the partners. Violent swings from dependent love to murderous loathing are commonplace when containment is failing and the opposites are being unleashed from each other.

The opposites, then, cannot be brought together for integration too suddenly until the necessary containment has been established. Only a certain amount of excitement can be held and bound, otherwise explosion or blackout (inhibition) occur. Before lovers can contain the excitement and passion engendered by gazing into each others' eyes, eyelids are turned down, the gaze averted, neutral conversations used to dilute the excitement, and supporting structures built up prior to the full experience of the potential passionate meeting. A weak container will readily result in the excitement of the awakening love turning to blankness, cut-off, or even hatred. Allowances have to be made for such shyness and waywardness.

The Relief of Exploding

Explosive behaviour and the violent projection of an unwanted or hated part of oneself often follow a period of mounting physical and mental distress. Headaches and other physical feelings, or feelings of unbearable tension, a feeling that something has to happen, all these indicate that explosion is imminent or wanted. If and when the projection or explosive behaviour can no longer be contained and finally occurs, the common experience is one of relief, notwithstanding any feelings of guilt or shame which the action engenders as a secondary matter.

The "successful" projection of a bad subpersonality is naturally accompanied by a feeling of rightness and moral integrity. The external person can now be wholeheartedly hated and fought, or wholeheartedly avoided or denied.

The physical relief of giving vent, exploding, speaking one's mind, blowing one's top, losing one's cool, confronting the other person, and so on, can be enormous. Murders have been known to occur so that this relief can be attained.

The conflict is no longer an internal one between good and bad subpersonalities or pros and cons. The enemy is now wholly outside, and wholehearted behaviour is much more possible.

Keeping the conflict inside and working on it mentally is part of the task of the containing person. The price may be feelings of physical distress, such as the knotting up of the insides, general pain, or specific pains and sensations exactly corresponding with what is being projected into oneself.

Obviously, bursting feelings in the body, chest, or head often precede explosion. Impulses to strangle, climb up the wall, kick, etc., may be felt directly or else experienced in inhibited form as numbness, paralysis, weakness, exhaustion, or sleepiness. The inhibited forms do not, of course, lead directly to explosion at the time.

If I cannot contain a projection, it feels like a projectile of some sort, so that I need to use my defences, or suffer wounds.

The relief of "acting naturally" is not for the therapist because acting naturally usually means escalating the problem. The natural response tends to be the one that the patient's parent had originally and which interacted with that of the patient to produce the explosion, impasse, or complex.

The therapist's main means of avoiding collapse or retaliation, while yet thinking and understanding the projection and the need for it, are experience and the ability to keep thinking and talking and maintain his analytical approach to the patient and toward the interaction. Sympathetic, affirmative feelings toward the projected subpersonality may not be possible at first in the therapist, but usually happen after time and work and are commonly followed by a corresponding change in the patient in his feelings about himself. This affirmative, containing feeling about oneself can be learned from one's parent or one's therapist and incorporated into one's ego or self-concept. When this is achieved by the patient, it is incidentally very heartening for the therapist.

Hopefully the containing function is learned from the parent and from society by example and by their treatment of oneself in childhood. If not, the cost of strengthening the ego in this sense in adulthood is relatively enormous. But it is nevertheless worthwhile because what else can one do? The same applies to group behaviour, including international relationships.

The holding behaviour of the mother toward the infant's destructiveness, her holding and facilitating attitudes toward the infant's instincts and activities, determine the mature person's holding and facilitating attitudes toward the corresponding parts of himself or herself. If the mother is rigid, the infant's holding characteristics will tend to be rigid. The child will develop a rigid character structure, like an explosive inside contained in a rigid armouring or container. This is a common cause of explosiveness, breakdown, breakup, sudden breakthroughs, and so on. The individual develops into a walking explosion waiting to be triggered off.

We have, in technical language, different sorts of potential explosiveness—schizoid, paranoid, obsessional, etc.—depending on the character defences—defences against alienated parts of oneself—which are in operation. A person with a schizoid personality has often not developed the requisite character structure to take responsibility for his violence, which is a bodily need and a bodily and psychic necessity. The paranoid individual needs to project his bad feelings onto others and is in hardly any better position to take responsibility for, contain, and turn into constructive channels his own evil side, the mote in his own eye. Of these character types, only the explosive rigid character is in some position to begin to take responsibility for his own violence and anger, which is fantasized as explosive bad/good bodily contents. No amount of preaching or exhortation can alter this state of affairs. The creative holding that can lead on to self-realization with self-discipline, like the mother's influence on the child, is a lengthy and sustained relationship. In adults it is more lengthy because adults learn so much more slowly than children. But in our adult patients we find that anything good that did happen to them in their infancy and childhood can be used and built upon, and the bad things and the missed good things can be grieved about and a melting and softening can take place in the violence or hardness, given time.

I am not suggesting that good mothers and psychotherapists are saints. Naturally one quite often feels that way – that our infant, our adolescent, or our patient would try or exhaust the patience of a saint, and that our own patience, tolerance, good will, and ability to continue and remain reliable are in doubt. Fortunately, at least in psychotherapy, our patients can sometimes themselves adopt a patient, helpful, encouraging, or supportive and reliable role at least for a time, when our own resources run out. The same is true even of very young infants. One is grateful to them at such moments.

The holding capacities of the people who care for the child will to some extent determine the way in which aggressive and other instinctual tendencies are contained by that person when he grows up. It will also determine to some extent how containers are perceived and used by him. The house, the family, the automobile, the group, the law, the state, all are endowed with containing properties. One's attitude toward these concrete and symbolic objects and institutions can vary enormously according to what one is projecting onto them, of course.

We must not forget that houses can actually be thick-walled, thin-walled, have poor foundations, and so on, and that the family, the state, the authorities can actually be chaotic, despotic, repressive, or whatever. Our attitudes toward these things are not *all* projections resulting from childhood experience, any more than the patient's experience of his therapist is all distortion and transference projection. In therapy, and no doubt in politics, it can be disastrous to have one set of rules for the container and another for the contained. For example, to assume that the therapist has no unconscious, never projects his madness or his badness onto his patient, or indeed that he is in no part of himself mad or bad, would make it difficult or impossible to help patients who could not make allowances for, or tolerate and contain, the therapist's badness or madness. It would put too much strain on many patients to make these assumptions, as many analysts used to do and as some still do.

Yet such omnipotent assumptions about oneself are to some extent necessary in professional and even more in political life. We would hesitate to employ an attorney or a soldier who did not seem to be on our side and who impartially saw both sides of any argument in which we were engaged. And the same is true of the politicians (and to a lesser degree the diplomats) whom we employ on our behalf. Just as at some stages of regression our patient needs to feel that we are on his side, some social groups in a similar state of regression need their leaders to be deluded and paranoid in a fighting way, whereas other groups might be more healthy, mature, and fair-minded.

The Reality and Use of Power in Containment

It is important in the building up of one's character as an infant that our parents have a vast preponderance of real power over us, and that this is the more so, the younger and more uncontained we are in ourselves. A temper tantrum in a child of between one and two years of age is a formidable event, difficult enough for the mother to cope with fairly, firmly, and lovingly. But a similar violent eruption in a grown-up, physically powerful adult is another matter, when physical injury and great damage to property are a real possibility. Even the six-or seven-year-old child can cause painful injury to the therapist at times.

It is important for our self-confidence and for our ability to trust and to love that the demands of reality and of the external world keep pace with and do not outpace our own capacities to give up our childish fantasies and infantile omnipotence. It is important that our parents and later parental figures do not presume that we have more responsibility and more social realism than we actually have.

The mother or beloved other person, for the child who is still at the paranoid stage of development, or for the paranoid subpersonality in all of us, becomes a hateful witch or murderess when she is perceived as withdrawing herself or her love or the things that symbolize her love. We wish her dead even if we do not act in a hostile way, and we are greatly reassured later, when our rage has subsided, by the fact that she is still intact and that she still loves us. If our murderous selves were omnipotent (for example, if we were omnipotent tyrants), we should have no opportunity to discover the external reality of others and their needs and wishes. A mother who is too inflexible or unrealistic in her expectations of her child damages the omnipotent self of the child, whereas a mother who is too compliant, not firm enough, damages the realistic self of the child. A creative dialogue between internal and external reality is the most important prerequisite for mental health and social behaviour.

The containing, facilitating, and frustrating behaviour of the mother toward the child's impulses and wishes is incorporated into the child's character and determines the child's attitudes toward his inner needs, perceptions, and intuitions. If the mother is experienced as a positive and supportive person, her containing and facilitating attitudes to particular sorts of behaviour are likely to be incorporated into the personality in a positive sense. But if the mother is a negative figure, her attitudes may be negatively incorporated, for example, as standards and ideals to be avoided or opposed.

Volcanoes, Fountains, Eggs, and Bombs—Different Relationships Between Container and Contained

An infant subjected to rigid standards of right and wrong in relation to, for example, his bodily impulses and instincts, is likely to develop a rigid character structure. Standards and principles, mostly taken for granted and not necessarily conscious by any means, have the defensive function of keeping subjectively bad or dangerous contents (bodily impulses experienced as coming from deep inside the self) in check. Illness, fatigue, heightened sexual excitement, the suggestions of naughty peers, etc., all tend to heighten the explosive charge – to increase the pressure from within and the strength of the defences. Early psychoanalytical theory postulated an id deep within, a superego incorporated from parental prohibitions, and an ego attempting to mediate and decide between the two, but on the whole tending to oppose or postpone instinctual gratification.

The model of the psyche chosen by an individual or group is a reflection of the predominant state of affairs, the predominant relationship between the ego (more accurately, the subjectively experienced I) and the nonego (not-I) part of the personality. This predominating model of the psyche may be represented by the differing images of the volcano (hot and dangerous emotions seeking release), the fountain (creative, life-giving forces seeking to enrich consciousness and needing harnessing), the egg (new life needing to emerge and break through a rigid conscious attitude), and the bomb (strong internal forces and strong repressions and rigid standards). Of course, other models are relevant at various times, and no model is permanent and unchanged. The model is changing from day to day in most ordinary individuals, usually without being consciously perceived or represented. Nevertheless we discern a predominating self-image or self-representation of these and other kinds (e.g., the plant or tree, the lake, various animal-human interactions) which expresses at any one era of a person's life his prevailing attitude toward his unconscious. In therapy we have to devote a good deal of attention to this relationship between I and not-I. An attitude of hatred and/or fear toward his unconscious parts (in practice, his behaviour), e.g., a situation in which he perceives his insides as volcanic or explosive, has to be modified by analysis before therapy can become safe and creative. The analysis of the explosive-prone personality in which the image is that of aggressive contents with a rigid body armour or containing shell usually involves the analysis of anal impulses and of the defences against them. The contents are felt to be bad, dangerous, and morally contemptible ("shitty"). They represent an attack on the morally superior parent, whose contempt is incorporated into the rigid armouring against the dangerous "shitty" impulses wanting to get out.

In society, of course, the dangerous, despised contents are usually projected onto "inferior" castes, repressed sections of the community, necessitating increasingly rigid protection and armouring and an increasingly explosive social situation. We have a combination of consciously high and elitist standards and unconsciously shitty behaviour that characterizes the anally defended, potentially explosive self-model and society structure. The self-model of the members of a social group and the social structure of the group bear a close relationship with each other. Usually it is similar, sometimes complementary, certainly in some degree. Utopias and idealized self-models are closely related, as are also actual social structures and "realistic" self-images.

The dangerous, despised content is often reversed and transformed into a treasure or holy kernel. In this situation the explosive and despised kernel goes with the idealized, protected kernel – we do not encounter the one without the denial of the other in practice. So when we have a community owing allegiance to a model of society with a holy treasured kernel and strong defences, we know from therapeutic work that we are dealing with an unconscious kernel of shitty, despised, and dangerous repressed pregenital impulses and actual behaviour.

The rigid shell and explosive contents, whether we take this as a model of society, of the family, or of the (resulting) individual self-models of the members of that family or that society, presupposes a lack of communication between contents and container. The fountain model is one of communication and fertilisation. In therapy we usually feel wary about conversions, reversals, and breakthroughs and feel happier when we have a fountain situation in which we have a steady flow of intercommunication between consciousness and unconscious material and a capacity on the part of the I to cope with the emerging contents. Repression or avoidance, interlarded with periodic clashes and confrontations, characterize the explosive individual and no doubt the explosive society.

CHAPTER 6

Trees, Fountains, Eggs, Volcanoes, and Bombs

Symbols of Renewal or Breakthrough of Varying Degrees of Violence

At the beginning of therapy, a patient of mine dreamt of a tiny plant appearing in a concrete pavement. Slowly it grows and slowly the concrete cracks and yields to the inexorable force of life.

It is not difficult to understand that, as the therapist, I would be encouraged by such a dream, particularly in view of its appearing at the beginning of our working relationship. Nor will the reader be surprised that the subsequent progress of treatment was steady and slow, and that it depended on the therapist and patient being in contact with each other, for when the contact was interrupted, the plant lost its vigour.

Another patient, after a period of therapy, dreamt of a system of underground waterways. The engineer in charge of the flowing waters was the man she loved. When I asked her to do a painting about the dream, she painted fountains issuing from the underground cisterns, and as she did the painting, she experienced living energy swooshing upwards and outwards in and from her body. Following this dream, several months of intense creative energy flowed from her unconscious into her consciousness – dreams, poems, paintings, psychic energy in many forms.

Another patient, more fearful of the energies within, might dream of a volcano in danger of erupting. The therapist would then suspect that fears preventing contact with the life forces within must first be understood and respected before it is safe to do things which increase the

100

internal pressures. Anger, destructive feelings, uncontainable passions are the emotions suggested by the dream image of the lava, which threatens to erupt and destroy the mother earth or the town or the people nearby.

Again, the image of the egg, with the new life within, occurs repeatedly in therapy. The shell may be too thin, or too thick; the egg may be protected, or possibly more often not protected or accidentally or purposely smashed by the parental figures whose instinct and function would, one imagines, be to protect and hatch the egg.

Tree, plant, fountain, egg, stream of living water, and above all, child, as we shall see, are all obviously symbols of new life within. Whether we are religious or not, and whatever our religion, we all worship these forms, unless we are too ill, or too depressed, hardened, or embittered. They naturally evoke our love and hope, unless these natural reactions are being inhibited by temporary or permanent pathology.

In practice one finds that the dream of the healthy plant, the unpolluted water, the thriving baby means that the dreamer is able to react positively to the external plant, baby, or whatever. So there is a correlation between a positive response to the external object and the occurrence of the inner symbol in its positive form. There is a similar correlation between a negative response to external objects and the occurrence of the inner symbol in a negative form.

Of course, none of us is completely healthy, or healthy all the time. There are almost always difficulties, defects, or dangers threatening or preventing the new life, the new flow of energy. These difficulties have to be understood and worked on as representing real external and internal resistances to the emergence of the new and potentially dangerous and endangered life. A harsh or critical parent with withering words may, in the past, have withered the young plant. But the dream, if it occurs in the course of therapy, means that the withering is still going on. The withering parent is present in patient or therapist or in the interaction, and it is only when the patient gets in touch with the withering parent in himself and can feel remorseful about this part of himself, as well as forgiving this subpersonality in himself, that the thriving plant or baby can emerge.

Where the precious potential life is symbolized by the egg, the shell may be felt as some kind of barrier between oneself and the outer world. The barrier is obviously necessary because it is needed to protect the embryo within. The shell prevents too much emotional contact.

Too much or too direct contact can be threatening or overwhelming. But the egg image suggests that it is only a matter of time before more direct contact can be achieved.

Taking the container or protective shell one stage further, it is important to understand the container as fulfilling a holding, maternal function in relation to the vulnerable, infantile, precious, emerging aspects of the self. If the container is rigid and cannot abandon its protective role when new life and energies and free movements need to burst forth, then the secure, safe haven and container become an intolerable prison, inside which only half a life is permissible. Yet the person inside the prison is usually unable to dare to break out. Being in prison has its compensations in terms of avoidance of dangers and responsibilities.

As in the case of the withering parent, the rigid, imprisoning container-parent, as it is functioning all the time and particularly in the present, has to be recognized, understood, and forgiven as part of oneself and one's own defences. For example, meanness and fear of loss of the precious loved one may be the part of oneself that is preventing one's own escaping and bursting forth. In other words, the prison is one's own rigidity, one's own need to control and organize, which is preventing the living, energetic subpersonality from making deeper contacts with life outside and life within.

The prison image is, of course, not merely an image but is the living everyday existential experience of the person having the image. If I dream of being in prison, it does not mean that I always feel imprisoned all the time – the dream may reflect feelings that were not fully felt during the waking hours and can be related to feelings that are specific to certain situations. But frequent dreams of imprisonment would obviously reflect a recurrent or continuing problem of a rigid, life-preventing aspect of the self projected onto authority figures.

It is not difficult to extrapolate one stage further and understand the bomb experience, the bomb image, in the same way. Here the life within, the energies within, have an even more negative relationship with the containing, parental, controlling, inhibiting functions. Only a revolution, a breakthrough, a reversal of some kind, perhaps a religious conversion of a tables-turning kind, an orgy or orgasm of destructiveness, can now liberate the life energies within, so strong are the inhibitory forces.

The explosive force depends upon both the amount of energy within and the strength and rigidity of the container. These factors vary, not entirely independently of each other. Both depend on the degree of vitality in the person concerned and on the strength and force of the instincts in that person. The spirit can be crushed and withered; depression and apathy can replace anger and tension. The phenomenon responsible for a certain degree of correlation between the energetic charge of the contents and the strength of the container is the finding that ultimately both the libidinal impulse involved and the psychic counterforce preventing its expression derive from the same instinctive roots. For example, anal eroticism and puritanism are, at one level, exactly opposed to each other within the psyche and, at a deeper level, both are powered by the same instinctive impulse.

Although I say that apathy, depression, and chronic loss of vitality may reduce the explosive charge, apparently permanently, we find that in many cases vitality slowly returns during therapy, almost invariably at first in a negative form (which was the reason it was alienated originally). Bodily vitality may return in the form of pain and hypochondriasis; depression, when it first begins to lift, gives place to irritability and outbursts of temper; anxiety and timidity give place to bravado and bullying, and so on. The therapist, and more especially relatives and friends, doubt the worthwhileness of the whole therapeutic endeavour and of its effects, at least in the short run. Parents may withdraw their children from therapy at this stage. Newly elected liberal governments are tempted to put back the lid of social repression. Yet explosions are not uncommonly a sign of life at this stage.

The awakening spirit has been dormant or has been alienated because of a negative relationship, a negative interaction, with the containing or holding forces (usually carried by the parental parts of the self). Positive parenting instincts see the contained life as baby, plant, a person to be nurtured and encouraged and validated. A negative parenting instinct will see the child part as a cancer or devouring monster, as monstrously deformed, rubbish, or a disgusting or chaotic threatening creature. It is important not to be complacent about these negative aspects of the inner vitality – these negative feelings are, as a rule, not at all unjustified, and the therapist, too, has to struggle with them as the negative infant in the patient dares to emerge and test the real good will of the therapist.

The words and images we use to refer to the hope of renewal and the life forces within (or without, at the disposal of the deity) can be divided into two categories: first, those referring to a precious object or person that represents potential life and has to be protected and nurtured; and second, images of force and energy of a more or less omnipotent character. The two aspects cannot in clinical practice be separated, any more than God the Son and God the Holy Ghost can be separated in the final analysis. The point most relevant here is that immense psychic energies are potentially involved and that we relate negatively to the infantile part of ourselves (with its omnipotent energy) at our peril.

In some kinds of therapy the emotional release caused by breakthrough of defences is sought and encouraged. In abreactive therapies the intense emotion of the traumatic memory is produced by encouraging regression and increasing the intensity of the situation, sometimes by asking the patient to replace his normal defensive or avoiding attitude toward the emotion with one of acceptance or nonavoidance. Sometimes drugs are used to stimulate the emotions or weaken the inhibitory forces in the brain. Similar techniques and similar results are obtained in the climax of the evangelical religious conversion and in the "rebirthing" and "primal scream" therapies. Such emotional climaxes may also occur without any outside agency, especially in people ready for a reversal of their normal bias or outworn persona, and in patients with epilepsy, particularly temporal lobe epilepsy.

After the climax the patient may be especially open and vulnerable to others, as the avoidance and rejection reactions of the personality have been temporarily swamped and inactivated. A person in this state is particularly susceptible to the implantation of new notions and attitudes quite different from his previous ones. At these times, a person is particularly close to God or, to put it another way, is in particularly intimate contact with the part of himself normally kept at a distance from his feeling of I.

To obtain a vivid impression of what this state feels like, the reader might do worse than read Dostoyevski's first-hand account of it in his book, *The Idiot*. (Like Prince Myshkin in this book, Dostoyevski was epileptic.) Repeated epileptic seizures (that is, repeated ruptures of the I-non-I defences) had changed the prince into a Christ-like figure whose avoidance responses were virtually nonexistent. He was unable to respond in a nonloving way even to very harmful and dangerous situations and people, so he was prey to the most painful and intolerable experiences. He was viable only because he was protected by others, as a child is, and when he lost this protection, he soon came to grief in a hopeless stupor. (Incidentally, this sort of behaviour is shown by some animals when the temporal lobes of the brain have been removed. These animals respond affectionately even to very injurious stimuli. It is as if the repeated overwhelming of the defences produces a temporary paralysis of the temporal lobes, which function to enable one to avoid too intense stimulation either from without or within.)

To return to the prince, he was very close both to heaven and to hell. Moments of intense awareness, of the highest mode of existence, flashes of dazzling illumination, yet of harmonious joy and calm, were his. He knew these moments were associated with his disease, but he decided at last, "What if it is a disease? What does it matter that this is an abnormal tension, if the result, the moment of sensation, remembered and analyzed in a state of health, turns out to be harmony and beauty brought to their highest point of perfection, and gives a feeling, undivined and undreamt of till then, of completeness, proportion, reconciliation, and an ecstatic and prayerful fusion in the highest synthesis of life?" (Dostoyevski 1871, p. 263).

I have had patients who, when they came to therapy, were ripe for such experiences, involving a radical change of the personality in which previously unlived parts of the self demand to be heard and integrated. The therapeutic problem is one of protection, and of learning, with the patient, to keep the experience and the flow of inspiration within safe limits, to avoid actual fits and stuporous incapacity, and to help the patient cope with his life problems while not interfering too much with the life-giving and life-transforming experiences which the patient will remember with gratitude for the rest of his life.

But normally the therapist prefers the fountain to the egg, the volcano, or the bomb. A fairly steady, even a desultory flow of infantile material or archetypal experience can be more easily integrated with the conscious, normal I of the patient than an outbreak or explosion. The value of the previously alienated parts of the self is, by this means, more likely to be acquired and not lost. It is a matter of working with the patient toward an accepting, and at the same time objective and critical, attitude toward the parts of the personality previously alienated and experienced as not-self, rather than being totally (and often merely temporarily) overwhelmed by the alien subpersonality or subpersonalities.

Tree, fountain, egg, and bomb are all aspects of the divine child, and the divine child is an aspect of the child subpersonality in us. The child subpersonality, at least the child image and the child we adore in reality, has to do primarily with the parenting feelings and instincts we all possess. It is the parent in me that adores, protects, and worships the image or reality of the child, including the divine child, and who sees the new life and new potential in the developing life of the self, and who can therefore nurture and protect it and, like a gardener, be glad of its growth. If it is the infantile part of the self that contains the new potential, it is the parenting part of the self that sees this and that can hold, contain, potentiate, and feed this new self.

The reason I link all these symbols of the emerging new self together to some degree is not at all theoretical, but empirical. It stems from the fact that, in therapeutic practice and in the imagination and the dream experience of one's patients, those symbols are to some extent interchanged and intertransformed. A patient dreams of a jewel that explodes, but when asked to meditate on it and paint it, she draws something that looks like a tree, and in subsequent paintings it changes into a definite tree which is also a fountain and is also an upsurging bodily feeling and impulse. In some ways the unconscious has little respect for the clock time we use for boiling eggs and catching trains. A growing plant, a fountain, a fireworks display, and an exploding jewel have a great deal in common, particularly if we slow them down or speed them up or take time itself out of the image.

Continence, in the sense of ability to contain, and mental capacity stretch the apparent time scale of experience. Premature ejaculation is a psychic phenomenon not confined to the narrowly sexual sphere. The explosion represents the shortest possible time scale of the growth of excitement. On the other hand, there are some experiences, for example, some of the experiences of true love or of religious revelation, which last forever as living experiences. Time may stand still: death is conquered, immortality is experienced.

Increased awareness slows down apparent time. This can be achieved by training the attention, so that the more-conscious person becomes aware of emotional changes occurring one after another in a meaningful sequence. He can, when awareness is achieved, modify or change the pattern or the response. Talking about feelings may help this sort of development of self-awareness and responsibility of action. I do not know if the slowing of apparent time produced by hallucinogenic changes, which some musicians used to say they found helpful in the performance of rapid complex movements and the achievement of increased extempore creativity, depends on a related neurophysiological mechanism or not. Hypnosis and trance states, in so far as they may enable attention and awareness to be focused and pinpointed, may also stretch out or contract the experience of apparent time. Finally, going to sleep, dozing, or succumbing to anaesthesia may completely change the apparent duration of both external events or internal sequences. I remember dreaming of an alarm clock bell ringing while I was under a general anaesthetic in the dentist's chair. As I awoke, the individual pings of the alarm bell sound slowed down more and more, until, when I fully awoke, they became the slow pings of a tap dripping into water, the actual source of the sound. Consciousness enables us to separate and discriminate between events and stimuli, whereas unconsciousness pushes events toward each other so that eventually events may compress and elide to the point of being experienced as an explosion overwhelming consciousness altogether. If we can only experience God as an explosion, it is because we have not attuned ourselves enough to this sort of numinous experience.

This is not an argument that hallucinogenic drugs should, or indeed that they should not, be used to increase one's awareness of the deeper truths. There are many ways of activating the inner voice. How intently and seriously one listens is another matter. It is like the distinction between daydreaming and creative imagination or constructive action. I have no experience of the serious use of hallucinogens as part of a training in spiritual awareness, but I have no doubt that this could be one possible path, in the right trained and disciplined hands.

Seizures Replaced by Painful Memories During Therapy

Many years ago a woman in her late twenties came to me for psychotherapy. She was suffering from attacks of drowsiness and vomiting, screaming spells in which snakes and other horrors tormented her, and prolonged periods of dissociated, regressed behaviour during which she seemed to be living in a child's world, when it was clear at times she was reliving bits of childhood experience in a rather fragmented way, as often happens in the delirious utterings and behaviour of sick and febrile patients. At this time, she had an electroencephalograph "consistent with the diagnosis of temporal lobe epilepsy," and suitable medication had been prescribed by a neuropsychiatric colleague. She had refused to have anything to do with the medication insisting that she must integrate, own, and derive value from all these experiences. She insisted on seeking a psychotherapeutic approach and, in spite of only being able to see me once or twice a week, succeeded in her aims after about three years, having worked through a great deal of highly emotionally charged experience and through very powerful feelings about the therapy and about me as therapist and as real person.

My reason for describing briefly the therapy of this patient is to illustrate how explosive phenomena and apocalyptic visions and experiences, when faced courageously with or without the help of a therapist or another person, can gradually give place to bearable actual memories and to more loving relationships with real people.

She came into therapy because her previous way of living was no longer possible for her. Her life had reached a crisis point, and she had to find a more real self in order to carry on with life. She used me as mother, midwife, and baby in the birth of this new-and-old self. I am not romanticizing but simply describing her actual experiences during therapy, not merely her daydreams but shattering bodily and emotional experiences and events.

A vivid and colourful person, she had had a turbulent childhood and an even more turbulent adult life before coming to the dead end, when the only thing left was the breakdown leading to therapy.

As a child she experienced her mother as cold, intellectual, and reliable, her father as warm, flamboyant, and religiose. She felt he was sexually frustrated and rather overdemonstrative toward his daughters, especially the patient, who felt herself to be his favourite. He would often thrash her out of sheer frustration, for example, if she had not learnt a Bible passage perfectly. The thrashings would quickly be followed by maudlin reconciliations which she found contemptible as well as somewhat endearing.

She led a barefoot tomboy life on the family homestead, where her father was cruel to the animals and made her help him with slaughtering and mating and mucking out. She was sexually abused on several occasions by older boys and men, all of which incidents she kept secret from her parents and repressed until the time of her breakdown and therapy.

She became an art student and a commercial artist and led a bohemian life in the city, during the course of which she made a disastrous marriage to an inadequate, degenerate man by whom she had two boys. The marriage broke down and was followed by many affairs and part-time prostitution. By her late twenties, she felt that her life had come to a cul-de-sac. She lost her sexual appetite and soon went into the anorexic and acutely neurotic state in which she came to me. Her periods had ceased, she was grossly emaciated, and was being looked after by her mother and father, who were also coping with the grandchildren.

Readers will be aware that the task of therapy is usually to encourage the unconscious to yield its secrets, to support the new child until it is strong enough to get along on its own, and to interpret apparently unadaptive behaviour patterns in terms of unconscious feelings and habits. In her case, everything erupted or exploded in the acute breakdown and the task of therapy was to support her wish to understand all this emotion and terrifying apocalyptic experience and to help heal the profound split and warfare between the two halves of herself which she portrayed concretely in her initial drawings as the right and left halves of herself.

In chapter 2 I showed how, very often, atom-bomb dreams symbolize a clash between opposing parts of the personality. The opposition and the clash are not experienced consciously but are represented in the dream. In the patient I am describing here, however, the opposition and the conflict were not only conscious but were experienced as an unbearable split in the self. One of the ways she verbalized her aim in therapy was that she had to bring together the split halves of herself. She experienced a split in several ways. At some times, she felt the two sides of her mind or brain were splitting apart, and at these times headaches or splitting sensations in the head occurred. At other times, she felt the split as a division between lust and love, or as a war between body and mind, between body and spirit; sometimes, bizarrely, as a conflict between the two sides of her body. At still other times, the battle was between her grown-up self and her infantile self. Finally, the split and the opposition were felt to be between the lively, vital part of herself and the dark, depressed part. In short, a war between moral and emotional opposites had erupted within her. It felt like a cosmic battle in which the main battleground was her own body, experienced as a microcosm and as the cosmos itself.

All these experiences she attempted to draw and paint, so that they were conveyed very vividly to me in various ways, and my participation was very real.

However, I mostly felt like a privileged and somewhat awed witness to a profoundly integrative process in her. I would guess that my respect for her and for what was happening to her was a source of some support, and indeed of satisfaction to her, after her initial suspicions about my "rubbishing" her, as she was wont to expect of men.

For the first few weeks I encouraged her to go with whatever feeling was there, not only during sessions but also when painting or writing or simply experiencing between sessions. Although I was not providing much emotional holding, I felt her to be a basically healthy, indeed remarkable, person who might well be able to experience and integrate a great intensity of mental and emotional content. However, we were idealizing each other at this time, allowing the regression to go too far. Her drawings became more wild, fragmented, and unorganized, mere motor expressions, mere scraps of abreacted infancy, mere explosions or smears. At the same time she became more and more childlike while doing them, until the point came when she had to retire to bed in one of her semistuporous infantile states and be nursed like a child for several days. When she recovered, she was very properly angry with me for letting her go too far and too fast. I acknowledged my quantitative misjudgment, and together we set about monitoring the intensity of flow of the explosion/volcano/fountain so that it became much less the explosion and much more the fountain. She learned to regulate her imaginative and creative activity so that maximum value was derived from the therapy sessions. Some sort of routine developed, and routine itself helps to contain and make safe. Poetry, painting, and imaginative and bodily experience outside the sessions were limited to what was safe and practical, depending on family demands and family resources. This material and dream material was brought into the therapy session, where discussion tended to bring a reliving of a childhood experience, often leading to screaming or other intense vocalisation. This childhood experience was the repressed content; the core of the complex being worked through at the time, around which the poetic, artistic, and bodily experiences were circulating, so that they came as near to the repressed memory as was bearable for her at that time, given the amount of holding she was experiencing. Following the intense abreactive phase of the session, there was a partial collapse, followed by a quiet period before she left, when we would comment briefly on what had occurred. The work would be interrupted if, for example, I behaved too much like her father or her mother. My behaviour, the transference onto me of her childhood attitudes, and the blocks and misunderstandings resulting therefrom then had to be sorted out before the main work could be resumed.

For several months the content seemed to centre around the coming to life of her body and bodily experience. There were vivid experiences of giving birth and being born, of her body as the earth, the cosmos, as Christ being on fire on the cross, and of strong sexual excitement with oneness with nature. Her memories of being taught whole passages of the book of the Revelation by her eccentric and overstimulating father would be expressed in vivid paintings of her visions and experiences, and the painting would further stimulate memories and bodily experiences, hypochondriacal, revelatory, disinhibiting, and terrifying. Her own experiences of giving birth were relived in a tender and moving way, experiences she had not "properly" had at the time, given the degraded nature of her relationships.

This first phase was necessary in order to establish a close working partnership combining intimacy and respect, involvement and professional continence. Birth and rebirth experiences, after all, combine the opposites of merging with and separation from the mother, whether the mother is experienced as the unconscious, the body, or the therapist— being all three at different times.

After this there were other major areas of therapeutic work. The disinhibition of the creative use of her hands and their growing strength and mobility followed fantasies and dreams of her hands sprouting like vegetation. The bladder was another important psychological area. Specific childhood traumatic memories of rape and of her discovery of the suicide by hanging of a neighbour were relived after weeks of work in which poems, drawings, bodily fragments of memory, all circulated closer and closer around the core of the complex until the core was finally revealed in a climax of raw emotion and behaviour during therapy sessions.

This actual psychotherapeutic work is an example of how the bomb, the volcano, the fountain, the tree or the world tree, the child or the divine child are all images of how the unconscious creative and growing core can present itself to consciousness as well as how the unconscious (the nonego) can actually in a sense behave in relation to consciousness or the ego. It can erupt, explode, flow, be born, or grow like a tree encompassing underworld, world, and upper world, past, present, and future. The unlived part of the self—the complex, the repressed memory—is unlived or alienated because the relationship between that part of the self and the ego is negative. The emerging bit of unconsciousness is inevitably experienced—imaged—in this negative way because that is why it was alienated or repressed in the first place in the history of the individual or the history of the social group. Intimately related to death-and-rebirth fantasies and experiences, these symbols are the stuff of the world's living religions throughout the millennia.

Parallel with the longing for refreshment and rebirth reflected in these images of the unrealized self, there has been the need throughout the ages for these new, primitive energy forms to be contained within mental structures, understood by the mind, and kept within safe limits. Otherwise madness or explosive destructive social changes ensue. Just as in classical times a new city tended to be planned or thought of in terms of a circle, or a square, with a radial or quadrate street plan, so the new life has to be guarded and prevented from destroying outside things by structures of ritual, habit, and dogma, and by limiting it to a definite location in space or time or both. Of course, these necessities may be carried too far, so that the new life is suffocated or gradually strangled; or else it may break out in violent paroxysms and spasms. The picture frame, the stage of the theatre, the sacred precinct, the university, the religious ritual, the holy day are all ways of channeling and disciplining the potentially dangerous new life energy. The artist is one conduit for new life. Being both bellwether and scapegoat, he is a specialist in communicating with the unconscious or at least in relaying its oracular statements to the rest of us. He may not at all understand what he is doing and perhaps he *has* to abandon understanding as his primary aim before he can express "himself" (actually the communal unconscious) sincerely and passionately.

The Bomb Image and the Cancer Image as Negative Aspects of the Unrealized Self

It seems a far cry from the divine child image to the cancer image – as far as from the divine egg to the atom bomb. The divine egg gives rise to the world or the world saviour; the atom bomb hatches the death of the world. The cancer is a malignant, growing parasite which destroys the parent body, whereas the divine child brings light and goodness.

The fairy tale of Beauty and the Beast is relevant here. The Beast, when loved, turns into the prince-lover. You might say that, in an exactly analogous way, the cancer, when "loved," turns into the divine child, and the atom bomb, when loved, turns into the cosmic egg. But what would this mean? There is some truth here, as well as some nonsense. It is a very important practical matter. It is just not adequate to say that beauty is in the eye of the beholder, because it is not entirely or merely in the eye of the beholder. There are a thousand ways in which the way a thing or person is seen can transform that person or thing and many levels of experience at which this is true. In other words, the beholder may to some degree exert an influence on the beheld.

In the same way, if the unrealized self is seen as dangerous, e.g., as an atom bomb or a cancer, by the conscious I, we are up against a very real problem which is not just a psychological one. We can attempt to psychologize and say: "It is just a matter of how you regard the unrealized part of yourself. If you fear it, it will present itself as a tender infant or a miraculous vision of life as it could be." In a way, this is all quite true, but completely inadequate. It is inadequate for the Christian to be told to love his enemies, and it is just as inadequate for the modern person who fears, and who is nevertheless producing, cancer and atom bombs to be told to take a positive attitude to the alien not-I part of himself. What *is* adequate will be discussed in later chapters.

A normal person distinguishes between an imaginary cancer, or a cancer phobia, and the real thing. But if real cancers can be influenced for the better by imagining them and working mentally with such images, then we cannot say that a cancer image has nothing to do with real cancer. We are very ignorant about such questions. But let us confine ourselves to discussing the image without claiming to understand its relationship with the real thing.

A young man I was working with was struggling with an overpossessive mother both as a real problem and as a psychological problem in himself. He dreamt that for once he dared to express himself and tell his mother the truth about things and in particular about the way he felt about things in general and his parents in particular. The trouble was that every time he began to tell it as it was, his mother developed a cancer of the face, which got bigger the more freely the son expressed his anger and his true feelings.

By this time in therapy, he was beginning to realize that his depression and his fears were to do with bottling up all this cancer-producing anger in order to protect his mother. Knowing this, the problem of working out something with the real mother yet remained a very real and virtually insurmountable one. But at least he was able to forgive himself and her for not being able to resolve it.

If the atom-bomb image is usually to do with the feared coming-together of opposites in the psyche, it helps to know that a change in attitude toward the clash could transform the fear into a revelation, but it does not help all that much. Talk is cheap, and such a pronouncement is mere talk. The building up of strength and capacity to the point where the union of the relevant opposites can be creatively contained may take a great deal of work. It may take generations for a social group to perform the necessary assimilative work, but it is more common for the dark one of the pair of opposites to remain projected for centuries. That is, perhaps, until now.

CHAPTER 7

Atom Bomb and Divine Child

Regression and Responsibility

I first wish to restate the biological basis of the child and the parent subpersonalities and how they change in the course of therapy. The child subpersonality is of special importance as explosion is a special form of birth; the parent subpersonality is important because of the role of the container and the one who takes responsibility for the new life that results from the meeting of opposites.

Subpersonalities are the working units that make up the dynamic structure of the mind and the total personality. They manifest themselves as prevalent ways of behaving or as commonly occurring dream symbols. If we had innate, fixed instincts, we would have uniform, fixed subpersonalities – they would be two ways of speaking of the same thing. We do not have inborn, unchanging, instinctual behaviour patterns, but we have patterns of feeling, emotion, and behaviour that serve as the bases for biologically essential, adaptable, and virtually universal kinds of human interaction. The various possible interactions between caring, holding, and nurturing parents and dependent/independent, obeying/rebelling, respecting/despising children are not exactly instinctual – they are endlessly variable in one sense, far from stereotypes. Yet, fortunately for the biological success of the human race, we are genetically endowed with parenting wishes and feelings that can be adapted to social conditions, and we are also genetically endowed with the needing, depending, and trusting wishes and feelings that, when we are babies and children, enable us to append to our parents and make it easy or at least possible for our parents to look after us as long as necessary. In life, as in psychotherapy, the parent and child subpersonalities in their protean forms are the most important ones. Second in importance, perhaps, are those pertaining to sex and mating.

Naturally, babies and babylike creatures, things, and images are what cause us to feel parental and behave in a parental way. Feeling parental causes us to say "Oh, how adorable," etc., and want to hold and care for the baby or babylike creature. A picture or dream image of a baby or babylike creature evokes the same sort of response in us. The child archetype and the child image, in other words, have primarily to do with one's parental "instincts." This is as true for the dream image as it is for our waking responses to a real child. The real parent, the real parent-figure, and the dream parent-figure evoke our child instincts, our dependency needs, and so on. They evoke respect, obedience, trust, dependence, etc., or their opposites (rebellion, contempt, etc.).

Our parental feelings, or lack of them, are in fact not purely instinctual. Although based on innate potentialities, they are very largely dependent on what we have learnt from our own parents and parent-figures, on how we have been parented. How the child or child-image appears to us, and how we feel about it, is a reflection of what parent feelings we have, which depends on how we ourselves have been parented. When the therapist talks to his patient about a baby in a dream, he may legitimately interpret that baby as the baby subpersonality of the dreamer for the reason that the health and lovableness of the baby part of ourselves and the loving, caring, responsible parental feelings of the good parent in ourselves are mutually causal or interdependent—you cannot have the healthy child subpersonality constellated without the loving parent subpersonality functioning well.

The dream image of the relatively healthy and happy child is not particularly frequent in patients at the beginning of therapy. Crippled, stunted, unconscious, or dying children are more the rule. Such images represent the problems facing the development of the healthy baby and the adequate parent in the patient, and reflect what happened to the patient as an infant—how his baby self is handicapped and how his parenting instincts (learned from his parental figures) are being distorted. In the course of psychotherapy, the patient identifies with this not-very-healthy child in himself in his relationship with the analyst. In other words, he learns to trust the analyst with his injured or deprived baby self while at the same time tending to project onto the analyst features of the previously (to some extent) unsatisfactory parent. This is a stage of regression in therapy; at first regressive *behaviour* without much awareness or insight tends to predominate, but later, such beha-

116

viour is replaced by *feelings* of helplessness, isolation, depression, or sadness (the abandoned child). The reader will recognize such circumstances as the mythical hero's origins. From such an unpromising milieu the hero or the divine child, the precursors of the individuated self, may come more into prominence in the dream content. Now therapist and patient have to cope with the grandiose or inflated ego states, in which the ego identifies to some extent with the hero or divine child, and the humble or depressed states, when the ego is disidentifying with hero or divine child and projecting these mythical images outwards. The child image and the parental images gradually become more healthy and, at the same time, more human. Now the patient is able both to be and to deploy the loved child subpersonality in himself and to assume adult and parental roles and responsibilities.

If I dream about a neglected child, the dream is not only saying something about my own neglected feelings (neglected child subpersonality) but it is also saying something about the neglectful parent in myself. Perhaps I am beginning to have insight into this aspect of myself—that I neglect my own roots or my own irrational, childlike, nonadult parts.

To summarize, the form and nature of the child image in my dream depends on the sort of parent I am, or would like to be, or would like not to be, and so on. The child subpersonality cannot be considered in isolation from the parent subpersonality in a person. We are dealing with the vicissitudes of the child-parent interactions within ourselves.

If the unlived part of the self is experienced by the grown-up ego as a cancer or a bomb, it is a reflection of the fearfulness and helplessness of the parent in oneself toward the invasive, greedy, destructive part of oneself (the cancer) or the omnipotent, explosive, destructive subpersonality (the bomb).

At the same time, it is obvious that growing up involves freeing oneself from the parents or the parent-images in oneself. Hopefully this happens with the parents' cooperation at every stage of one's development. Autonomy is not an event but an endless succession of stage-appropriate interactions between parent and child. Moments or phases of defying, confronting, or breaking away may all play their part at times. At such times, the parents may be ignored or forgotten or metaphorically disposed of. But if the parents are "killed off" in this sense, they stubbornly become part of the underworld, shadowy, negative part of oneself. The attainment of freedom and autonomy entails the painstaking and detailed working through of the child-parent interactions and not simply attempting to wipe out the parent-images.

If the parents (or the derivative parental subpersonalities) are too controlling, possessive, crushing, or indispensable, stage-appropriate autonomy – normal growing up – cannot occur. In therapy, blocks preventing the full realization of the potentialities of the person are usually due to fixed (fixated) negative interactions between parental and child subpersonalities in the patient (or the therapist, or in the patient-therapist interaction).

Normal growing up entails good self-parenting. The healthy child dream image implies good self-parenting potential. The crippled or inert child, or the child as cancer or atom bomb, indicate problem areas in self-parenting of the type I have indicated.

The Child Image Arises Out of the Meeting of the Opposites

The child, and the dream child, are born out of the union, and the bomb image out of the clash, of opposites in the mind. Typical opposites in the case of the child image are, of course, man and woman, and these are also typical opposites in the case of the bomb image.

The emergence of the child image in a therapeutic relationship signifies the possibility of self-parenting in the patient. It also says something about the patient's ability to relate to the therapist. Therapists talk about the child of the analysis because, like a real child, it is in many ways the product of the interaction of therapist and patient at a deep level. I suppose this sort of interaction tends to be stronger between therapists and clients of opposite sexes, but this is not markedly the case.

The precise moment of the psychic conception sometimes becomes evident. It is in some ways analogous with religious and other conversion experiences – sometimes like lightning or fireworks, sometimes like fire, wind, or an invasion by a spirit. More often it is simply to do with a realization or, more prosaically, with something significant about a date or a previous experience at a certain time.

I am stressing here that the impregnating experience may be a shock of some kind, a kind felt to be good though sometimes painful.

I attended a lecture by an attractive and sensitive male analyst in which he was movingly describing how much hurt and suffering women have experienced in our patriarchal culture. He was recounting one of his patient's dreams of a woman crippled in the legs to make her a more successful beggar, as she had heard happens to children in some countries still. The whole audience was deeply moved, and a woman amongst us emitted an audible wail or groan. Afterwards she said that at that moment she felt a flash of lightning strike her—a flash of revelation rather than destruction—and she heard someone groan, but it did not feel as if she herself was doing the groaning.

The reader will also have related these subjective experiences with those of the psychic orgasm as well as those of conversion and revelation. The idea of psychic impregnation is very close to that of being shattered—one might almost say that it is merely a matter of severity or degree.

In his essay, "The Psychology of the Child Archetype" (1951), Jung links the child and divine child of mythology and dreams with early indications of the individuating process in analysands and, of course, others not in analysis.

The child (emerging new self) motif tends to take both negative and idealized forms at first—serpent, crocodile, etc., on the one hand, or divine child or king's child on the other. I am also adding the cancer image and the atom-bomb image to this list. The negativity and idealization represent a kind of mood swing or enantiodromic transformation into its opposite. Parts of the self emerging from repression (negative attitude by the I) naturally take on negative forms, or else idealization protects them from this hostile I. The same applies to sensations, when the body is coming alive in therapy out of a state of deadness or paralysis. The first signs of the body coming to life are almost invariably negative—pains, hypochondriasis, spasms, and irritations.

The fear or the unbearable feelings or sensations that may be experienced when these lost parts of the self are being recovered are the reason why those parts of the self had to be sacrificed in the first instance, usually in childhood. If a child has been badly hurt, he may have to keep going by becoming hard, tough, cruel, or neurotic. In therapy, feelings of closeness, warmth, or dependence encourage the child and the childhood memories to emerge, and there are often violent reactions against this at first, related to prevailing character defences. These reactions protect the hurt child but cripple the adult. They have to be understood before the core of the hurt can be exposed. Each complex has its own such nucleus of hurt, and each complex behaves like a person who wants to be approached and loved, but who also freezes, runs away, or explodes when one gets too close. It is not the function of the therapist to approach these tender cores in a clinical or confrontative spirit, or even in the manner of a hell-fire preacher who is terrifying and cajoling by turns. He needs his full humanity and this includes an honest admission of his limitations, particularly of his limitations as a parent or lover of his client.

The patient cannot be simply talked into being the good parent toward the child in himself or herself, or the child vis-à-vis the parent in himself or herself. He is this in any case, only he is repeating the pattern of his own childhood and repeating the blocks between parent and child which arose in his own childhood. The emergence of the healthy baby or child image in his dreams usually means that he is now potentially capable of positive, creative self-parenting. This means he is now potentially autonomous and, more important, potentially able to assume genuine caring and authoritative responsibility toward himself and others. This kind of personal responsibility is not something that rules, regulations, or laws can produce. Force and legalistic manoeuvrings attempt to make up for the lack of such responsibility. The therapist, like the parent, knows how this kind of responsibility has to be worked for from both sides – the parent's side and the child's side – before the image of the healthy loved child and the loving, effective parent can be constellated and enacted.

It may be disgusting and obscene to place these two opposite images of the divine or the healthy human child and the world-destroying bomb side by side. If the atom bomb is taken as a symbol of the dark and destructive side of God and the divine child of the light and creative side of the deity, the opposition might still be theologically unacceptable to many. The atom bomb is omnipotent as well as destructive, and we have, I think, to understand omnipotent images and feelings as reactive to and compensatory for feelings of helplessness and separation, feelings which are induced more in the unloved or nonunderstood child than in the loved child whose parents introduce reality in suitably graded doses. The omnipotent destructive feelings and fantasies of the narcissistically damaged person are rapidly becoming better and better understood by therapists, who can therefore really help others understand this particularly important subpersonality of ourselves and our society.

Fat Baby, one of the nicknames for the first atom bomb, was one concrete form of the infantile, omnipotent, destructive, narcissistic subpersonality of the self, present in all, but nurtured and augmented by hurtful social forces always acting on and through individual human beings.

CHAPTER 8

History Seen Partly as Concretized Mythology

The Interaction of the Subpersonalities of the Self

If we visit a strange and distant people, we discover that their account of what is happening now and of what has happened in the past is very different from our own. We can understand their views and their behaviour better if we know more about their beliefs, customs, folklore, religion, and their apperception of history. Otherwise much of what they do and of how they see things is either meaningless to us or else we project our own ideas and fantasies, our own meanings, onto them. Is it permissible to use some such word as *mythology* to cover the beliefs, customs, folklore, religion, history, etc., of a group of people? One pitfall we must obviously avoid is to use the word *myth* in a dismissive sense, contrasting it to "the truth," or "historical or factual truth," which is, of course, merely our own view of what is true and real, a function of our own personal or collective myth.

Could it be said that my truth according to my reality will not necessarily, indeed will necessarily not, be yours? You would have to see my truth as my mythology in a sense, without being at all disrespectful or dismissive of it. The same must be true of your truth, your reality, from where I stand. A partial exception to this obvious fact might be people who are in telepathic or mystical union or unity with each other, but even so the same content even when shared has different meaning or significance for the several persons concerned.

In other words, my truth, my history, my science, will be from your standpoint my mythology. That is evident; the difficulty, having admitted this, lies in becoming aware of one's own mythology. We are virtually unconscious of our own mythology, which to us comprises our behaviour, our unspoken customs, unspoken beliefs, our self-evident truths, the religion not so much of ourselves as of our forbears – simply the way we are and the way we have been brought up. It is quite a struggle, and a very worthwhile one, to discover as much as possible one's own mythology. Dreams help a lot here.

It is generally conceded that we all convert the "facts" of history into our own mythology – this is true of both persons and groups. But it is equally true that one mythologizes the present, even one's own perceptions. Sensory reality is meaningless, and we have to arrange and select our sensations and memories according to what is meaningful. An event acquires meaning through the filter of our mythology. As we retell it to ourselves, the event becomes more and more purely mythical.

This is not the only point about the myth in our lives. Not only do we perceive and structure the world according to our myth, but we act on the world in such a way as to bring the world, and particularly other people, into line with our myth. We all act in such a way as to try to bring about the world that is most real to us (this is not at all the world we actually want, of course). We work and vote and go to war under its influence. Our leaders lead us through our mythologies, our popular stars and heroes embody and help to fashion them.

Many of the generation of British men who took part in the 1939–1945 world war refer to it as "Hitler's war." That is part of our mythology. We do not doubt that Hitler had a vision about a lordly people, that a sufficient number of German people shared it, and that they tried to make this vision into a reality. How true this is is not important to our present thesis. What is important is that we are all trying, largely unconsciously but partly consciously, to realize our mythologies.

Part of the thesis of this book is that, historically speaking, we are all engaged in behaving in myth-realizing scenarios of which we are, in fact, largely unconscious. The apocalyptic myth is competing with other myths and mythologies to realize itself. It has a religious and psychological validity that I have tried to illustrate, and this increases the danger of its concretization unless we become more aware of its mythological power.

The somewhat idiosyncratic definition of mythology I am using here, where I am stressing actual behaviour and unspoken assumptions more than consciously verbalized ideals and stories, helps one remember that it is the actual behaviour of nations and individuals we should

look at in order to formulate the nature and the motives of the subpersonalities in charge. By their behaviour shall they be known. The ideal
or even the conscious intention may bear a reciprocal or compensatory
relationship with the behaviour, and the myth becomes mere hypocrisy
or wishful thinking around this point.

The notion of history as a vast setting for the interaction on a
socially significant scale of subpersonalities of the human self is in some
ways the same as views with other areas of emphasis, and I am not
claiming that history should only be looked at or studied from the point
of view I am delineating here. But I do feel that this point of view is
unbelievably neglected and important.

The classical Greeks, or some of them, saw history in terms of the
conflicts and interactions of the gods – the Greek gods in this case. In so
far as the gods are seen as powerful or important forces working on the
human psyche, this view of history would not be very different from
mine, and, of course, many Greeks would see their gods in this way. In
so far as the gods are seen as real, concrete, external beings or persons
outside humanity, there is some discrepancy in theory, but perhaps not
so much in practice, for subpersonalities usually act *as if* they were
outside forces working in their own way within us.

A view of history as the stage of interaction and conflict of heroes,
kings, leaders, and other key people (often mythological) also makes
sense if these partly mythical characters see themselves, and contrive to
be seen, as embodying historical, social, or religious forces or aspirations
of the mass of their followers.

If we say that one Marxist view of history emphasizes the conflict
between socioeconomic classes or groups, say, a class of those who
control the means of production and those who man the means of
production, here again we can recognize these subpersonalities as
images or embodiments of parts of ourselves with very real historical
and social significance. If we see people struggling for survival, or for
power or wealth, we may develop a theory such as Marxism to account
for this. This theory should be carefully distinguished from the behaviour, hence the underlying mythologies, of ourselves when we go to
work or employ people.

Clearly any particular god or idealized type of person would be
included under my definition of subpersonality. It must be stressed that
a subpersonality, such as the Christ-like potentiality of the self, may be
experienced as very much superordinate to the I. Indeed, to identify
oneself with Christ or God the Father would be inflated, even psychotic.

We can regard history in terms of movements and clashes of gods and ideals, but a moment's reflection shows that gods and ideals, although they influence social movements and sociopolitical dynamics, are also influenced by them and by all the concrete aspects of life which they themselves influence or determine. If I am a primitive farmer from a primitive farming culture, cycles of death and rebirth and ways of influencing will dominate my religion – in the direction of the mother goddess – and my religion, rites, and customs, ways of living and of bringing up my children will all tend to perpetuate and make more successful my farming life. Lore will tend to be farming lore rather than hunting or fishing lore. Metaphors will be farming metaphors.

Let us group all this under a heading of a farmer subpersonality, thereby making the assumption that the farmer in oneself is not, or at any rate not quite, one's complete and natural self. For example, patience, the ability to take a long view, fortitude and doggedness, and certain nurturing qualities might be at a premium, whereas quite other ideals and aspects of the human potential would be at a premium for the hunter or the nomad.

If there were such a thing as a purely farming group, those potentialities which ran counter to the farmer ideal would be repressed and would take on a negative significance. A group of hunters, if they came into competition with the farmers, would embody many of these negatively toned characteristics, and then we have a potential for struggle or war. The struggles between cattlemen and sharecroppers in western films constitute a modern case in point. This oversimplified fictitious example will suffice to explain the thesis that history and historical movements involve a clashing of opposing subpersonalities of the Self or a compensatory swinging from one position of imbalance and repression to another. An equilibrium position is hypothesized, but this would be a subject of hot debate at any one time. Swinging between a self-indulgent ethos and a self-denying one would be an example of an inherent instability in a group, with a cycle whose duration might be expected to be one generation.

If a group or culture is moving dangerously away from this hypothetical stable condition of what is most natural or human, so that disintegration, explosive expansion, or backlash is imminent, we should expect to be able to detect this in the neuroses and psychoses, the dreams, the countercultural groups, and in individual and group behavioural and subjective explosions (art, science, religion would show distortions or explosions). Many of us discern such tendencies at times. I do not claim to be much better than the next man at this sort of divination, but it is possible that the therapist has something to offer here. The therapist is cast in so many different roles (subpersonalities) and acts and feels like so many different persons during the course of each working day as he relates to his different patients that he learns to use himself and his feelings and actions as indicators of the reciprocal subpersonalities at work in his clients. One client makes him feel grand, or upper class, or clever, or masculine, while the next makes him feel lower class, or stupid, or small, or effeminate or whatever, according to which subpersonality (social or historical role included) is in charge of his patient. The therapist, at least in his therapeutic work, cannot indulge in airing his social class, political, religious, racial, sexual, or historical views and opinions without much more attention and consideration to the needs and projections of his patient, and above all to the effects of such self-indulgence on his, the therapist's, part, than he needs to show in everyday life. He cannot be a neutral mirror in the Freudian sense, but he has to pay full attention to his own feeling responses and think carefully before foisting them on his client. In other words, he aims at an unusual degree of awareness of the myths by which he himself lives.

In his work, the therapist is continually confronted by issues concerning the balance and the relationships between the various important subpersonalities of the self, for example, the parent and the child, the old and the young, ruler and ruled, teacher and pupil, rich and needy, and, of course, male and female. The therapist has to deal with all these conflicts and issues primarily as issues between parts of the patient's own total personality, whereas the sociologist, the historian, and the politician tend to try to deal with these issues in an extraverted way, as issues between old and young people, males and females, haves and have-nots in society, and so on. The inadequacy of both the introverted and the extraverted treatment of these issues is obvious. For example, we cannot possibly regard the present movement toward the greater power and influence of women and of the feminine as solely an issue between women and men. It is a change in balance occurring in the personalities of men as well as women. It seems clear that feminine subpersonalities are respected and heard more and that there is a shift in both balance and harmony between male and female parts of ourselves—on the whole.

Subpersonalities Resulting From and Causing Social Interactions

We regard subpersonalities, the basic interacting units from which the total personality is constituted, as being partly genetically and partly socially determined. The social element is, of course, mediated largely at first through the family of each of us. An unloving parent will usually result in an unloved and probably unloveable view of oneself and will reinforce unloved subpersonalities in our repertory of behaviours and feelings toward others. If one child in a family is preferred to another, the second may take on various shadow aspects of the first; one child may be clever at school, the other rebellious and stupid at school. Differing social roles and different subpersonalities will be formed in the different members of the family. The different roles in the family will reflect the division of labour in the family, and this obviously applies also to larger social groups.

The social groupings, the class structure, the division of labour within a society will follow lines of commonly occurring subpersonalities in all of us – good parent, bad parent, good child, bad child, teacher, learner, priest, doctor, merchant, artist, prisoner, possessor, wanderer, divinity, hero. Our dreams may tell us which of these is strong or weak, healthy or damaged. The structure of a society reflects that society's myth about itself, just as each person's personal myth is a reflection of the subpersonalities within himself or herself. In both the individual's or society's case, a rigid personality structure or a rigid social structure represents a primitive, concrete expression of subpersonality. If I "happen" to be a teacher, and I am only capable of acting in a pedantic way toward all and sundry, I am fixed, stuck, in a very concrete way, in one subpersonality out of the many that are present in me unconsciously, some of which are pressing for recognition or expression.

A special kind of division of labour concerns phenomena such as scapegoating, persecution, and the concrete enactment of shadow aspects of ourselves by criminals, neurotic and psychotic people, in so far as they are fixed in those social roles, and nowadays by terrorists or freedom fighters who use bombs and guns on the rest of us. Perhaps only the therapist who is familiar with the power of projection can feel the importance of the need to take responsibility for the criminal, the madman, and the terrorist within himself as an essential part of dealing with those problems of modern society which are, in a sense, *solutions* for each of the rest of us. Looked at in this way, the nuclear bomb would be a way for each of us to avoid taking personal responsibility for those omnipotent destructive feelings or wishes which no doubt we all have had at some stage in our lives. The bomb would be a kind of scapegoat onto which we could all unburden ourselves of responsibility for our destructive feelings. In our nuclear dreams, it is our narcissistic defences that are threatened, but we feel as if our whole world is in danger.

The Social Evolution of the I

If the nuclear threat is a sort of mass projection of fears of I-disintegration, then what can we say about the I? The awesome power of the bomb threat can only be compared to that of a malign God. What can we say about God in this sense, and does this have to do with the I?

The helpless and vulnerable I of the infant under coercion or threat could certainly be psychologically related to an omnipotent God either as a compensatory reaction or in terms of projection of the part of the self which the I feels itself *not* to be.

We can view historical events and changes as acts of God or of the gods, blessings or punishments at the hands of omnipotent gods or vague forces, for example, as the interplay of heroes such as great world leaders. Or we can view them as events determined by the acts of people for which we are collectively and to some extent personally responsible. Which view we take may well determine our fate. If I do not have an I, a sort of metaphorical container within which is a person like other persons with feelings, memories, stories comprising history, and ways of communicating with the not-I part of the totality of my experience and personality, then my role in relation to planetary issues and decisions must remain that of an unconscious contributor to the fluid tides and explosions that characterize our present social behaviour. The nuclear bomb and the other things which threaten human life can be seen as things we are actually creating, or we can remain irresponsible (a state without an involved I) and die.

I have explained how the psychotherapist and his client are vitally concerned with the I of the client and the amount of energy at its disposal in containing conflict and relating to the subpersonalities of the self (instincts, habits, internalized persons, complexes, structures of the mind, brain structures and functions, and what have you). This Western sort of I is a special kind of complex or subpersonality which, like other subpersonalities, has a history. By this I do not mean to say that there is a Western I and an Eastern I and an African I, but that there are all kinds of I and that they differ enormously, and that cultural history is the important factor determining the kind of I we have.

Taking the family as an early cultural phenomenon, there is considerable differentiation of function and role but that does not require an I. I can be suckled, cleaned, held, and loved by my mother and fulfill my baby instincts of dependence, obedience, naughtiness, worship, or admiration without differentiating my actual mother from my thousands of experiences of her—which constitute the mother subpersonality for me.

I may continue to be the child to her mother until she dies and even after that if I preserve her actual body or successfully replace her with an effigy, and I need some such way of communicating with the mother subpersonality.

The mother goddess and mother figurines of early human history, looked at this way, can be used to free me from my actual mother, alive or, even more so, dead. Of course, while freeing me from my actual mother, they may embed me further in the larger social group, if the group mother goddess rather than my personal mother goddess is the more powerful for me.

If my life is devoted to relating to cows and I need to use my mother experience for this, the cow as mother is an early form of subpersonality that I may experience in projected not-I form. This goddess will tell me how to conduct my life or will tell the group to which I belong (usually by hallucinated speech) how to conduct ourselves for our mutual (cow and human) benefit.

Speaking as a modern Westerner, when I refer to a cow-mother-goddess instructing the chief persons in the community in matters of concern to us all, such as husbandry, culling, group movements as related to pasture and rainfall, etc., I am not saying that the cow-goddess statue was possessed of superhuman knowledge and wisdom. Rather, the knowledge was gained by the members of the tribe and the hallucinated instructions and commands were projections, perhaps group projections of the maternal subpersonality resulting from learning by the individual human members of the group.

The early family and small groups were presumably dominated by a father, a powerful male, if present primate groups are similar to human ones. No doubt his leadership was needed in itself, but even more by example and internalization. The male god as ruler and as potent male animal would therefore be a step in the direction of freeing man from his actual father and leader, but of binding him to the group with whose god he is communicating. For the larger groups, he or she who controls communication with the gods and goddesses (or who communicates with the chief gods) controls the group. But to speak of control and power is the language of a later age.

To truly assimilate the notion of the man-made god statue "speaking" to the group may be difficult for the reader at first, but it is vital if he or she is to understand the nature of subpersonalities and how they interact with the I. There is ample archeological evidence that god statues were felt and thought to be living persons – they were fed, dressed, and washed like humans. To enable them to speak, their mouths were often washed out – later in a ritual fashion. But this does not help us much with the actual experience of projecting a subpersonality which is experienced as a person. Perhaps the reader remembers having quite genuine conversations with an imaginary companion as a child. Perhaps he or she has had the genuine artist's experience of getting into the creative state when what one creates becomes a separate person and speaks back to the artist, so that the work of art – picture, poem, pot, statue, or sonata – creates itself or, better still, is created out of the dialectical relationship between opus and artist. This is the not-I part of the self speaking to the I. Thus is the I informed and enlivened. It is an experience we all can have in one way or another, if we are not embedded merely in the I. Add to this the fact that subpersonalities were experienced much more concretely in the past.

God speaking to man would therefore be a precursor of not-I communicating with I. In a refreshingly lucid book, the psychologist Julian Jaynes advances the thesis that in right-handed persons the gods "speak" from the right (nondominant) cerebral hemisphere and are "heard" by the speech centre of the left (dominant) hemisphere. This book has the formidable title *The Origin of Consciousness in the Breakdown of the Bicameral Mind* (Jaynes 1982).

Jaynes uses the *Iliad* and the earliest unadulterated book of the Bible, the book of Amos, as examples of literature before the modern I was present in human psychology. At the beginning of the last millennium before Christ, God spoke directly to man whether he was hero, ordinary man, or prophet.

Jaynes's definition of consciousness accords well with the one I am using here. He points out how little of our lives are spent being conscious. Consciousness is not necessary for reacting to situations, for the performance of skills, for simple thinking, for reasoning. It does not copy down experience, it is not necessary for signal learning. It is not the seat of reason. All these things are what it is not, and human life went on long before consciousness in Jaynes's sense came into the world. Consciousness *is* to do with using metaphors. Indeed, the mind itself as conceived by us, and the self-aware I in particular, might be said to be metaphors.

In this sense, then, there is no consciousness in the *Iliad*. There are, in general, no words for consciousness or mental acts. Words like *psyche, thymos, phrenos, nous*, which have been translated as psychological terms such as *soul, mood, mind, consciousness*, were at that time purely concrete words referring to bodily events or life substances such as blood and breath. The gods are the ones who motivate and command and to listen to them is to obey. A character in the *Iliad* could not say that he was angry. A god would simply tell him what to do or what not to do. It is gods who start quarrels among men and who cause war. One god urges Achilles to go into battle, another urges him not to, and another screams through his throat and rouses ungovernable fear in the Trojans. In other words, the gods take the place of the conscious I.

The book of Amos (ca. 800 B.C.) is almost wholly pre-I. There are no words for "mind" or "think" or "feel," no hints of any understanding of such things. His thought is all done for him by the voice of the Lord. God speaks to him in an angry, admonitory, condemnatory torrent which simply pours out of the mouth of the prophet, who probably does not even understand much of it.

At the other biblical extreme is the most recent unadulterated book, that of Ecclesiastes (ca. 200 B.C.). The mind of this book is that of a fully developed subjective consciousness. Time is spread out in a metaphorical mind-space, as in our modern consciousness ("To everything there is a season, and a time to every purpose under heaven . . ."). Ecclesiastes considers, is considerate, compares one thing with another, is kindly, concerned, and mellow. Amos is fiercely righteous, absolutely assured, relaying a blustering God speech similar to the rhetoric of Achilles.

For Jaynes, the modern self-conscious I arose when the ancient civilisations declined and the voices of the gods were no longer clearly and concretely heard. The I develops when the directness and easy intelligibility of the voices of the gods decline. This took place in the Mediterranean area during the millennium before the birth of Christ. The Mycenaean and Minoan civilisations broke up at the commencement of this explosion, and tremendous migrations of people occurred during this entire millennium.

Prior to this, in the ancient civilisations of Mesopotamia, Anatolia, Egypt, China, Central America, and the Andean highlands (later in time but of the same nature), we have god-kings or theocracies in which the chief god is housed in the central god-building (often a multitiered pyramidal structure), receives offerings of food and obeisance, and speaks to the community or to the priests or steward-kings of the community in the direct speech of the divine command. Jaynes believes that the divine subpersonalities are located on one side of the brain and the human subject on the other. This type of god-based civilisation is termed *bicameral* by Jaynes because it is based on the two chambers of the brain functioning as two persons. But when the members of the community no longer think with one mind, and other gods compete or clash, the subjective I emerges as the container for the conflicts that result. The main factors causing the many-mindedness which could not be contained in the bicameral ancient civilisations might have been:

(1) Trade and other exchanges between diverse cultures, some of which were not necessarily friendly or like-minded.

(2) Others not recognizing the authoritarian hierarchy based on the common mind of the stable community.

(3) The weakening of the divine authority with the development of writing. This weakened the hallucinated voice of the original cuneiform tablet and the direct experience of the god, but provided codified laws and commandments that for a while helped perpetuate the stable structure of the state.

(4) In times of social chaos, the gods cannot always tell you what to do and tend to become a Babel of confusion.

(5) When other city-states become enemies, the human tyrant/paranoid ruler emerges, as in Assyria.

(6) In times of oppression and conquest, defeated individuals may survive by means of trickery and deceit (pretending to be friendly or even to worship the same gods as the conquerors). Lying and deceit are potent enhancers of the subjective I with its boundary between I and you or them.

If god has ceased to speak directly, simply, and mandatorily to the individual with the emerging I, then, says Jaynes, the individual adopts the following partial and residuary ways of achieving divine guidance (the modern therapist might substitute the idea of the unconscious or the not-I in its creative and life-enhancing aspects):

(1) prophecy – the emergence of "specialists" in divine communications;

(2) divination and the use of oracles;

(3) prayer;

(4) trance;

(5) poetry and music; and

(6) schizophrenia, also a vestigial form of bicamerality.

The success or otherwise of the communication with the divine depends on the collective authorization, the belief system, the ritualization of the means of contacting the divine, the depth of the trance state, and, of course, on physiological factors such as fasting and hormonal balance.

According to Jaynes, then, bicamerality of the mind is the fact underlying, but also producing, the growth of civilisation and the explosive advances that produced the great early priest-governed city-states. Bicamerality evolved as the individuals in social groupings – the villages of the Natufian and later cultures from about 7500 to 5000 B.C. in the Near East – ceased to know each other personally. The dead rulers were immortalized and their hallucinated voices used for guidance, and the imaginary voices of other living people (rather, their internalized images) and of effigies, idols, and figurines were used in the same sort of extensions and extrapolations of the personal communications of village life.

The price paid by the individual for his enrichment and consciousness is the loss of the certainty of "knowing" God's will and "hearing" His voice directly. In other words, the experience of inner conflict in a container called I replaces the conflicts of the gods (nowadays, states, political groupings and loyalties, ideologies) of which now one, now another takes over the person or his behaviour or both, together with his companions'.

From what I have already written in previous chapters it will be clear that I am more impressed by our present depths of unconsciousness than by our consciousness. But having said that, I think the weight of Jaynes's evidence indicates that massive increase in the capacity of the

I, in its powers to tell stories in space and time, to create metaphors and therefore be less subject to the concrete acting-out of instinct and emotion, took place in the first millennium B.C. Before then the instincts, the traditions of the group, the experience of other people, the emotions, the ancestral images, and so on, were experienced in purely extraverted form, including the voices of the gods, ancestors, the souls (or, in Egypt, *Kas*) of other human beings, and so on.

As an academic Harvard psychologist, Jaynes shows some regret at being imprisoned in his left cerebral hemisphere, and some nostalgia for his right. This might make him ready prey for the divine lightning, but we cannot doubt that his heart is in the right (correct) place. We do not have to accept the split-brain theory of the divine voice in its simplified form, but we have to accept that (a) in the right-handed person, the I may prefer to reside in the left, dominant hemisphere; (b) the various main subpersonalities may have their main residences in different parts of the brain; and (c) the boundary between excitation in one area and inhibition in a neighbouring area (or neurally linked part of the brain) may produce excitation in the inhibited area sometimes amounting to the lightning flash of the epileptical discharge. But all this is for the neurophysiologists to dispute.

Psychotherapists take a somewhat different view of the development of the I in the modern Western individual from that inferred by Jaynes's thesis, although some of the discrepancies are due merely to differing emphasis on different aspects of the I. Here, I wish to emphasize the following aspects of what one might term a normal modern Western I, always bearing in mind wide cultural and personal variations.

(1) The experiencing I, besides having the quality of being a metaphorical container of metaphors, as Jaynes so beautifully substantiates, is basically very much bound up with bodily feelings and sensations, i.e., with a direct experience of the body, its well-being or otherwise, and of the various parts of the body as experienced as background. The experiences of depersonalization, in which one feels alienated, with a disembodied I, amply illustrate the vital component of embodiment, of body feeling, in the total experience of I. There is a strong correlation between the ability to feel and to contain feelings and the embodiedness of the I. When therapy is advancing satisfactorily, there is a progressive increase in the aliveness of the I and this coincides mainly with the degree of embodiment of the I.

(2) Although there are differences in how therapists define I, ego, and self, there is general agreement among them, I think, that the I gradually becomes more a personal I in childhood and arises as the child gradually differentiates himself from his environment (mainly the parents). Before this happens, i.e., before we can talk of a resilient I who can know what it wants and can differ from the parents and stand on its own feet and stand up for itself, we may have a situation where the I, the body-image, the world-image, and the maternal body-image are not at all differentiated. Pleasure is fusion and undifferentiatedness, pain and anger are cosmic disintegration. At this stage, before the angry I is a resilient ring or ball with firm boundaries, the angry baby has to be affirmed and held by the parent, otherwise it never proceeds to the stage of resilient independence.

Thus the containing, nurturing, and affirming parental images, often a mother image, constitute a vital stage in the development of the I in its earliest form. The development of autonomy, combined with ability to relate and to negotiate, goes on throughout life, of course, with important steps during the latency and the adolescent periods and throughout adult life, too.

But the I cannot contain emotions, instincts, passions, feelings, and impulses, i.e., be responsible for these parts of the self, while it is yet contained either in the real parents or the group. If the mother insists on containing the son or daughter because she cannot tolerate difference in values or physical separation, therapists often talk of a devouring mother, or a son or daughter with a mother complex.

The container may be projected onto the family group as a whole, onto the tribe, onto the state or the organized religion of the group, or onto the image of the leader of the group—priest, king, or dictator.

I do not need to spell out what tremendous differences there are between individuals in the same group as regards their autonomy, their responsibility, and their dependence on parent, family, local group, or religion, etc., in our culture. I have analyzed only a limited number of persons from the Levant and the Far East, but it is very striking how different their I's are from those of Westerners. I remember one patient, a wealthy man from the Indian subcontinent, whose I was so little differentiated from those of his family unit that he could not quarrel or allow himself to become conscious of genuine and powerful divergences of interest between himself and other members of his family group. Doing so would have exposed him to painful feelings of separation and exposure. Situations involving such conflicts always made him physically ill rather than angry or consciously conflicted. This degree of immersion of the I can occur in Westerners, of course – it might be regarded as normal in close-knit married couples, for example. But it is much less frequent than in the East.

So much for the immersed or enwombed I. A second dimension along which the I can vary, with profound historical consequences, is that of omnipotence versus realism. The infant's real impotence and dependence and the power of his needs give rise to omnipotent screams and demands. The child needs to have these states respected rather than crushed, because it needs to have a resilient rather than a fragmented I. But one parent may tolerate and meet the child's omnipotence where another may demand a greater degree of compliance or realisms – accepting the parent's values and the world's laws and realities. If the conflict or paradox of impotence versus omnipotence cannot be understood and respected, there is the strong possibility that omnipotent/impotent subpersonalities of the self will be repressed and projected onto the not-self, where they will contribute to the vast oceans of historical and religious movements and omnipotent gods of all kinds that history presents.

The omnipotent part of the self is not all temper tantrums and selfishness. The magic of childhood and the beauties of love and of romanticism, the splendour of music and the joys of spring are all part of this side of the human being. The suppression of this side for the sake of realism or conformity makes for the dullness and envy of the compliant individual. The psychologist Donald Winnicott called the compliant subpersonality the "false self," but he admitted that we all need some degree of false self to adapt to other people at all. Jung had a similar concept for the socially adaptive subpersonality which he named the *persona*, after the mask worn by players in classical times. There has been, and still is, a rather quaint dichotomy among therapists according to whether they encourage the magical, omnipotent, romantic self or the realistic, socially adapted self. Recently, in a public discussion, I spoke with approval of Winnicott's emphasis on the need of the infant to have his or her omnipotent side met and respected (although not necessarily indulged, of course). A well-known Kleinian (a follower of Melanie Klein, another pioneer of child therapy) who also spoke disagreed sharply, saying, "It is important not to 'stroke' (approve of) patients' omnipotence – it makes them unbearable to live with and is hell for their families." All of which is very true and points to a painful human dilemma which has apparently existed as long as humanity has tried to live in groups.

With this dichotomy in mind, we can compare the psychologies of the earliest humans. Joseph Campbell (1976) describes the mythology of the paleolithic hunters even as early as Neanderthal man, with his bear or lion cults and the ritual magic of his hunting practices, both for killing the animal and, when killed and eaten, of magically restoring it to life and avoiding guilt and punishment. The magic power may often be a kind of phallic pointing, and the sun, the Great Hunter, may be a prototype of this magic pointing with his rays.

The paleolithic cave paintings and engravings, for example, those of the Dordogne region of France from the Upper Paleolithic, also suggest that the vital magical link both for killing and immortalizing, through whom the hunter attains mastery, is the Ruler of the Animals, with whom the shaman or specialist in magic and in the conquering of death, identifies, for example, by donning the skin and head of the dead animal and imitating the animal in ritual dance or shamanic trance.

The same sort of magical solution to the problem of mortality is suggested by the practice of ritual burial, sometimes in the foetal position, dating back, again, to Neanderthal times.

The mythology of the primitive farmer differs in important respects. One of the fundamental mythological ideas of the primitive planting communities of the world, as we all know from the poem "Hiawatha," is that plants originated from a death, usually a murder, and that the death needs to be ritually reenacted in order to ensure the continued growth of the plants. The maiden, the young couple, and in later times the king, might be sacrificed in this way.

Thus, from the hunters the specialist mediator is the shaman-magician, while from the planters have evolved the priests, gods, and rituals of sacrifice, and eventually of descent and resurrection. The shaman develops his own solitary path to his unconscious through personal and lonely privation. The priest obeys and interprets the gods and from his studies the high ancient civilisations evolve. The Titan Prometheus, the defier of the gods and the bringer of the boon of fire to mankind, would be the heir of the early shamans. Nietzsche, Jung, and many others have drawn attention to this polarization of the Western mind.

The mother goddess, or the female figurine, suggesting the projected power of the female subpersonality, is not confined to planters or hunters, and she dates back at least to mammoth-hunting times. One does not have to be a farmer to have a mother, any more than one necessarily has to be a primitive hunter to have to deal with one's animal subpersonalities (I remember dreaming of being suckled by a polar bear when I was three years old, at the time my younger brother was born).

I am not blandly asserting that the history of the development of the consciousness of mankind parallels in any precise way the development of the consciousness of the individual modern person. There must be something in the idea, but there is also something in the idea that the same themes and the same subpersonalities continue to crop up throughout human history, in different era-appropriate forms.

Freud's work on the Oedipus complex in the development of the individual and its mythological and historical-ethnological correlates suffered from a distinct Procrustean tendency, just as his psycho-dynamic theory was strong at the Oedipal level of development but not so strong at earlier archaic levels corresponding to human psychosis as distinct from human neurosis. Subsequent psychotherapists have explored these deeper levels more fully, and there has been a consequent broadening and deepening understanding of mythology (and possibly of history, too). However, the same Procrustean temptations reoccur, partly owing to the exigencies of teaching and explanation.

In the Oedipus myth, the hero Oedipus, fulfilling a divinely decreed fate, kills his father and later marries his mother, all unawares. His kingdom is blighted, and when he becomes aware of what he has done, he punishes himself in a terrible way. In the Oedipus complex, the developing boy goes through a phase of genital desires for his mother, is jealous of his father, and has castration fears centred mainly around the father and his imagined punishment. Thus the Oedipus complex applies classically to the genital stage of development and to triangular relationships. The longings for the mother occur at all stages of development (they may be anal, oral, or even cannibalistic and involve desires to merge with, devour, or burrow into her and regressively seek the enveloping womb). Fears of retribution and punishment occur even when a jealous father, or any third person, is not involved. I do not wish to be unduly controversial on these matters. Some would prefer to say that the anal, urethral, and oral impulses (the acts and behaviour to do with feeding and elimination) need to be met and validated by the mother and need to be part of the relationship with the mother and other people. It is when these impulses and behaviours are presumably not satisfactorily integrated into an easy relationship with the I that neuroses and perversions arise, and it is mostly the dreams of unmet and alienated parts of oneself later in life that the therapist meets in everyday practice. The dreams can be taken as metaphorical expressions of these primitive impulses, or they can also be taken as opening out possible ways in which these alienated parts of the self can attain creative expression. For every boy and girl, there could be said to be regressive longings for the mother or her symbolic (metaphorical) representative, on the one hand, and heroic-feeling needs for self-sufficiency and real relationships on the other. A stronger I is one that can resolve these twin needs.

In his book *The Origins and History of Consciousness* (1954), the Jungian analyst Erich Neumann asserts that there is a strong correlation between the stages of the individual's development and the stages of the development of human consciousness which are reflected in the history of the mythology of mankind.

Neumann's essential thesis is that the great myths of mankind represent and describe the development of human and individual consciousness. His stages are: (1) Creation myths that describe the original self-generating and self-devouring unity of the self, the Great Mother in both her beneficent and devouring aspects (this would correspond with very early experiences of the mother in the life of the individual) and the separation of the World Parents and of all mythical opposites. (2) The birth, the struggles, and the life-and-death transforming achievements of the hero; the hero represents the individual I emerging from the primitive states of identity and of immersion in the archetypal mother, the mother goddess. In his struggle, the hero, often with divine help, overcomes the regressive temptations such as the dragon (the devouring mother) and slays both mother and father in their negative forms before attaining the treasure, which we might possibly describe as incest in its positive forms of winning the maiden and founding an empire. Facing the negative parents and the fears of the incest taboo is thus seen as a necessary part of normal, successful, individual development. Every boy or girl is a hero or heroine, and the hero and the heroine myths are constantly being brought up to date, as they must be in helping new generations of boys and girls (and who is not a boy or girl in this sense?) imagine and try to attain their life's goals.

Neumann's understanding of the Great Mother and the evolution of the divine mother and maiden seem to me, as a practising therapist, particularly illuminating. The relationship between these myths and my patients is borne in upon me every day of my working life, just as are the ramifications and variations of the Oedipus complex at a later, higher level of the psyche. In other words, the Great Mother myths speak to a level of the psyche present in all of us, although largely unconscious.

The relevance of the mother and maiden deity to my present historical perspective is that she evolved directly from paleolithic times and was prominent in the neolithic priest-dominated cultures, where she was associated with the increased knowledge of astronomy which played a large part in the growth of the high civilisations.

Part of the task of the hero or heroine is the facing of the devouring Great Mother in the form of a death, the cave, the forest, the underworld, the world of the dead, the ocean, or whatever. The Sumerian naked goddess Inanna is one of the first to undertake this perilous journey, where she meets the dark side of herself, the sister-goddess Ereshkigal. Persephone and Psyche make the same heroic journey later. Tammuz (Adonis), Osiris, Orpheus, Jesus, and countless other male hero-divinities also represent that part of ourselves which, one hopes, can consciously and deliberately undertake this regressive temptation with its perils and punishments, and be rewarded with, usually, the very thing whose tempting, seen in a negative light, had to be resisted in the first place. This is the paradox of regression in the service of the ego, which is so different from regression as simply being swallowed up by the devouring mother of temptation. As noted, shamans had to undertake the journey alone, facing death, or the fantasy of death, as an essential part of their training.

For Neumann, the mother in the form of Great Mother, the earth, instinct, and the unconscious represents the polar opposite of the masculine principle, which has the attributes of spirituality as opposed to instinctuality, heaven as opposed to earth, consciousness as opposed to unconsciousness. The father helps the boy free himself from the mother and become a man. The male gods of sky and plain, the men of the community, and men's societies function in the same way. Earth Mother and Sky Father form a neat couple, once earth and sky have been differentiated from each other in the creation myth. Earth Mother and Sky Father unite at the apex of the ziggurat, the focal worshipping and ritual building of the early cities. These pyramidal, layered structures are amazingly widespread in the priest-astronomer-dominated cities of the early high civilisations (Jaynes's bicameral cities).

All this is a little too neat, of course. All myths by their very nature are too neat and specious to fit all they mean to fit. Generalizations about myths and religions (which is, I am afraid, what we are doing here) necessarily suffer from two such orders of Procrusteanization, not one. But I blame my oversimplifications on my need to be clear.

For our present purposes, it is sufficient to remark that these early gods and goddesses, god-kings and goddess-queens played a vital role in freeing people from identification with the actual parents and the small group of persons known in the flesh. It is easy to see how these subpersonalities could emerge over untold thousands of years from the cult animals and the dead relatives who were both feared and needed as continuing figures by the living. The dead chief would be especially important and specially kept as an actual person, becoming to some extent immortalized and deified (which in fact often meant being murdered at the appointed time). These changes have been thoroughly documented and discussed. But for the purposes of this book, we need to pay particular attention to the sudden explosion of civilisation more or less as we know it, for example, in Mesopotamia and the Middle East, and to the dehumanizing violence involved in abstract thought and schematic imagery.

CHAPTER 9

Human Sacrifice

I would like to distinguish two psychologically different forms of human sacrifice, namely, that of the primitive farmer and that of the first city dwellers.

Farming requires planting and waiting. Waiting involves a degree of inhibition of one's natural spontaneous impulses and needs for immediate gratification. This entails a sacrifice of one's feelings. Also, reaping the reward or bounty of the harvest after the seed is planted makes one feel that the crop has to be paid for, and this is another powerful incentive for sacrifice. Fertility and farming are under the aegis of the mother goddess, who primitively demands concrete human or animal sacrifices as her price for the harvest. The connection between planting and harvesting on the one hand and human sacrifice with subsequent death and resurrection mythology is too well documented to require much emphasis in this volume.

It is the second kind of human sacrifice on which I will concentrate here. It stems from the sacrifice or inhibition of feeling required in the achievement of abstract thought, social administration, and military and engineering projects. These are the first achievements of civilisation, living in cities.

Writing, the wheel, mathematics, the astronomical calendar and the discovery of the planets, kingship, the temple priest, taxation, and many other aspects of civilisation suddenly emerged around 3200 B.C. in the south Mesopotamian riverside towns. My purpose here is not so much to describe these interrelated changes, which are a source of wonder to us all, but to draw our attention to the dehumanization involved in abstract thought, in social administration, and in the organization of great enterprises, all of which are essential to the advances of that time. The title of this chapter refers to the sacrifice of one's humanity involved in becoming a thinker or a specialist in a civilised society, as well as to the actual human sacrifices often undertaken apparently willingly by the actors acting out the mythical basis of the sacrifice. This is not a sentimental plea for a Golden Age, but a statement about the dark side of civilisation.

Living in cities requires order: orderliness and structure. These are potentially explosive states of mind, as they all do some degree of violence to what one might call the natural, animal human being. The ability to think and carry out ideas and plans involves the sacrifice of feelings and bodily impulses. My thesis is that this sacrifice of feeling and embodiment was originally possible only when actually accompanied by concrete sacrifice of, say, the maiden or the child as a representation or projection of one's love and feelings. Quite early, of course, a doll or pottery figurine would be used for minor undertakings like the construction of small buildings, so that we find many figurines in the foundations of buildings of all sizes from around this period of history.

The new cities were modelled on the new image of the cosmos with its sun, moon, and the newly discovered planets. In keeping with our thesis that body, self, community, and cosmos all stand for each other (to a varying extent), Joseph Campbell among others asserts that in some mystical way the notion arose that the laws governing the motions of the planets should be the laws governing the life and thought of man on earth. The whole city was conceived as an imitation and reflection of the cosmic order. The king was the centre and was the sun (or moon); the walled city was designed as a quartered circle centred around the palace or ziggurat; and there was a calendar to regulate the seasons of the city's life according to the passages of sun and moon among the stars. The wheel appeared at this time. The most amazing parallel between state and cosmos was the enactment of the ritual death of the sun-king with his wife and all the planetary ministers and the whole cast of characters in the mythical pageant that the life of the city was and was made to be. The moment for the deaths was astronomically determined by the calculations of the astronomer-priests.

The ruthlessness, the human sacrifice, underlying order emphasizes the cost at which civilisation was achieved. The violence underlying order is a function of the killing off of embodied feelings (hence the killing off of the embodied person) underlying depersonalization and the formation of abstract images (the circle being an important one). The sun-city-wheel-king is the kind of self-image which is a symbol of order, and because it is founded on violence and blood, the violence and blood of the sacrifice of embodied feelings and (primitively) of actual human sacrifice, the sacrifice of loved persons, we can begin to have some idea of the potential explosiveness of the order and abstraction underlying our civilisation.

The assertion of I is a defiance of the gods. The circle, the walled city of circular design, the house even, the wheel, the calendar, and the armed state are all concrete forms of the symbol of the developing I. Civilisation carries this huge Promethean danger, the danger of a back-lash of the gods, and we see the gods exacting the penalty in periodic violence and hideous behaviour. The atom bomb by the same token would be a concretized form of the omnipotent destructive I.

The circle, like the developing I (or more likely expressing the developing I) has an inside and an outside: it is a boundary, a container. If it represents the self, then it is a protection from the outside world. But it can and does often also represent the cosmos, the whole of the ordered universe of experience, and the I would, in this case, be but a dot in all the vastness of the cosmic unity.

Circles, with dots in the centre, appear as designs in pebbles in Paleolithic caves and are among the first abstract patterns to be found. The beautiful Halaffian pottery made in large Mesopotamian villages antedating the city by several millennia has circular motifs as well as the dove, the horn, or crescent of the moon bull and the maternal double axe, all of which are prominent in later millennia. The sphere and other circular images and objects figure prominently in the process of bound-ary formation and the emergence of the defended and separated self, for good and ill.

I am only too painfully aware that the simple assertion that a great deal of violent psychic energy is "locked up" in these symbolic images may not convey very much. It is hard to see how it could be supported by archaeological evidence alone. I can best illustrate the kind of energy I mean, and bring the images to life, from a case. It illustrates the role of the image of the sphere and one of its meanings for a patient of mine.

She was a married woman in her forties who had been an only child and who remembered only hatred for her parents. In her mind, her father was an aloof disciplinarian and her mother a timid nonentity who always sided with him. Rose, my patient, was paralyzed with fear into meekness and submissiveness while in the parental presence, but away from them, she became a spirited, cheerful, and often naughty person. This cheerful side became her normal, usual self. It persisted several years after marriage, but gradually her husband and mother-in-law dom-inated her, and she became meek, submissive, and hating, whereupon she broke down with severe neurotic anxiety. For years after this, Rose had the same contempt for her husband that she had had for her father. It was clear to me that her cheerful subpersonality had been developed on the basis of a denial of her father's existence. At first she was very hostile and belittling toward me but when I took her up on this and interpreted her behaviour along these lines, she developed a strongly positive attitude; I became a benign, even somewhat godlike figure, able to allay her fears by merely existing; her husband, however, remained negative for her.

Two years after commencing psychotherapy, she had a terrifying dream of separation from me. "I was in your kitchen; someone said 'Come this way' and ushered me into a place like a theatre. There was a wide, carpeted staircase and this person got a long way in front. Then an excited child ran in front of me and fell over and over backwards downstairs, like a ball. I screamed to the person in front, 'Don't just keep on walking, that's a child, not a ball,' and a man came to me and asked what I was waiting for. I said I was waiting to see you. He said it was five o'clock. [Five o'clock was a "hideous time" that was associated with the end of the analysis for her.] My mind had gone." Her other associations brought out nothing relevant to the present paper, except her fear of separation from me.

A year later she brought another dream. "I was on holiday with my husband. We were in Africa. He said, 'Don't eat that fruit, it's poisonous.' He offered me some messy coughdrops, saying they would do me good. I refused, wanting something local and exciting to eat. Then I saw the local population doing a ritual penance. They all wore white and were high up on steps, each step being as high as a room. They somersaulted off these steps backwards. It was a religious ceremony. If they arrived at the bottom, their sins were forgiven, but if not, bad luck." So there again we have the rolling-over-and-over image. About her holiday with her husband, she said, "I felt as if I were on a lot of rocks, being thrown back into childhood. Everything was real, horrible; he treats me like a fool," and so on. In the next session, she told me about a dream she had just had about being with me and another doctor. The other doctor was trying to force some unpleasant medicine on her but she wasn't having any, and I seemed to be neutral. She went on to talk about her dislike of a certain woman who was always on the side of authority. I murmured something about this woman having good feelings about her parents and she said, "That's right, she's always talking about her parents."

After that there was a silence, after which she said, "I can't stand your silences, they make me think you're saying 'I can't do anything for her' and you wouldn't say that, would you?" When I didn't give an immediate assurance she shouted, "Why don't you say something?" I said, trying to be a proper neutral mirror (this was 25 years ago), "I think we should go into that." She immediately screamed "Say something!" and, in an amazing gymnastic feat, she somersaulted rapidly backwards, over the back of her chair onto the floor. As I pulled her up, her backwards motion reminded me of the child falling backwards in the first dream, the ball dream, and I asked (I didn't need to ask, really) if I'd turned into a rejecting parent. She said, "My father was very slow and pondered things. The child in that dream rolled over and over down the stairs and that's what I've done." I commented that it was practically the first time she'd reacted to me as if I was a bad parent.

The interesting thing to me is that the regressive piece of behaviour, the turning into a ball, was foreseen as an image of a ball two or three years previous to the actual behaviour and in the exactly relevant dream context of separation from the protecting parent figure. Is it not remarkable that her bouncy, cheerful, ball-like nature is illuminated by this dream, as is the underlying, hating, angry, resilient self-sufficiency, forced on her by the pain of separation and the sheer need to survive? And is it not even more remarkable that the bouncy resilience, the movement patterns in the dreams, and the much later spontaneous emotion-driven movement over the back of her chair expressed, and for many years contained, her angry despair? So the dream image of the ball-child "canalized" (in Jung's term) her angry, abandoned child feelings. I believe that it is with such a relationship between feelings, impulses, and images that we are concerned in the vicissitudes of the child subpersonality and the parent subpersonality in ourselves. The ramifications of such imagery and mental content, particularly when ritualized and used in social institutions, form a fascinating subject in itself. When we successfully catch a cricket ball, we are not very much aware of holding our baby selves and protecting our emerging autonomy. Indeed to become aware of this would no doubt ensure that we dropped the catch. But I feel quite sure that the invention of the wheel and the ball originally came about from the same imaged separation-anger that I came to understand in Rose. Such separation-anger, like individuation itself, has its good as well as its bad aspects. The child subpersonality, with its twin motifs of abandonment and of omnipotence, expresses the combination of opposing tendencies in the most cogent way, and for this and other reasons, its image constitutes a most important therapeutic symbol in our clinical experience, and one that is vital to understand with all its polarities and paradoxes.

Returning to the significance of the circular designs in the early pottery, it occurs to me that the beauty and order of these designs may make it difficult for a reader to contemplate how in any way anger, sadness, or violent feelings of any sort could be involved in the production of such images (and feelings) of order and beauty. As the previous clinical example does not deal fully with this point, I shall present another patient (the second patient mentioned briefly in chapter 6) in whom the most violent and murderous impulses were expressed, or rather disguised, and contained, by beautiful and orderly images.

At one stage in her analysis, my patient was going through a difficult time with her husband, who, unknown to herself, was having an affair with a woman he was eventually to marry. Alternating feelings of love and anger toward him, corresponding with moods of happiness and hopelessness, possessed my patient according to how things seemed to her to be going in her relationship with her husband at that period.

At this time she dreamed of underground waters being liberated by an engineer. The engineer was her husband. She had a picture of light and dark fountains which she painted, and this picture was the first of many in a torrent of creativity over the ensuing months, a torrent which had to do with the unlocking of the opposites, one might say.

These pictures vividly expressed both feelings of beauty and harmony, and opposite feelings of violence and hatred. For example, one picture was a beautiful circular design containing flowers and intertwining branches, while in another the same flowers were crocodile mouths whose stamens were crocodile teeth. Pictures and dream images like these, and hundreds of others, have amply convinced me of the fact that underlying many of the beautiful, stylized, and orderly traditional ceramic and architectural forms are impulses of primitive violence, violence locked up but easily able to be liberated by a change of mood or a socio-historical reversal of "us" and "them." It is obvious to any observer that the pageant of history is a continuing and bloody game of "us" and "them" – which, of course, is to do with the location of the I in relation to the total personality. But perhaps only a privileged observer of human nature could feel in a real way, i.e., in his own body, the relationship between, say, dentate elements in an architectural feature and impulses to bite or devour which are being reversed and hopefully harnessed by the people concerned in their use. Jung talked of the canalization of

instincts in the process of civilisation, and Freud talked of the sublimation of instincts, while here I stress the creative and potentially explosive
nature of the binding-together of opposing forces in the psyche in the
furtherance of mental structure and civilisation itself.

Returning to my patient and her beautiful, circular, mandalalike
paintings, it will be clear to the reader that I regard these paintings as
containing and denying (by reversing) certain emotions and feelings
which she would have regarded as violent and destructive in relation to
her husband and the marriage. (For a further discussion of these mandalas, see chapter 11, page 217. The true mandala contains or combines
opposites rather than emphasizing one side only.)

At the time that her marriage was on the point of breakdown, she
was reliving and expressing some of her feelings through her paintings
and drawings brought to me as communications continuing the dialogue
of our regular therapy sessions. These paintings varied with her mood
and particularly with her feelings about her husband and about me. At
times when she felt loved, loving, and secure, the paintings were often of
a beautiful, circular, symmetrical, and concentric arrangement of identical floral elements. But on the day she learned of her husband's infidel-
ity, the picture she painted looked not like a floral mandala but an
exploding bomb, with torn fragments shooting out from the blast in the
centre. One of the pictures is reproduced on the frontispiece of this
book.

It is perhaps necessary to emphasize here that the paintings done
by a patient in analysis as part of the analytical communication process
are not trivial, thought-up illustrations. Like the deepest work of an
artist, they can lay bare one's very soul and may reflect more fully,
perhaps more so than dreams, where the person is at in relation to his
important subpersonalities (his deepest emotions and his active archetypal driving forces operating at the time). So the contrast, the oppositeness, between the mandala image and the bomb image, which I suppose
is the most succinct way of expressing the theme of this book, was not in
this patient a superficial or melodramatic affair. The image of explosive
disintegration was the most profound and heartfelt expression of her
anguish, yet, in keeping with my contention that behaviour and awareness usually are reciprocally related rather than going hand in hand with
each other, she did not go to pieces or even explode behaviourally at the
shattering news, but managed to continue on and behave well.

The mandala and other circular, containing, and defending images
reflect the need of the nucleus of the self to become mobilized when

disintegration is feared. Jung and his followers have tended to regard it as an image of the wholeness of the personality and have rightly drawn attention to its divine and cosmic associations for the individual human being in keeping with its use for prayer and meditation in Eastern and other religions. But my purpose, while reemphasizing the profound meaningfulness of such images, is to draw attention to the defensive and particularly to the abstract and formal nature of these images. They represent to some degree a disembodiment of feeling. I have heard Freudian analysts such as Donald Winnicott and Clifford Scott express a certain degree of mild horror at what they regard as Jung's idealizing blind spot as far as the dehumanized, abstract aspect of the mandala and of similar images of the cosmic, the divine totality, the wholeness and harmony of the personality are concerned. In other words, they were emphasizing the downside of abstraction, as am I.

In his autobiography, *Memories, Dreams, Reflections*, Jung described how he painted his first mandala in 1916, without understanding it. By 1918–1919, he was sketching a mandala almost every morning. Those mandalas, he felt, were cryptograms concerning the state of the self which were presented to him anew each day, a living, dynamic conception of the changing self of very great meaningfulness to him. By then he had understood the connection with the mandalas of oriental religions in terms of the collective unconscious and the self in a wider personal sense. A feeling of harmony and wholeness of the self correlated well with a mandala expressing such a feeling, while a feeling of upset and irritation, caused by a letter from a woman he had hoped he had successfully broken with, was accompanied that morning by a mandala whose peripheral defensive boundary had burst open and whose harmonious symmetry was destroyed.

I have been asked, "Why are some of these early boundary phenomena circular, and others square?" I can only refer to what produces the image, and that is the underlying feeling. A square does not feel the same as a circle. It is not bouncy and rounded, it is foursquare. It is an image of a feeling of wholeness and independence, no doubt, but the feeling is different from that conveyed by the circular image. Of course, one can elaborate the difference between circles and squares in many profound ways, as Jung has done in his many volumes on the subject.

I have had sufficient experience with the drawings and paintings of my own patients to confirm that such products of the imagination do vary from one time to another according to the vagaries of the self. Little extrapolation is needed to understand how traditional patterns and designs reflect the personality of the group on a long-term basis. In therapy I rarely if ever make interpretations as to the "meanings" of details of these patterns but try to arrive at the situation in therapy where the patient is in sufficiently close contact with himself to know the "meaning" in a direct way and feel it in his own body, as well as projecting it onto the drawing. The genuinely creative artist produces projections from a similarly deep level of the psyche, but may be (often needs to be) relatively unaware of their personal meaning.

The circular, firmly bounded visual image with symmetrical structure, then, reflects a reasonably well-defended, intact, and harmonious state of the self. If highly defended, it suggests a relatively vulnerable state in which the individual needs to be relatively impervious to the external world. Schizoid individuals under some stress may often produce these images as part of the necessary mobilization of defences and the need to remain in equilibrium, and we can assume that Jung was in such a state when he was isolated from his colleagues and was having to work out his own theoretical and personal understanding of his own psyche and those of his patients. The well-defended mandala, like the strongly walled city, keeps safe the "good" while keeping out the "bad." In this sense it is like an extension of those bodily defences of closure, rage, immune-reactions, and glandular and plain-muscle responses which Nature uses to defend our lives from conception to the grave. I do beseech the reader not to imagine that I am merely using analogies. The ball, the circle, the image of the walled city, and so on are reflections and expressions in imaged form of actual bodily (body-image) vicissitudes. Only to us are they metaphorical. At first in history they are enacted concretely, as I keep saying.

In childhood, the ability to use abstract concepts and images and to be motivated by abstract ideals develops rapidly during the latency period. The anxiety attached to actual bodily impulses, especially where taboos are involved, is no doubt one major cause of the depersonalisation and abstraction involved. Another cultural factor in the fourth millenium B.C. must have been living in cities—places where people do not know each other personally and where depersonalisation is necessary for administrative reasons. Persons have to be felt as things to some extent, and this is the essence of human sacrifice. The sacrificed person or animal represents (i.e., is a projection of) the feeling part of the self (the subpersonality) that is having to be sacrificed (put aside, etc.) in the administrative, engineering, military, building, or farming project involved, the group activity needing to be motivated. Abstraction, depersonalisation, and thinking as opposed to feeling were all developing apace at the birth of civilisation.

My thesis is that the nuclear-bomb image, and in a sense the actual bomb, is the opposite of the mandala (the containing, harmonious, balanced, circular image) and that both reflect opposite states or aspects of the self. Both the mandala and the bomb image are somewhat abstract – things as opposed to persons – in other words, depersonalised. The relationship between persons and things needs to be examined in more detail here, apart from the merely historical aspects.

What Is a Person, What Is a Thing?

In his meditations, Thomas Traherne asks, "Can you take too much joy in your father's works? He is himself in every*thing*" (emphasis mine).

It is a truism that good human relationships involve treating other people generally as persons rather than as things to be made use of. My clinical observations over many years convince me that the same applies even to things. In successful relationships with things, they are generally felt to be persons. I am in no way referring to the mere sentimentalisation of things.

For example, if a craftsman is to be a good craftsman, he has to know his tools and his materials intimately in their every mood and in their good and bad aspects *as they are*, rather than as he hopes they are or wishes they were. He has to know these things as multidimensional wholes and not as wishful projections of himself. Thus, respect and caring, also, of course, mixed with ruthlessness when appropriate, are sentiments just as appropriate to things as to people. Knowledge, letting the object talk back to him in a real dialogue, give and take, loving union at times . . . all these considerations apply to the creative craftsman and artist as much as to the successful parent or friend. Furthermore, just as there is often something less than healthy about using people for one's own ends, there is a similar failure in a craftsman or an artist, or even in a business man, who uses his craft or his art or his business in that way, merely as a means to an end, however justified that end may appear to be.

Furthermore, I have found that people treat things in the same sort of way as they treat people. There are notable exceptions to this rule: for example, some schizoid and autistic people may treat things more like persons than they treat people. I am of the opinion that in the natural, primitive, way of psychic functioning, things are in fact persons. Primitive animism is not the name of a peculiar religion that Stone Age people follow. It is a basic truth about ourselves and the real world which we all need to relearn.

I do not think one can define a person as a human being. In our own society it is doubtful whether slaves were considered persons a century and a half ago. And we might say of an inhuman criminal: "He is not fit to be treated as a human being." A person is therefore someone or something with whom one has, or could have, a personal relationship. This does not get us very far. Obviously it is easier to have a personal relationship with a thou or you, a second person singular or plural, than with a third person singular or plural. However, a second person singular is not always a person and even the first person singular is not always a person either. In the state of *depersonalisation* one has lost the essential feeling about oneself of being a person.

In seeking to differentiate between things and persons, the extroverted approach would be to seek the difference in qualities or attributes of the thing or person. On the other hand, the introvert would emphasise differences in the way one feels about or relates to the thing or person. The emphasis here is introverted in that it is about personalisation and depersonalisation as psychological processes.

In order to illustrate how things become persons, I will describe my own quite commonplace experience with a boat, a kind of person for many sailors. I had had my boat, *June Folly*, for about three months. My wife, son, and I were beginning a summer cruise in her, but only three days after starting our holiday, I had a bad accident. I inadvertently put my foot down the open hatchway and the propeller shaft caught my ankle. My leg was broken, and I had to spend the rest of the holiday first in hospital and then on crutches.

Such an experience could hardly fail to affect my feelings about the boat. Actually, *June Folly* had not really become a person by the time of the accident, as she was a new boat, but the accident made the boat *more* of a person to me rather than less; she seemed like a hard and murderous and destructive great-mother type of figure, a sort of Iron Lady. I felt she had seduced me into feeling (unrealistically) safe in her. Machinery is, of course, like that. But it did not make me want to get rid of her; instead, I spent a lot of money and time putting in shields and making her safe and sound in that and other respects, so that no one else could have a similar kind of accident. Other sources of danger and sailing vices were gradually eradicated in the next year or two. It felt as though I was taming her; the nearest expression I can find is "making an honest woman of her." I mean that in the sense of making her sound and wholesome rather than unsound and fraudulent or appearing to be something she was not. It was a challenge, a personal relationship which had to be put right. Only when all that was done, and after a few more years, was I ready to part with the boat and have good feelings about both her and the person I sold her to. A big help to these feelings occurred when we made a successful cruise in her and completed the journey we had been intending to make on the original disastrous occasion.

There is no doubt that I was, in a very important sense, relating to this boat as a damaging and damaged female person, as one of my subpersonalities, perhaps trying to put something right inside myself in my relationship with the boat. People work out the same problems in themselves through things as they do through other people.

An acquaintance of mine was trying too impatiently to teach his son about decimals. The child became frightened and intellectually paralysed. The man became more and more vehement and finally exclaimed: "Do I have to knock it in with a hammer?" A few days later, the same man was repairing his car when a nut would not yield. He became angry and in trying to force it he sheared it off. He yelled and swore and ended up, almost in tears, addressing his car in very violent, personal language.

On the other hand, I know many men who have more patience with their children, and with their cars, too. We even find that such things improve with analysis! Personal and impersonal symbols of union and intercourse tend to become more positive *pari passu*. There is no question that internal conflicts are worked through just as much with things as with people, provided that the passions are involved. If it is said that it is regressive or animistic or irrational to treat things as persons, one can only reply that this is, in fact, how we operate, that we operate best in this way, and certainly we operate naturally this way.

Personalisation and Reification

Just as in some respects we sometimes personalise things, so at other times we depersonalise or reify persons. By reify I mean to convert mentally into a thing. Personalising things means imbuing them with warmth, life, and feeling, or projecting these affects onto them. Depersonalising persons and things means taking away warmth and life and feeling. I wish to use the words *embodying* and *disembodying* for these two opposite processes. In some of its most creative aspects, the unconscious seems to personalise things, and it often happens that archetypes and complexes are made into persons such as god-persons and trance-state subpersonalities even if they only represent parts of ourselves. When I was learning to give the Rorschach test, I seem to remember that it was considered a healthy sign if patients saw the ink blot or its various parts as animate or animal or even human. A lot of "human responses" were considered more emotionally healthy than a lot of nonhuman responses. If our unconscious tends to personalise and humanise, it has to do with being in contact with one's feelings and one's own body-self.

On the other hand, there are times when depersonalisation or reification is a helpful and necessary process. This process of removal from feelings or disembodying is a necessary part of imaging and, *a fortiori*, thinking and abstraction. I shall argue that it may enter into activities such as architecture, engineering, and science and into much of what we regard as adaptation to reality. It has to do with separating and sometimes with alienating from the person in one's self. It has to do with simplifying images and symbols. There are many human situations in which depersonalisation is necessary. For example, in government and administration we have to extract certain qualities and properties of people and use these in order to make the mechanisms of administration possible. In law we have a perpetual tension between the person and the reified person. I have given other examples at the beginning of this chapter. Modern warfare seems to require the depersonalising of enemy populations in my experience. The bomber pilot is just "doing his job" when he is engaged in his slaughtering work. He preserves his sanity in this way.

Possible Origins and Nature of Personalising Tendencies

We might say that the tendency to personalise, particularly on the part of the unconscious, seems to be a natural function, but that, according to the results of the Rorschach test, this tendency to personalise, at least to personalise ink blots, is not equally present in everyone; it is present to a greater degree in those people who are more in contact with their feelings and with their humanity. It is arguable that the prototype of the relationship between ego and nonego, between I and not-I, is the early relationship between baby and mother. It might then follow that if the relationship between baby and mother were human, warm, and kind, then the tendency to personalise later in life would be stronger than would be the case with a baby whose mother was more impersonal, less warm. What sort of nonego figures would occupy the mind of a child brought up by monkeys or wolves or put into a cage with a robot mother as the unfortunate baby monkeys were in the Harlow experiments? How much personalising could go on in people brought up in that way is a matter for conjecture. I think the indications are that for normal sociali-sation and creative relationships with things and people, it is necessary or at least very helpful to have had warm early relationships with humans. But let us not take that too much for granted. How "human" the womb is in this sense is something we shall no doubt be finding out much more about. From birth, the baby learns to recognise and respond in detail to more and more differentiated, human qualities of the mother. Both emotional atmosphere and details of caring and interaction may contribute to the humanising of the baby's environment, which becomes the thou, and which is also incorporated into the "myself."

Part Objects, Persons, and Things

When some analysts talk about the child's first relationship being with parts of the mother, such as the breast, rather than the whole person of the mother, what bearing has this on the matter of personalisation and whole-person versus part-person psychology? Is the breast experienced as a thing or as a person? Are we not dealing with a period before there is a differentiation between persons and things? Or is this a cunning way of avoiding the question? Certainly we know that later in life, the child has a tendency to regard parts of his own body and parts of the mother's body as people or little people. So breast-person may well be more nearly what the breast is to a baby than breast-thing. We might suppose that if the mother is warm and loving and gentle and so on, the breast is experienced as a warm, loving, and gentle kind of person by the baby. Preperson might be a more accurate word for it than person. Later in life, as I have said, the unconscious sometimes transforms parts of the body and parts of one's self such as instinctual patterns, zonal patterns of functioning in the body, etc., into images of people. For example, the erect phallus is transformed into, or symbolized by, the toy soldier. But quite often the obverse process occurs, so that parts of the mother's body such as the breast and insides figure in dreams as landscapes, mountains, buildings, furniture, even machinery; hence there may be movements either toward personalisation or toward reification at different times, operating on these primal images. It is deceptively easy when we are theorising to say that each part of the infant's life or each part of the mother's body is felt as a part object, and that later these part objects are united into some sort of a whole person. While this may be so in one sense, experientially the process would probably be more like the unification of wholes rather than of parts. Then, and only then, would the former wholes be seen as parts. The word *part* has no meaning unless it is in reference to a whole, but if there is no integrated and differentiated whole there, then the parts are in some sense experiential wholes. What we as adults refer to as part-object psychology, that is, relating to people as if they were parts of people, as if they were breasts, or receptacles, or other parts of people, as if they were entirely good, or as if they were entirely bad, may all be easily confused with depersonalisation, but is quite different. Treating persons as part objects in this sense is perhaps regressive, but it does not mean that there are things rather than persons in the baby's first experiences.

I cannot overemphasise the fact that I am making a clear distinction between the part-object/whole-object dimension of psychoanalytic psychology and the thing-person dimension I am discussing here. The person in this dimension is seen as a primary way of experiencing and not as the result of holding the opposites, which is relevant to part-object/whole-object psychology. The achievement of holding the opposites is a later achievement for the child and for the adult, too.

We probably have instincts to do with union and unification, and instincts to do with alienation and separation; when our instincts for unification or union are in operation, then objects are naturally treated as self-projections or representations of the self, and this self always seems to have a bodily configuration. Much of our art, for example, and our design of things are based on projecting bodily features onto the objects which are being designed. Objects are fashioned to imitate and express the self and particularly the bodily self. This applies to the design of furniture and the design of houses and cities as well as to visual and sculptural art. The infant relates readily to objects at first as if they were people, so the mother trains the child to care for objects as if they were people. If the child is damaging a table the mother will say,

"Poor table, don't hurt it," and the child will learn a more considerate way of behaving toward the object. If what I am saying is correct, it would follow that there may come to be different ways in which the child perceives the breast; either as more of a person or more of a thing. There are certainly different ways of feeding at different times, for example, a playful feeding, a sort of lovemaking relationship where the baby is gazing up into the mother's eyes, as opposed to other times of more hungry feeding when the baby might be ruthlessly locking on to the breast. There can be no question that the breast and the mother are perceived quite differently in differing internal states. A patient of mine dreamt that when she was feeding her baby she had three breasts; there was a sexy breast on one side, with playful, sexy "grown-up" feelings; the other, normal breast had non-sexy feelings, simple to do with the satisfaction of the baby's hunger. But also she had a breast in the middle representing some process in herself that aimed to combine these two ways of relating.

Possible Origins and Nature of the Tendency to Depersonalise

Readers may know of the indescribably terrible state of mind known in psychiatry as depersonalisation or the depersonalisation syndrome. It is a state in which one does not feel oneself to be a person but more of a thing, perhaps a robot, sometimes more of a two-dimensional entity than one of three dimensions. This feeling or state of mind sometimes spreads from one's feeling about oneself to one's feeling about other people who also become depersonalised, and perhaps especially to important other people like mother, father, wife, husband, and so on. It is not quite so well-known perhaps that this feeling may sometimes affect only part of the person – part of one's body, for example. Or it can start in one part of the body and spread and radiate to the rest of the body or self-image and then to other people and perhaps to everything in general. It is important for my argument that things – from treasured personal objects to the whole world schema – are often also affected by this depersonalising change. For a person suffering in this state, there is usually a feeling that one will never get over it, never get back to a normal world. A normal state of personalisation is an ineffable blessing that we take for granted until we have suffered from its absence. Depersonalisation is a state which feels like madness or alienation and is a fundamental disorder of the embodied self and of personal identity.

It is hard to describe the essential feeling of this state to someone who has not experienced it. Many or most people experience it to some degree in the course of their lives. One may lose altogether the feeling of *I myself in my body*, with all the normal, taken-for-granted bodily feelings that one associates with this image of oneself. Instead, there may be something like a detached observing ego or eye looking down on oneself from a height, or down a microscope or tube, as if the normal I is just a thing, an object viewed with tortured but objective detachment. So depersonalisation is a state in which cold clinical detachment has burst completely out of hand and has not only spread to objects but even to one's self, who now seems to be an object, a thing. Such a degree of cold clinical detachment, when applied to oneself by another, is experienced as a very hostile and chilling act.

I am reminded of a film of a child who had been abandoned for some weeks by his mother. I shall never forget the look of cold clinical detachment on the face of this child as he scrutinised his mother on her return. It was a very chilling thing to see. This state of detachment may follow a state of conflict and anxiety and supersede it; it is as if the anxiety has been replaced by deadness. In fact, we might say that in the fantasies underlying the state of depersonalisation we have the same fantasies as in anxiety, that is, fantasies of separation, damage, annihilation, and so on, but in the state of depersonalisation the feeling is that these have happened, this mutilation of the body or this separation has actually come to pass, rather than being in the balance or in the future. Anxiety always involves some hope, whereas depersonalisation involves the abandonment of hope. I mentioned that a feeling of depersonalisation can actually affect a part of the body rather than the whole, just as in anxiety mutilation fears can affect part of the body and not the whole. This form of anxiety can go on into depersonalisation of part of the body-person. It may seem odd to talk about the depersonalisation of a part of the body, but this is a very real state of mind; it is as if the personality, the livingness, of that part of the body, and one's identification with it, are now lost, and it becomes an alien thing. Degrees of depersonalisation that are often found in a schizophrenic or pre-schizophrenic state of mind are described in the Schreber diaries. The schizophrenic patient, Schreber, saw the doctors and attendants as "miracled up, cursorily improvised" puppets moving around, not as human beings (Schreber 1903).

The state of depersonalisation is sometimes described as loss of soul. I had a patient many years ago who illustrated some of these features. He was an engineer by profession; his engineering interests had developed as a defence against the anxiety of perceiving his mother as a biological, sexual person. His interest in his mother's body was first converted into an interest in biology, but this was still too anxiety-provoking, and eventually, in order to experience even less anxiety, his interests became mechanical and engineering in type and he lost all his sexual and his biological interests in turn during the latency period. He became depersonalised in his early thirties. He read a book by Jung in which mandalas and individuation were discussed, and he started drawing his own mandalas. One had an eye in the middle and he felt compelled to go through this eye in his imagination. He masturbated and abandoned all control over himself and his sexual feelings, and this was the same as going through the eye, plunging into himself, one might say, or plunging into another world. At that moment, he felt that he had lost his soul and he became depersonalised. He felt that his heartbeats were harming his little niece, and he tried to commit suicide. During psycho-therapy, he recovered from this state of depersonalisation, which he often described as like being in a pit (swallowed up in himself or swallowed up by the hostile great mother image). His recovery from this state was heralded by a dream of a machine which went wrong: a furry little animal, a baby creature, scurried away from the machine (Chapter Two, page 21). The dream was followed by his falling in love with the girl he was going out with, marrying her, and having his own baby. The fur of the animal had been associated at the time of the dream with the girl's genitals. Thus it was through his sexual, tender feelings that he once again became an embodied person loving an embodied mother substitute.

Of course, it is not always possible to say that clinical detachment and the scientific attitude are pathological, but my hypothesis is that they represent alienation and separation from the mother and that the mother-image is turned into something less personal; the image of the mother's body is turned into something less personal, or even into a machine or into an abstract mental image. It is not just the image of the mother's body which is changed in this way: one's own body-image and one's own feelings are altered at the same time. Archetypally, reification, disembodying, and the cutting-off from affects belong to the masculine archetypes, while personalisation, rebirth, reuniting with affect, and reuniting with the body tend to belong to the feminine side.

In 1919 the psychoanalyst V. Tausk wrote "On the Origin of the 'Influencing Machine' in Schizophrenia." He described patients who had ideas that they were being influenced paranormally or persecutorily by various objects around them. He showed that these objects were modified images of body parts and the composite influencing machine was, in fact, a human body that had been depersonalised and made into a mechanical thing by the schizophrenic withdrawal and detachment. This same transformation of the body-image may be involved in normal scientific, engineering, and architectural activity and imagery. In primitive times, as we saw, ritual human sacrifice may have accompanied the founding of buildings or the beginning of great projects. This is, in fact, the concrete, behavioural form of the psychic process that is necessary in order to achieve mechanisation or this engineering type of transformation of the mother's body, this liberation from the mother and from instinct. Primitively, one had to enact these things in the external world in order to bring about the necessary internal psychological change. I am suggesting that in the process of depersonalisation and of certain cultural achievements involving abstraction, mathematics, science, imagery, and so on, these achievements are brought about by depotentiating the body and cutting the mental image off from feelings and that the unconscious or semiconscious fantasy involved is a kind of reification of the maternal image at a level where the mother's body-image and one's own body-image are identified. It occurs when direct motor instinctual discharge is prevented in a tolerable way, such that motor discharge is replaced by mental imagery.

Abstracting certainly often obviates anxiety and pain. For example, a patient of mine who was working through intellectual defences dreamt of a little bird trying to get into her room. The bird was prevented from getting in by a glass partition and the bird changed into a blue wavy line that was a sine wave. So the feared phallic invader became an abstract mathematical symbol. Once the impulse is alienated from the ego and becomes a mental image, it becomes subject to the simplifications worked out by the psychologists in their tachistoscopic and remembering experiments. (A tachistoscope is a device for showing a picture to the subject for a very short time so that only a fleeting glimpse is obtained.)

Some of these points are illustrated in the dream of another patient of mine, a middle-aged woman in a high administrative caring professional role. She dreamt of a middle-aged man and his twenty-year-old daughter who were digging around the base of a building, partly to strengthen it and partly because of a bad smell. When they went to replace the earth, it was clear that there was not enough earth to replace what they had removed. This was because underneath the building there was a cellar; the building stood over it and had no foundations of its own. It was discovered that underneath the building there was another woman who was both dead and alive. She was dead in the sense that when the building was put up, she had been buried under the foundations in the way the ancient cultures used human sacrifices in the founding of buildings. She was alive in being intensely evil and able to move around. She pretended that she would help the other two by holding up a wooden door for them to throw earth on. But she reached over this door and embraced the man in a way which was crushing him to death. She was the same as the daughter who was digging or she was another daughter of the man. In reality, this woman, in her childhood, had had the most intense murderous feelings toward her father who, it seems, entirely deserved them. She transformed these murderous feelings into conscientious, socially directed wishes and idealised healing and helping attitudes toward people. In this way, the "evil murderous daughter" was buried and the artificial erection of her character defences and career was founded. The living bodily affects, felt to be evil, had been transformed into the nonliving, maternal-type building, the reified body.

Energy Transformations after Depersonalisation

In the case of this patient, it was clear that originally murderous repudiation of a parent may have been transformed into working toward an ideal of what relationships, and society itself, *should* be like, as unlike the parent as possible. This kind of transformation is commonplace in character development. I can murderously repudiate and triumph over my image of my actual parent. The resulting fantasy image, often semi-abstract in the form of political or ethical principles, because it is imbued with the transformed energy, may have a beautiful, shining, or otherwise energised quality.

In schizophrenic and pharmacologically hallucinated perception, objects in the environment may be seen as depersonalised and energised in this way. The Beatles song, "Lucy in the Sky with Diamonds," illustrated the depersonalisation, the disembodiment, and the imbuing with energy (bejewelling) of the maternal image which may have occurred in Lennon's LSD intoxication. Separation from the mother may involve this type of transformation of the maternal image or be helped along by it. I described earlier in this chapter how sadistic oral and phallic impulses experienced in a dream were transformed into mandala images during awakening, the images developing into beautiful formal patterns incorporated into the mandala. The mandala itself is therefore a typical result of the depersonalisation, abstraction, and energy imbuing of the body-image/maternal-image described here.

In drawing attention to the schizoid, disembodied aspects of the mandala, I am not devaluing such experiences. Art in general is schizoid in the same sense: it cannot take place without some disembodying from affect. Individuation occurs through succeeding cycles of disembodiments and reembodiments. I know of no neutral, nonpejorative word for healthy, physiological splitting of this kind.

This theory (of the progressive transformation of the image of the mother and of the connections with one's feelings) is an alternative way of looking at the phenomenon subsumed under the psychoanalytic theory of sublimation, whereby the sexual instinct is deflected from its primary target onto other, more practical or more acceptable ones. The emphasis here is on transformation rather than deflection or aim-inhibition, in line with the usual difference in emphasis between psychoanalysis and analytical psychology.

Imitation, Synaesthesia, and Personalisation

By synaesthesia I mean the transfer of perceptions from one modality to another by virtue of affective correspondence. Thus a sound may be seen as a colour with the same feeling-tone. In all human interactions, affects are transmitted from person to person. It is as if they are infectious. The transmission may take place via affective expression and synaesthesia, or by a process we might call primal imitation. How far transmission at this level, e.g., from the mother's expressions and actions to the baby, has to be learned and how far it is a natural or innate process is no doubt being gradually elucidated by patient observation by various research workers. However, there is no question that imitation, synaesthesia, and affective communication are present at a very basic level in the mammalian psyche. The communication at this level is sometimes quasi-telepathic, as, for example, in phenomena coming under the heading of *participation mystique*. This sort of communication is actual and not to be confused with illusions or delusions of oneness by either party. The nature of such primitive communication is very difficult to study or to pin down. But we can observe that a baby sometimes echoes or imitates emotional facial expressions of the mother, or more often vice-versa. This illustrates the fact that there is an intimate connection between sensory data, i.e., from the mother's body or facial image, thence via the organisation of such data by one's perceptive processes, through one's own body-image, and through this to one's affects and motor expressions. In some psychotic states, imitation is automatic and compulsive, and even the common phenomenon of negativity in schizophrenia may well be due to a reversal of this normal process of primal imitation.

Whatever the exact mechanisms involved, it is quite likely that here we have two or more human people communicating at a primitive level, where bodily motor expressions are integrated in a not necessarily conscious neurological stratum that subserves the body-image. It is my belief that the self at this level is a body-self, just as the ego, which is based on the self, is a body-ego. I am here suggesting that personalisation is rooted in these unifying affective experiences at this primitive level of the psyche. The destruction of links of this sort, the fragmentation of this integrate of affective communication and the primal self, and the phenomena of so-called schizoid mechanisms and defences (suicidal and matricidal attacks on the body-world-mother-self) are also mechanisms belonging to this level. They develop by degrees into "normal" patterns of thinking, abstraction, and depersonalisation, if they are not made to occur precociously in psychic development by impersonal mothering, and so on.

Disembodying as the Basis of Schizoid Defences

In schizophrenia and schizoid state, we continually encounter situations in which mental images are split off from feelings. Jung's thinking type of person shows this tendency, but here it has not necessarily yet been carried to an incapacitating degree.

The language of feelings is the language of bodily impulses, move-ments, postures, etc. It consists of how one stands in relation to external or internalised objects or images. The internal images are often visual images and in any case they may develop into thoughts that are usually located subjectively in the head. The subjective distinction between upper and lower – both as feelings or as a description of location within the subjective image of the psyche – is much to do with this disembody-ing split between image and affect.

When the inner living mother affect-image is sacrificed in the founding of the great engineering project and her body literally or meta-phorically placed in the foundations, the sacrifice of feelings for the purpose of enhancing the capacity to think is what is happening psychi-cally. If the sacrifice is carried out in consciousness of love, inevitability, and remorse, as, for example, perhaps in the sacrifice of Iphigenia by her father Agamemnon in order to launch the massive project of the Trojan Wars, it is perhaps not madness but greatness we are talking about, allowing for the beliefs then current. But when the destruction of the lower is carried out unconsciously, compulsively, in hatred, fear, envy, or contempt, we are talking about a schizoid situation. The split-off feel-ings, represented by corresponding images, may force themselves into consciousness autochthonously in a distorted, haunting, or obtrusive form – the return of the repressed. Usually it is when the love object or the Kleinian breast or other affect-image becomes overwhelmingly excit-ing or engulfing that she/it has to be dealt with in this potentially destructive way.

My example of the patient's dream of the woman buried in the foundations illustrates another kind of return of the repressed, but in a therapeutic setting when the patient was becoming more aware of the schizoid defences. Much of therapy consists of reestablishing the con-nection between ego and affect – realising that images are images origi-nally of affects, so to speak – and reembodying the affects into the body/ ego/personal identity. In practice, in the same way as much of the holding, conflict-withstanding, personal-identity ego consists of intro-jections from the affirmative, conflict-holding mother, so the establish-ment of connections between affect and images, between these and the body-ego, depends on the successful introjection of the affirmative ana-lyst's attitude.

Autochthonous, nonholdable, or uncontrollable images and men-tal contents are, of course, at the root of the schizoid problem. This is why the "as-if," metaphorical attitude is lost and thinking become so humourless and concrete. Autochthonous contents are disembodied affects and affect-images bursting through into the thinking consciousness as alien thoughts and images – hauntings, I like to call them, because they are unresolved and unredeemed parts of the self, often in reversed or other bizarre forms, distorted by a made sense of humour, as it were.

In the event that this seems too abstract, let me illustrate it by means of a dream I had when I was working through some of my own schizoid defences in analysis. In this dream, a huge, mighty semigod or hero took hold of a Charlie Chaplin-like comedian (who in the dream was very sad and humble) and hurled him with murderous contempt and shattering force down the cellar steps of my parental home. After a while the bones of the comedian came to life at the bottom of the cellar steps as a dancing, mocking skeleton to haunt the murderer, and a voice explained to me, the dreamer, "This is schizophrenia."

I am not pretending that we can ever really understand these archetypal relationships between one's omnipotence and one's sense of humour, which when repressed tends to obtrude as schizophrenic content; the dream still says it all as far as I am concerned. However, I am very much aware that this is my personal way of understanding these schizoid defences of which depersonalisation seems to be a prototype. How is disembodying represented in image or fantasy? In the above example, it is represented by the hero's attempt to rid himself of the comedian, perhaps even get rid of inferior affects altogether. The avoidance of affect, and the projective attribution of all kinds of affects to others, is typical of schizoid patients. Affect can, of course, be represented by animal figures. And depersonalisation can be represented by the progressive abstraction, mechanisation, geometrization of the human, biological mother-image described herein. Images of decapitation, hanging, and other cuts or blockages between upper body parts and lower ones are relevant here, although I think they do not refer to depersonalisation as such but to splitting, repression, or numbing of part of the body-self (rather than the withdrawal of narcissistic libido from the whole of the self- or body-image as in typical depersonalisation). On the other hand, blighted landscapes, ruined buildings, images of world destruction are all very close to depersonalisation. In these images, we have destruction or blighting of the world-mother-self image. The cosmic matricidal quality of T. S. Eliot's early poems, such as "The Waste Land" and "The Hollow Man," is a case in point. (It was only in his later works, such as "Family Reunion," that the matricide became more personal and less cosmic.) The landscape represents the Great Mother at the level where what happens to Her is very close to actual (somatised) happenings in the imaginer's actual body. Even at the mundane social level, it is now obvious to all that what we do to our landscapes we are doing, inside so to speak, to ourselves. We cannot hack away at the earth all our lives, as a miner does, without something happening to our souls. The same applies to factories and assembly lines, of course.

Complex Interactions of Affect, Objects, and Images

Supposing that a human, actual, biological mother causes me to experience unbearable affect. For example, she may cause me to experience affects, e.g., sexual feelings or aggressive feelings, that she could not recognise or tolerate. Any such affects might cause unbearable conflict or anxiety in me. An image of a human biological woman would give rise to such affects. And so the actual mother would be treated as a nonsexual, nonhateful person, and the image of the mother would be modified so as to provoke less anxiety, less affect. In this way, images would become less human, more mechanical, etc., corresponding to the splitting-off or denial of affect that is occurring in the personal relationships. The degree of reification in objects of interest, dream images, etc., would be a reflection of, a pictorial description of, and a result of, the affective splitting. However, the split-off affects would, in some circumstances, tend to give rise to their own corresponding affect-images, perceptual distortions, autochthonous mental processes, and so on. These in turn would be subjected to the same processes of affect-suppression, denial, projection, and other schizoid and postschizoid defences, until images emerge that carry tolerable or pleasant affect and a new interest, a new tolerable object or person is found, a new toy or a new pet is cathected. The resulting complexity and variability of humanisation/ dehumanisation in our interests, sublimations, and imagery account for the richness and complexity of our lives and cultural patterns.

The separation from the maternal image of anxiety-provoking affect proceeds alongside the ability to maintain an affect-experiencing personal identity. It is this personal identity, the omnipotent precursor of which (the primal myself as it were) employs the narcissistic defences, which finally produce feelings of me and not-me and then of inner and outer worlds.

Meaning, Symbolisation, Affect, Transitional Phenomena

Let us try to clarify some of the relationships between the above terms with the use of concrete examples.

In my account of my relationship with my boat, I suggested that the boat represented a damaged and damaging mother to me. My actions and interest in her can be compared with the behaviour of a normal or an autistic child who shows interest in a boat (or, more likely, a doll-house), taking contents out and rearranging them to the child's satisfaction. Let us suppose that for the normal child the boat or dollhouse is a transitional type of object. We – normal adult, normal child, autistic child – can all be said to be dealing with reified mother-images. The house or the boat can, in each case, be said to represent the mother's body.

We can all be said to be behaving practically and adaptively with our "toys." I am treating the boat as a boat, arranging and modifying it so that it sails better, is safer, more comfortable, etc. The same might well be true of the children with their dollhouses. The practical, mechanical manipulations and skill would be right-handed affairs, assuming we are all right-handed, and would be carried through by the left cerebral hemispheres.

The meanings of a referent can be divided into those practical or scientific or cognitive ones about which accurate objective definitions, even quantitative ones, are supposed to be applicable, and those meta-phorical, affective, or attitudinal ones about which we can all happily argue. We might call these two types of meaning the realistic type and the affective type. Thus the realistic meaning of the object could be the same for the autistic child, the normal child, and the normal adult. Also shared by the three of us is the fact that the object can be said to represent a reified mother's body. Where we differ mainly is in the ways or in levels at which the three of us relate to ourselves and to objects in general. The autistic child, while showing intense interest in the object for a time, may, for example, apparently not care if he has to leave it or lose it, and on occasions may evince signs of fear of it. He seems to be avoiding the personal both in the object and in himself – for example, he may use the third person singular for himself. For him, the thing or the "it" is much less upsetting than the "thou" or the person. The normal child and the adult are relating to the object in a personal way, and the adult has, or so we might hope, worked through more conflicts about possessiveness and loss than the child.

It is clear that each of the three is using the object as a symbol, in that he is working through fantasies and conflicts about the mother and the self through the object. However, the symbolic value and symbolic depth of the use of the object will be different in each case and will, of course, depend on the maturity and richness of the ego-self and ego-object stage of development reached by the individual. As analytical psychologists (Jungian analysts), we often say that such-and-such a patient or such-and-such a type of patient is not using symbols or is not using psychic material or content in a symbolic way. This is hardly ever true if it is intended to mean that the patient, even the autistic patient, is not using the mental content, objects, or persons to work through psychic conflicts in an unconscious or conscious way. It may be true if it means that the patient is not able to use symbols and mental content in an aware way in the therapeutic relationship or in some other sophisticated sense such as writing or group discussions. The primitive situation means that the metaphor is enacted in its concrete form rather than experienced *as metaphor*. It does not mean that the brain is not functioning in a metaphorical way.

But the fundamental question is to do with the individual's power to contain affect and tolerate paradoxes, incompatibilities, separations, loss, despair, etc.

A strong body-ego identity can do this. It is this that determines how symbolic experiences can be. There is an important connection between reification, distancing, and (thereby) creating sufficient space for oneself to enable oneself optimally to work through symbolic content, in other words to optimise emotional involvement. Play, cultural phenomena, working through conflicts with transitional objects (for example, my boat) depends on one's ability to create the necessary space, and this in turn depends importantly on the space originally allowed by one's personal mother and mother-figures. Reification is another way of speaking about increasing the space between the "myself" and the thou, the mother originally, and optimising (often decreasing but not to the point of meaninglessness) emotional involvement. The accretion of more and more successive layers in the growth of our complexes is a result of this course steered between overinvolvement and meaninglessness.

Containers and Containers Within Containers

For Jung and for many who have followed him, the alchemical vessel stands for the ego-function of containing and holding archetypal interaction and conflict so that further syntheses and resolutions come about. That the vessel itself is a reified mother, and that originally it is the actual mother who holds and reflects, now needs no arguing. The frequency with which the earliest jugs and containing vessels were given breasts suggests that our ancestors arrived at the jug by the process of reifying the maternal image and abstracting the holding and giving qualities to a degree necessary for their purposes.

The *temenos*, the theatre, and the picture frame are further abstractions of the same containing/splitting function. Remembering is itself another important example of the same thing on a more microscopic level. As analysts we talk about being swallowed up by a mental process and also of getting outside it. Some ability to get outside, i.e., contain an affective experience, is necessary both for reflection, for thinking, for imaging, and for working symbolically. My being aware of myself in some context is the same mental trick. Often intellectual and schizoid defences are represented by successive containers, such as dreams within dreams, even containers within containers within containers, and so on. Each level of containing represents a further stage in the distancing of image from primal affect, a further safety boundary against unbearable affect. A patient of mine dreamt that she was calling her husband. She then woke and her husband, who had been lying awake beside her, told her that she had just been shouting out "Mummy" in her sleep. So the remembered dream image was several layers nearer to consciousness than the more archaic affect/action of the shout. There was no question that her husband was very much a mother-figure to her.

What I am suggesting here is that what we experience as our minds is built up by successive layers, and that each comes about by this very important psychophysiological process of the image-enhancing/disembodying of affects/affect-images.

The tremendous increase in the ability to experience and use abstract images that occurred at the end of the fourth millenium B.C. in the Middle East must therefore have been accompanied by a separation, in the persons concerned, from embodied feeling; and as embodied feeling has to do with the early relationships, particularly with the mother, it is often linked with or represented by a mother- or animal-figure who has to be sacrificed, or a couple (king and queen) who have to play their role in the march of civilisation. Other kinds of sacrifice, in other cultures, can be viewed as the splitting off of other parts of the collective self. The bloody sacrifices to Kali to the accompaniment of chants of peace would be an example of the splitting off, with acting out, of violent aggressive feelings.

Robotic Self-Images

Today we are living not so much in a world of plants and animals and enduring landscape, or an ordered world of the movements of stars and planets, as of technical marvels, computers, and robots. These are the images of much of modern mythology, and an important source of active modern subpersonalities. Fashions and styles reflect the movements of prevailing subpersonalities. Robotic dance, robotic dress styles, and robotic ways of speaking suggest a sacrifice of feeling and humanity according to the law that world, group, art styles, and self are all related to each other and represent each other in the mind. Polarization and countermovements reflecting opposing subpersonalities also abound, and this is part of the turbulent working out of the dehumanising forces of the present time, with the danger of human sacrifice on a lavish scale which has never been absent for long in recent centuries.

CHAPTER 10

The Rise of the Male Gods and the Separation of the Opposites

Let us recapitulate the findings so far.

(1) The end-of-world image occurs when an important split-off subpersonality, in conflict with the "normal" habitual attitude, is ready to be reintegrated. In other words, when the split-off opposite is ready for healing, when the paradox or contradiction is ready to be faced and confronted.

(2) The coming-together of opposites generates subjectively intense psychic energy which is often difficult or impossible to contain and harness.

(3) The containing function can be looked on as ego strength and is a maternal function often learned from the real mother. The mother image in personal or abstract form is concerned with this. These containing, holding functions are usually introjected from the mother in early childhood, but can also be learned later from respected parent figures, including therapists.

(4) Conversely, the splitting-off of subpersonalities is accompanied by acting out and projecting the unacceptable part of the self. This is often violent and explosive and is the *reciprocal* of the explosion image (which occurs when concrete explosive behaviour is foregone).

(5) The image of the opposites combining creatively is associated with images of new life such as the child, the divine child, the secret of eternal life, the heart's desire, the goal of life, etc. If the energy cannot be contained, the image of the new creation takes the corresponding negative form, such as cancer, dead child, or atom bomb, etc. Work can often convert the feared image into its opposite or

into an integrated image. Rubbish and *prima materia* can be converted into valuable things, intrapsychically speaking.

(6) The ability to contain conflict and make something valuable is a function of the ability to suffer pain and not project it as sadism or aggression. This is a function of loving and of feeling loved. Self-love and self-respect reflect ego strength in this sense.

(7) The mother's function of holding and reconciling opposing and conflicting parts of the self was integrated into the self historically during the long period of the female figurine and the mother goddess and her consort.

(8) As the early self integrates the maternal functions it is able to have images of container and wheel, have an existence to some degree independent of the group, and have an image of a walled city or temple which is a projection of the self and which is now defended and able to contain value. At the same time, we have the beginning of narcissism and individual self-awareness as opposed to the group self.

(9) The ability to have abstract images occurs when the mother and her body are disidentified with. Thinking is now embarked on a course separate from feeling. Abstract thought carries the penalty of loss of conscious feeling, depersonalisation, and sacrifice of humanity. Early engineering and military projects requiring planning and the putting of ideas into practice therefore necessitated ritual sacrifice of humans or animals, symbolizing the feeling side of the self. The human sacrifices of the mother goddess period concern mainly planting and fertility and the sacrificial persons seem to represent the death and renewal aspects of the heavens and of the agricultural cycle. But planting and cultivation, like engineering projects, require considerable will-power and sacrifice of feeling, so the same considerations apply partly here as to scientific, engineering, and military endeavour.

(10) The image and the aim for self or cosmos of the perfect circle containing the opposites in creative combination is an abstraction that is orderly and which splits off feelings of disintegration, chaos, and destructiveness. Mathematics, science, and administration carry with them this inherent danger of alienation from the body and bodily feelings and of explosive behaviour.

A Biologically Based Notion of the Opposites

The opposites whose combination or splitting-off from each other is so energetic in the human psyche are love and hate (Eros and Thanatos in Freud's hypothesis); goodness and healing as opposed to evil, destructiveness, and disease; and the opposing twins of male and female, parent and child, inside (the boundaries of the self that is) and outside – in other words, I and not-I, and so on – but that is sufficient to stimulate the reader into adding to the list.

The opposites that matter are not, repeat *not*, based on mathematical or conceptual abstractions such as plus and minus, reversal of images, or physics. If hot and cold are opposites, it is because they are biological opposites – they produce incompatible, mutually inhibitory physiological effects. It is these physiological effects that are the basis of the idea that coldness and warmth are opposites, for example. It is *not* based on the "fact" that, taking a reference point of 15°C, 18° is 3° of warmth and 12° is the opposite, i.e., 3° of coldness. Of course, if I were to grip a metal bar whose temperature was 15°C, and if its temperature increased by 3°, it would feel less cold, and if it decreased by 3°, it would feel colder; but the feelings or sensations and the physiological responses of the body are very complex and involve many factors in addition to the temperature of a metal bar or even of the skin touching that bar.

One of the great pleasures of my academic life was my first encounter with Sir Charles Sherrington's classic book, *Integrative Action of the Nervous System*, which was written in 1906 and was a landmark in modern physiology. This book, as well as any other, describes simply but in detail how, in the integration of bodily functions from the "lowest" reflex level to the "highest" functions of the brain, opposing reciprocal actions have to be built into the nervous system by nature for anything to work at all. If I am to bend my arm at the elbow, one group of muscles (biceps, etc.) which bend the forearm has to shorten, while at the same time the opposing group of muscles (triceps, etc.), which stretch the forearm, has to relax automatically and at the right time. So there has to be mutually negative feedback built into the two sets of muscles, together with ways of overriding this negative feedback when necessary. A moment's reflection will convince the reader that reciprocal inhibition of opposing behaviours and emotions must be built into nervous mechanisms in the same sort of way for any action to be accomplished. One cannot relish and swallow a morsel of food and spit it out in disgust at the same time, nor would one act in a tender loving way and a murderously attacking way at the same time. The resolution of conflict, certainly when action is needed, means the inhibition of incompatible or opposing innervations and the sharpening up of boundaries, and Nature provides for these things to happen in the most marvellous ways.

Of course, further reflection soon leads to the conclusion that the nervous system is far more multidimensional than to be describable in terms of opposites and of their mutual inhibition. Yet it is remarkable how we are constantly reminded of opposites or, perhaps one might put it another way, how we seem to be most at our mental ease when we are oversimplifying things by using emotive, ethical, and moral opposites and when we are opposing I and not-I (inside and outside the subjective self) in the ways I have described in previous chapters.

In the world of action, from the simplest to the most complex, incompatibles have to be inhibited, boundaries have to be sharpened by the setting up of perceived opposition and conceptualized opposites, and the resulting opposites used to reinforce thinking and increase the efficiency of the action. Attitudes being but subliminal postural actions, the same tendencies prevail there, too.

For my own dialectic purposes, I am contrasting (opposing) the world of action with the world of containment, reflection, and conscious awareness, i.e., of holding as opposed to discharging mental experience. In the world of action, differences and boundaries usually must be clearcut or even emphasized; in the world of holding, unity, joining, and intercourse prevail. It is easy, perhaps a little too easy, to understand these two worlds of action and of the containment of conflict as the world of the father or the masculine principle and the world of the mother or the feminine principle, respectively. The principle or subpersonality is, of course, not to be confused with the person. We all know that fathers can contain and mothers can differentiate and act, and, in fact, the father can do a lot of holding when mother and children are disintegrating, as well as vice-versa. But as far as the baby, and therefore one's roots of experience, are concerned, the mother figure is the holder and container-in-chief, the symbol of loving and caring and provider of the experience of being loved that holds one together. She therefore provides the foundation and the springboard from which one can later make distinctions and differentiations (taught perhaps by father or by one's own daring independence).

Before "I" and "you" are separate, there would seem to be a stage of development where I, world, mother, mother's body, and one's own body are not differentiated. Primitively, world-image, body-image, and Great Mother (or Great Goddess) are not really differentiated. This can be inferred from a study of regressed patients and of the deepest layers of the unconscious. At this level the baby can be contented, distressed, and angry in turn, or the schizophrenic patient can have moods of loving and hating within a very short space of time, but these states or moods are not connected even as opposites with what *we* regard as opposites. Nevertheless, the withdrawn or withheld loved person or breast-type person is experienced as hateful or murderous, no doubt a separate person from the present and enjoyed person or breast, because experiences are separate from each other. In other words, the loved and the hated breast or mother are not connected with each other, even as opposites.

The late Neolithic and Bronze Age great goddess in her most powerful days in the Middle East and in Crete, whose consort is the immortal snake or the moon bull, sometimes has a dual form (queen of heaven and queen of the earth or of the dark underworld, for example, the Sumerian Inanna and Ereshkigal).

The great goddess is the mother and creatrix of all, the swallower and destroyer of all. Death and resurrection are the destiny of the consort and of the worshipper of the mother goddess. She swallows and conceives at night, and she gives birth in the new day. Paradise, fruitfulness, and immortality reward those with the courage to enter her portals and submit to her judgment. She is free and bounteous with her maternal, as with her sexual, favours, and she rules over sexual love as well as the earth's bounty, because her body, the earth, and her consort's body are not divorced from each other.

The great goddess moved mankind during the New Stone Age and the Bronze Age stages of civilisation, which, of course, were at different dates in different parts of the world. In the Middle East, her period lasted from 7000 B.C. to the dawn of the Iron Age about 1250 B.C. She presided over the basic early agriculture and the crafts and techniques of mankind, particularly before the era of the city-state, when the art of thinking was developed, with the splitting-off of feeling, the depersonalisation of the mother-figure, and the liberation of abstract thought. We could put this date at around 3200 B.C. The mother goddess corresponds with the integration of the internalized mother and the separation from dependent relationships. While one is separating from dependence, the mother-figure can be a snare and a temptation or a prison; her milk can be a tempting poison. The negative aspect of the mother goddess is that of Circe, witch, poisoner, ensnarer, seductress, and captor.

With the gradual rise and eventual victory of male deities over the female between 3000 and 1000 B.C., we see increasing separation and differentiation of the opposites, greater divorce between the I and the world of instinct and between I and not-I, and the separation of good and evil. The concomitant justification of mass slaughter and terrorism that characterizes the omnipotence of the one god who is all-true and all-righteous can be seen in Levantine monotheism to this day, and in Hitlerism and Stalinism. Counter to this has flowed the maternal stream of the mystery religions, the universal and loving aspects of religion, and, nowadays, those psychotherapies that are in line with the personally transforming mystery religions and in which regression and rebirth are experienced in one way or another.

Whereas regression-and-death–rebirth-and-renewal characterize the cults of the transforming powers of the mother goddess, inspiration and the thunderbolt or lightning flash characterize the transforming qualities of the male god. The atom-bomb image or dream may contain both feminine and masculine attributes, but in its aspect of sudden, shocking attack it has more the qualities of the early father gods such as Marduk, Yahweh, and perhaps Zeus. The positive transformative aspects of the lightning flash of the Buddha Vajradhara, who bears supreme illumination, is a less destructive and punishing version of this same masculine principle.

By the time the Bible was written, the power of the mother goddess was largely destroyed, although her resilience is shown by the violence and ruthlessness that were necessary to eradicate her shrines and her priests and the abhorrence shown toward her worship and worshippers. Eve and the serpent are but a pale remnant of the great mother goddess and her serpent-bull-consort-son-victim of the earlier times. But let us take an earlier stage of the Genesis story in the Middle East, namely the victory of the solar, law-giving god Marduk, the mighty Marduk, god of the law-giving King Hammurabi of Babylon, over the primordial mother and genetrix of all, Tiamat, and the story of her murder and her splitting into the upper and lower worlds.

According to this creation myth of the time of Hammurabi, later found in the library of King Ashurbanipal of Assyria, in the beginning was Tiamat, who gave birth to everything, Apsu, the begetter of every-thing, and Mummu, their son and messenger. Other generations of gods followed, until their clamorous turmoil disturbed the insides of Tiamat, and Apsu and Mummu conspired, against her wishes, to rid her of her disorderly progeny. However, the progeny learned of the plan, slew Apsu, and took Mummu prisoner. In her mounting rage Tiamat now spawned monstrous and frightening creatures. All the gods but the mighty Marduk were intimidated and overawed, but Marduk offered to be their champion if he were given sovereignty over all the gods. Thus the now hideous Tiamat was slain, and Marduk, the god of Babylon, reigned supreme just as his earthly counterpart, Hammurabi, ruled over the world of men. By this time, the king had learned to escape the double axe of the regicidal mother goddess and knife regicide of the priest astronomers. He had become both god and king, and his view of the cosmos and of the ruling of the state develop in some groups into the dominance of the hero king and the father god. We may be quite sure that Yahweh and Zeus reflected the same social changes. Indeed, the triumph of the Olympian gods runs closely parallel to the Marduk story. Here, again, it is not possible to say which is causal, history or mythology – changes in the external world or the concomitant changes in the internal world.

With the slaying of the universal mother comes the division of her body and those of her spouse and sons into heaven, earth, and the abyss. The victorious god defines the year and its twelve zodiacal signs, the days, the phases of the moon, the stations of the sun. He creates man from the body of the chief ally of the murdered Mother to serve the gods. And perhaps most important of all, he divides the gods into good gods (his allies) and evil gods (those who had helped Tiamat). He sets up his dwelling in shining Babylon with its wondrous ziggurat.

In the rule of the mother goddess, death and resurrection, good and evil, light and darkness, the cycle of the seasons, human sacrifice as the price of fertility are seen as opposite aspects of a unity. The unifying bond is the mother, and when she is murdered the opposites are split (or differentiated, depending on one's point of view). In his book *Occidental Mythology* (1964) Joseph Campbell, mourning the defeat of the matriar-chy, says that all is now strife and effort, defamation of what is alien, pretentiousness, grandiloquence, with a lurking sense of guilt. God is now quite other than man and the arbitrary maker of the laws that are henceforth what man shall strive to live by. All man can do is not to follow his own divinity and his own nature, but try with greater and greater learning to study the will of God through the holy books. This is the story of the Levantine religions. The price of competing omnipotent and all-righteous Gods is internecine turbulence and strife, as we see in the history of the Middle East.

A later, more differentiated stage in the law of the opposites is seen in the birth of ethical dualism in the Persian religion of the late second millennium B.C., ascribed to the vision of the prophet Zoroaster and his god Ahura Mazda, the god of truth, goodness, and light, who is destined after thousands of years to purify the world and defeat the corrupt, lying, diseased world of his evil counterpart, Angra Mainyu, the Demon of the Lie.

So by the late second millennium B.C. goodness and evil are firmly established opposing ethical principles at war in each of us, with each of us deciding, and eventually being judged and rewarded or punished for, the goodness or the evil in our deeds. In this kind of religion, ethical free will entails a Heaven and a Hell very similar to the vision of Dante, and moral principles are envisioned in personified form as angelic or demonic beings, the forerunners of the angels and demons of the Judeo-Christian religions.

The eventual, inevitable triumph of goodness over evil is now seen in historical, apocalyptic vision, with moral judgment of all human beings, each of whom is responsible for his own fate. Mingled with moral behaviour that we would recognize as good, we have the religious law of the time reminiscent of the Judaic laws – in the Zoroastrian case, next-of-kin marriage, disposal of hair and fingernails, purification of the evil of menstruation, provision of dry wood for the fire. The injunction to marry one's next-of-kin contrasts curiously with the horror of incest of the oedipal myth.

Ahura Mazda was god of Truth, Beauty, Goodness, and Love. He was the god of Cyrus the Great of Persia. Unlike the more mythical Joshua, whose god ordered the wholesale slaughter of defeated enemies and of their priests, and unlike some cruel Assyrian tyrants, who slaughtered, tortured, and moved whole populations from their homelands, Cyrus restored their gods, treated defeated kings kindly, and was thought great and good by friends and former enemies alike. We cannot say that Ahura Mazda was a projection of Cyrus in the same sense that Marduk was a projection of the Babylonian kings of the time of Hammurabi, because Cyrus post-dated Zoroaster by several hundred years. It is almost as if Cyrus was an incarnation of Ahura Mazda, an incarnation of the Zoroastrian ideal when the religion had reached maturity.

In the Babylonian myth, the battle of the opposites is between the ancient mother goddess and the modern male hero-god, who after his victory goes on to create the world as we know it. In the Zoroastrian myth, the apocalyptic confrontation is between the god of light and truth and the demon of the lie, and the inevitable victory of good over evil ushers in the final millennial period of future history.

There is hardly any ethical conflict in the Babylonian thinking, although there would be a conflict about whether to obey the law of Marduk or Hammurabi or suffer the consequences. In the Zoroastrian religion, behaviour and ethics are seen in terms of personal choice between good and evil: abstract ethical principles are personalised and seen as angels and demons. Personal responsibility is thus a very real part of the I of that time, and this, without presumptuousness, we can see as another great step forward in human consciousness. Love and goodness are now felt as motivating principles opposed to evil and hatred.

In the Vision of Arda Viraf, a late Zoroastrian work, the good man meets a beautiful woman who identifies herself as his own good thoughts and actions, whereas an evil man meets a hideous, diseased hag who announces herself as his own evil deeds. Just as the beautiful vision has been made beautiful by the first person's goodness, so the hideous, deformed hag has been made thus by the second person's misdeeds.

In psychotherapy the client may have dreams of a diseased man, woman, or child, a dead or desolate or a beautiful paradisal landscape, or a beautiful or ugly building. At first we have to discuss the beautiful or ugly images as if an impersonal outside agency was responsible for the creative or destructive effect on the person or landscape. It is a great and gratifying step forward in therapy when the client can feel the beautifying or otherwise as a reflection or even as an effect of his own love or hate, without condemning himself but with a feeling of responsibility and joy or sadness, respectively. The patient must not, however, be rushed or preached into this personal feeling of being the disease, the earthquake, or the atom bomb that has attacked the mother, father, baby, landscape-mother, etc. To interpret these things therapeutically rather than counter-therapeutically is one of those therapeutic skills which are elusive and mostly a function of one's own security and empathic good feeling.

If a patient dreams of a city devastated by bomb, let alone by an earthquake, the therapist has to accept that the client is not yet ready to assume personal responsibility for the destructive anger causing the damage to the depersonalized person – say, the mother figure or whatever manifestation in which the mother appears or is symbolized. We have no choice but to cope with this anger as an impersonal force far beyond the ego's capacity to contain or own. We cannot *force* responsibility for destructiveness onto people who cannot *feel* responsible.

We have to admit that mankind is in a somewhat similar helpless, immature, nonresponsible state with regard to political, historical forces and, in particular, with regard to wars and especially nuclear warfare. It is a simple fact that in collective conflicts resulting in immense suffering, death, and destruction, no less than in damaging and escalating conflicts of all kinds, the subject's "reality" is that he is the innocent victim and the enemy is the one who should be taking the responsibility for the evil. This is true for both sides, of course.

Nothing so clearly demonstrates my thesis that behaviour and awareness-with-responsibility bear a reciprocal, opposing relationship with each other. It is difficult for this reason to bring in historical examples without being untherapeutic, but many of us can feel ashamed and sickened on behalf of humanity in general and Europeans in particular on account of the rise of Nazism, its appeasement, and especially on account of mass slaughtering of Jews and others in the death camps. We are making ourselves learn more and more about how these atrocities could occur. The more we learn about what happened, the more we have to acknowledge that ordinary people like you and me could have become embroiled and involved in almost any of the roles played out by Germans and other nationals on the one side and by the victims on the other. From Eichmann down to the lowest-ranking railway official arranging the timetables of the death trains, all regarded themselves, and arguably were, ordinary people innocently but uncomfortably doing a job, carrying out instructions. There were sadists among the torturers and there were people around the camps who gloated at the fate of the victims, but they were not particularly numerous. Nothing evil or incriminating was committed to paper, but everyone knew what was expected of them.

Even more humiliating is the finding in experimental psychology that ordinary students, thinking they are participating in scientific investigation, can be instructed to administer electric shocks they believe to be of lethal strength to experimental subjects who are young people like themselves.

How can we go on believing that this wickedness is nothing to do with us? At an infantile level it is, of course, necessary for our peace of mind, our physical well-being, our functional efficiency, let alone our self-respect, to project all this evil into the not-I part of the Self. But at a more mature level and for the sake of the survival of the race, it is necessary for us to take on board some notion of shared responsibility and with it the hope of changing our fate for the better and of allowing love to work its self-rewarding way through our personal and collective transactions. The insecurely extraverted may need to deny any sadness, let alone any share of responsibility for where the world is heading, but such innocence and irresponsibility on the part of vast numbers of people is just another fact of life we have to recognize as such and cope with somehow. One cannot ram responsibility down the throats of our children, our clients, or our extraverted brothers and sisters. If they do not feel responsible, they are not responsible, although they will suffer innocently for their unconscious contributory roles along with the "guilty," if guilty ones could ever be found.

When I was a young man, I was preoccupied for a time with the battle between what I experienced as a good, loving part of myself and a rebellious, hating part. This was at the time my first marriage broke up and I became seriously ill. During my convalescence in the sanatorium for chest diseases, I was encouraged by a visiting art therapist to paint. One of my first paintings was of a Christ-like young man joining hands with an antiChrist, Anubis-like figure, both being held in the arms of what I intended to be a nature or mountain god, but who turned out to be a nature mother goddess. This, I now realize, illustrates the profound truth that at the level of the mother goddess the opposites, even the ultimate ones of love and hate, good and evil, are, if not identical, seen to be opposing and united aspects of an underlying unity in nature. For some Chinese, at least, it is not a question of the ultimate opposites of sun and moon, yin and yang, it is a matter of yin-yang. Yin-yang is the ultimate unity. I mention my own experience only for the reason that nowadays, in the West, we are experiencing a powerful resurgence of what we should for all practical purposes call the Mother Goddess. It is not simply a matter of revising our rational views about the sex of the Deity, but of a powerful rebalancing of the masculine and feminine subpersonalities which is going on in Western society, at a level far beneath the ordinary, conscious, rational level.

But for the worshipper of the male god, it is very much a matter of good versus evil, of differentiating right from wrong, or fighting for what is right, and of not being soiled or humiliated by weakness or compromise.

The mother goddess has her destructive, terrifying side, when love is withdrawn and death or engulfment threatens. The beloved who is withdrawing her love toward a person who is relating at this level of the psyche becomes a foul murderess or witch who must be destroyed or who will destroy oneself. Tiamat becomes hateful and monstrous when she is resisting the clamour of her descendants, and spawns pestilence and storm.

A person who sees things in terms of black and white, who always "knows" what is right, and who always does what he know to be right, is far too good to be true. Indeed the person who always "knows" what is true, good, or whatever, is a most omnipotent, inflexible, boring, and insensitive person. Such would be a caricature of the extreme devotee of a male (monotheistic) god. On the other hand, a person who is completely tolerant, morally indifferent, and who always sees similarities and is not able to respect boundaries or make distinctions is equally difficult to deal with. Such a person might be thought of (again in a caricature, of course) as under the spell of the goddess. At an even more archaic level would be a person who is so fragmented that he or she loves or hates in an unpredictable, moody way, and who, when hating, is totally unaware of anything good about the object of the hatred – and who is the same when loving, unable to see anything bad about the object of the love. This schizoid splitting occurs at the level of the good and the terrible Great Mother and should not be confused with the ethical dualism of the Zoroastrian, Judeo-Christian, or Islamic religions.

Clearly we need to respect both these aspects of ourselves and other people, i.e., the uniting impulses and the ability to distinguish. Does this mean that we need to relate both the masculine and the feminine deities in (or outside) ourselves? My answer is obviously yes, and furthermore, that the male and female parts of ourselves, or the male and female deities, need to relate to each other in human (including union and parenting) ways if we are to be mature and healthy. A person is to be judged by the gods he worships, so to speak, and by the way these gods behave (particularly in his dreams or visions) toward humans and toward each other. In successful therapy, the parental and other figures in dreams become more loving or easier to live with, and the nature of the primal scene fantasy (basically, the way the internal parent-figures relate to each other) changes toward the creative, the facilitating, and the nonexcluding. By the same token, the gods who are one's real objects of worship both reflect and determine the dynamics of the inner life and the outer relationships.

From the above, it might be imagined that, as a therapist, I try to prescribe the religion that I feel may help the patient most. A therapist would not be functioning as a therapist if he were attempting anything of that sort; indeed he tries to respect and learn how to relate in a positive way to the patient's inner figures, working at the blocks and difficulties preventing the full deployment of the various parts of the personality, the full instinctual and experiential repertoire of the whole person. But it cannot be denied that as a person changes, his god or gods change in a way consistent with the change in that person. He may worship a god he believes to be the same god, of course, but the way that god relates to him changes, hopefully for the better.

I am taking the liberty of crudely characterizing the aim of the believer in the case of the monotheistic Middle Eastern religions as being to love and obey a righteous and loving God, and the aim of the oriental as the realisation in oneself of the God within-and-without. We also have to recognize an all-important element of the realisation of the divine in oneself in the rituals and mysteries of the Hellenic world at the time of the beginning of Christianity, as well as in the mystical strands and sects of the Christian and the other Levantine religions. As a therapeutic transformation of the personality, modern psychotherapy is very much in line with these oriental religions and mysteries, without of course prescribing stages or ceremonies celebrating or imprinting those stages of transformation. The mysteries of Isis, Cybele, Mithra, and Demeter and the Orphic mysteries, as well as of some Christian groups, all involve personal confrontation with the unconscious depths of the psyche and an identification with the deity as a new self-realisation becomes possible. How much individual development was allowed for or catered to, as opposed to cult identity, I personally find it difficult to judge, but we need not explore that further here. The point I have to make is that in the oriental religions and in the mysteries and mystical experiences of the Levantine religions, "personal apocalypse" (ego-shattering, world-destroying) experiences are very much in evidence and are taken to be referring to the breaking up of the old self, with the development of a new self. Whereas, as we have seen, the apocalyptic myths and movements of the Zoroastrian, Jewish, Christian, and Islamic religions are, in the main, taken to refer to the outside world. There has always been a degree of understanding that the apocalypse or the millennium is "not of this world" in the concrete, literal sense, but this is a minority position I think. It is, of course, the thesis here that the apocalyptic image or vision must be taken to refer to an inner necessity in each of us and not taken as an outer fate for which we are not responsible. Here, again, the therapist finds himself between the introverted and the extraverted way of understanding the vision or the religious experience. The danger of the literal enactment is all too obvious.

The opposites of good and evil, and the closely related opposites of love and hate, are the ones concerned in the Judeo-Christian apocalypses, and in the dreams of patients. The involvement of the whole world is taken literally in the religious view perhaps, metaphorically by patients, in the sense of "so-and-so, or such-and-such, means the whole world to me." Even the cosmic wars of modern science fiction tend to involve these two basic ethical opposites of good and evil in relatively crude and simple form. The failure to recognize and take responsibility for that part of ourselves we split off and project as the evil in others is no doubt the main powerhouse of the present concrete world situation. This is why I think that a study of the origins of ethical dualism and its relationship with male monotheism and the God outside us is helpful in the present context.

The vision of the war of the opposites is not a reflection of a split mind. On the contrary, it reflects a mind that is becoming more whole in the sense that it is a mind aware of conflict and contradictions between warring parts of the self. The split mind is that of the person who *feels* whole because he is simply unaware of the opposite as a part of the self, and may be unaware of conflict or feel he has solved all conflicts. I have often said, and do not apologize for reiterating, that the *feeling* of harmony, wholeness, or freedom from doubt or conflict is certainly no attribute of a person who *is* experiencing the whole of himself, which includes his many part selves (subpersonalities), who cannot be all "of one mind." A whole person cannot feel all of one mind. Yet there are many occasions when we need to feel all of one mind, or wholehearted, at least for a time.

It follows from the last paragraph that a vision of the war of the opposites which ends in total victory of good over evil, or one's own side over the enemy, is a dangerous psychic situation, involving explosive, disruptive behaviour, psychological inflation with omnipotent self-delusion, or psychotic self-destruction. Of course, most published fiction or published visions are of this wishful type, but I can only hope they are censored or progressively distorted derivations from the original genuine dream or vision, with contradictory elements taken out in the telling. This is the sort of censoring and distortion that helps people go to war (or fight evil) while remaining apparently sane.

CHAPTER 11

Pavlov, Freud, and Jung
On the Meeting of Opposites

In Part One, I shall very briefly summarize the story of the main polarities and dualisms as I see them in human nature and in historical times and shall, in particular, examine how these polarizations have occurred in the history of medicine. I shall then discuss how the three great medical men came to play their respective roles in the polarizations of their time. In Part Two, I shall describe how each of them saw the dualism of the psyche and the nature of the interaction of opposing psychological forces, the thesis here being that the meeting of the opposites in love or destructiveness is the creative or destructive experience at the core of the self.

Part One

Do and Don't in Animal Nature and Prehistory

I hope the reader will bear with me if I reiterate some of the aspects of our early history which I described in relation to the development of the I. I will now attend to the dualities and polarizations which must have been important at these same stages in history and continue the story into later times. Does any true opposite exist in nature? Do good and bad, light and dark, cold and hot, pleasant and unpleasant have any scientific or physical basis? Are not positive and negative, plus and minus, merely useful mathematical tools for constructing machinery, computers, and models of the mind? Again, although man and woman, male and female, mother and father, are clearly not abstractions, are they truly opposites? Because two different things or persons fit together as a pair does not mean that they are opposites.

When all this has been said, it is still the case that the conflict between opposing or incompatible emotions and possible actions can shake us to our foundations. The wars between good and evil in ourselves, the war between love and anger, the various conflicts surrounding the oedipal situation and incest in general, the opposites of treasure and rubbish, of self-value versus self-contempt, the contrasts of beauty and ugliness, purity and filth, these are the opposites that we cannot often deal with by the expedients of relativisation, psychologizing, or even by detachment, although there are certainly times for such methods. The opposites I have listed are those that we see clashing or being resolved every day in our consulting rooms. They are not academic or even theological matters, but the grist of therapeutic work.

It is hard to imagine how a single generation of human children could be brought up without a "Thou shalt" and "Thou shalt not." The self-confidence that we need from unconditional love is continually being enriched and modified by the structure and self-discipline of rules and of mental activity. When we have learned the difference between "thou shalt" and "thou shalt not," and only then, is it practicable to modify the basic pattern of oppositeness and of clear-cut boundaries with reconciliation, love, forgiveness, and tolerance. Only then can one proceed to talk of uniting, reconciling, and of seeing both sides of the question; only then can one begin to understand the wisdom of the paradox. It is the function of the parent to establish the rules of safety, of conduct, and of social behaviour, and it is the instinct of the parent to mitigate these commandments with love, tolerance, and forgiveness. It is misleading nowadays to say that it is the father's task to establish and enforce the rules and the mother's function to mitigate and humanize the law. It is certainly the case that there exists in each of us a capacity to establish boundaries and also a propensity toward transcending them. However, it is not accurate to link these respective tendencies with the masculine and the feminine parts of ourselves. The mother does a lot of holding, containing, and setting of boundaries, and, of course, all this requires firmness and clarity on occasions.

Whether we establish these basic dos and don'ts by a system of rewards and punishments or rather by a system of rewards and nonrewards matters a great deal in practice, of course. However, it is important to recognize that even at the nonhuman level the organism protects and feeds and reproduces itself under the aegis of Nature's dos and don'ts, mediated by the hormones and the nervous system. It is a gross oversimplification even at the mammalian level to affirm that pleasure and pain are Nature's dos and don'ts, but it *is* important not to attribute dos, don'ts, oughts, and ought nots, entirely to the parents or to society.

186

At the mammalian and prehistoric human level, therefore, we have to postulate quite complicated and traditional dos and don'ts which were evolved according to the particular natural environment.

The Opposites in History

Consciousness of conflict and opposition has certainly preoccupied civilised people since the times of Zoroaster, Confucius, the Buddha, and Heraclitus. Before these real or mythological characters made their influence felt in the last pre-Christian millennium, it is probable that the most important human opposites had been experienced and integrated with the funeral and hunting rites and deities of the primitive hunters and the fertility rites and mother goddesses of the small farming communities. The killing of animals with whom one identified and from whom one needed forgiveness, the overcoming of death, the need for social conformity and the subjugation of individual liberty were all governed by elaborate rules in preurban man. The natural opposites of light and dark, day and night, summer and winter, the ebb and flow of tides, dearth and plenty, sowing and reaping, are all, of course, very much opposites in Nature as seen through human eyes. Farming, in particular, requires work without immediate instinctual reward and then waiting, and this necessitates the suppression of opposing short-term wishes and feelings and, primitively, this entails concrete ritual sacrifice to help in this inhibitory process. All these sorts of opposites are embraced, contained, and, in a sense, united in paradox by the mother goddess, whose worship helped to integrate holding, nurturing, and uniting skills into our consciousness.

Different ways of life require different social structures, different ways of bringing up children, in short, different sets of dos and don'ts. When we try to imagine the ways of life of the early settled farmer, the early nomadic farmer, and the first city dwellers, we cannot but wonder at the complex specialisations and divisions of labour already in place. Each specialisation requires specific habits and specific, more or less permanent, suppression of opposite tendencies. Rulers and ruled, administrators and administered, artists and mathematicians, soldiers and priests, all needed to have very different ways of thinking and sets of values to suit their different roles. From the beginning, the early cities traded and competed with each other, and soon they were warring and building defensive walls, defending loved ones, holy symbols and gods, and treasure from the onslaughts of the enemy. The need for administration meant the development of depersonalisation and of thinking as opposed to feeling. The need for the preservation of the city and its defences meant the accentuation of the paranoid character structure, the good being preserved inside the walls of the mind and the bad being kept out.

For the development of the calendar, mathematics, writing, the wheel, and the walled city, people needed to develop the ability to depersonalise and abstract. The mind had to be affectively freed from the body. It needed to take off from the down-to-earth. The body, and in particular the mother's body, began to be imaged as a circle, a building, a wheel, or whatever. Thinking and feeling were in opposition. A change had taken place similar to the change occurring in the latency period of childhood.

As we have indicated already, for the settled, unthreatened city-state based on agriculture certain things went together. The astronomer-priests ruled. They presided over calendar and zodiac, the orderly cycle of nature and the periodic sacrifice of the royal, fertility-bringing couple. The system of medicine, the division of administrative functions, and the architectural layout of the city based on the zodiac and the planetary movements all reflect the cosmos and the self in this unitary system. But when war, trade, and the population movements of the nomads threatened, there emerged the king who ruled in real leadership, with the help of the male god from whom he derived his authority and his code of law. The early empires, male monotheism, and extreme ethical dualism developed together in varying proportions, and consciousness of the opposites in terms of ethical choice and ultimate reward or punishment became more personal, painful, and prominent. Good and evil were in conflict in Zoroastrianism, with the eventual triumph of good preordained. But for the individual human being there increasingly seemed to be the possibility of ethical choice, with the black-and-white, carrot-and-stick approach to the individual typical of primitive male monotheism and its ethical dualism. It is as if the symbol of authority is a hard father who is not yet assured of loving and being loved, a narcissistically wounded or deprived person who, despairing of being loved, resorts to force and legalistic principles and reinforces this way of feeling secure by accentuating masculine-feminine polarities and subjugating females and female deities. As far as the kind of dualism is concerned, the dualism of the loving and the terrible mother goddess had been replaced by the black-and-white ethical dualism of the rewarding and punishing monotheistic god.

188

When we speak of the overcoming of the mother goddess by the father god and the triumph of fundamentalistic monotheism, we are referring to developments in the Middle East, whereas in Egypt, Greece, Crete, and Europe, the indigenous male and female deities were never so thoroughly suppressed, so that the family and the menagerie of gods and goddesses arguably perpetuated a more-balanced interaction between the subpersonalities of the Self. In the Western cultural tradition, the one male god of truth, light, and goodness was transformed above all by the mediating and redeeming love of Christ.

The adoption of Christianity as the Roman state religion, and its political exploitation in an attempt to unify and hold together the imperial hegemony, resulted in the political need to suppress heterodoxy and the consequent stagnation of religion and self-awareness. However, Rome's contribution to Christianity was a rich one. The treasures of pagan polytheism, Egyptian and Greek mysteries, and soldierly Mithraism all influenced the Roman version of Christianity and helped to preserve a lively underworld of the mother goddess of superstition and witchcraft, of gnosticism, alchemy, and personal heresy, of classical scholarship and lore, and, above all, of classical rational Prometheanism, which finally burst through in the Renaissance.

Joseph Campbell, in his book *Creative Mythology*, brings to life something of the spirit of the Renaissance and the role of Christianized Celtic pagan mythology. He writes,

> Of all the modes of experience by which the individual might be carried away from the safety of well-trodden grounds to the danger of the unknown, the mode of feeling, the erotic, was the first to waken Gothic man from his childhood slumber in authority; and, as Gottfried's language tells
>
> > A man a woman, a woman a man
> > Tristan Isolt, Isolt Tristan,
>
> there were those, whom he calls noble, whose lives received from this spiritual fire the same nourishment as the lover of God received from the bread and wine of the sacrament. (Campbell 1976, p. 42)

So it seems that we must not underestimate the role of the Tristan and Arthurian legends in the first stirrings of the Renaissance spirit. Neither must we ignore the role of the troubadours, and the way of courtly love they inspired and celebrated, as they made their way across Europe from their Arabic origins in Andalusia. But one should not be completely starry-eyed; I assume that for every heroic Abelard there must have been several hundred "liberated" priests having their discreet affairs of love and lust, and one assumes that the Protestant Reformation was an inevitable backlash against the corruption of the established Church, undermined in this and other evil ways. "Evil," in this case, is an example of the long-sightedness of the workings of the Self.

The Opposites in the History of Medicine

It is not possible here to trace the history of polarizations in the transition from the mediaeval to the modern in literature, science, religion, or social organizations. Freud, Pavlov, and Jung were all medical men. It is therefore in the history of medicine that a brief account of the pendulum swings of opposing tendencies, or in other words of opposing subpersonalities within the human person, will be attempted. For example, the healing power of faith on the one hand and the medicinal skills of the knowledgeable, reasoning physician on the other have always been at odds with each other in individual doctors and in the medical profession as a whole. In Egypt and Babylon, seers or diviners were employed to decide whether an illness was due to spiritual or cosmic forces (Jungians would refer to archetypal forces) or to natural causes. Depending on the opinion of the seer, the patient was referred to a priest or exorcist, in the first case, or to a general practitioner skilled in herbs and natural history if a natural cause was diagnosed.

In more primitive communities, the power to call on faith, or superstition, together with skill in the use of the trance state in himself and his patient, was combined with medicinal skills in the shaman and the witch doctor. Religion and science were not clearly in competition, as they were in more specialized societies.

The medical historian Henry Sigerist used to say in lectures I attended that the history of the theories of medicine is a history of pluses and minuses, of too little of this, of too little or too much of that. In the case of the oldest continuous system of medicine, that of the acupuncturist, there was too much yin, or too much yang, with tao as the position of balance. Yang and yin, light and dark, male and female, positive and negative, plus and minus, excitation and inhibition for Pavlov, life and death for Freud, and, for Jung, the light of consciousness and the dark of the shadow and of the unconscious—all are ways of describing the same fundamental antithesis. Do these pluses and minuses exist out there in the cosmos, in the body politic, in the organs of the patient, including his brain, or are they simplistic pictures in the doctor's mind projected out of himself onto his world? As with the computers we have fashioned, like God in Genesis, after our own image, the language of plus and minus is one we readily understand and speak.

For the ancient wisdom of oriental medicine, religion and science are integrated; there is no antithesis, therefore no synthesis is necessary. For the Western doctor, oriental medicine is pre-Hippocratic; that is to say, it is full of superstition, formalism, and magical thinking of a kind where outer and inner are simply confused with each other, because they have not yet been differentiated.

The Western doctor traces his professional ancestry, as he traces back many of the noble and rational, liberating attitudes of our civilisation, to the ancient Greeks and, in particular, to the age of Pericles. Many of the medical writings of that period we have ascribed to the wise Hippocrates. He it was who delivered us by observation, reason, and kindly common sense, out of the superstitious and magico-religious medical practices of the followers of the half-divine Homeric Aesculapius, whose power was in the healing dreams, the fear, the faith (or credulity), and the privations of the faithful pilgrim-patient. Aesculapius and Hippocrates are subpersonalities who are very much alive and at odds with each other in the modern Western healer, but in the late nineteenth and early twentieth century, Aesculapius was having an exceedingly hard time of it. The Apollonian, not to say Promethean, wisdom of the Greeks was the type of wisdom we learned to admire in our medical schools. The use of observation, reason, the senses of touch, sight, hearing, and smell in order to arrive at a diagnosis which is even then only a matter of probability – this is the scientific way. It is a way that throws open the question of the truth of dogma and established practice. This is a Promethean impulse that is exercised with great danger both to patient and healer in an art where faith is a therapeutic force in many illnesses much more powerful than science.

But the more powerful rivals of the magico-religious leaders of classical Greece and Rome were probably not the pragmatic followers of Hippocrates but the model-making, schematizing followers of the mathematical, mystical Pythagoras. (See, for example, Brian Inglis, *A History of Medicine*, 1965.)

The medicine of Pythagoras, which he practiced a hundred years before Hippocrates, sought to replace the all-too-human, infantile waywardness of the gods and their numinous or chthonic powers with a pure, mystical, mathematical-musical universe that, for him, was the true ground of the force for healing and for the purification of the soul.

He nevertheless was able, quite deliberately, to use the therapeutic, transforming energy of frenzy and the trance state, which he induced largely with the help of musicians. Even more important for Western medicine for the next two thousand years was his fascination for numbers, particularly the number four, and his adoption of the humoral theory of medicine, which may have been an Indian elaboration of the yin-yang hypothesis. This combination of the number four with the humours of the body became, a hundred or so years later, the doctrine of the four humours. As in the Indian and Chinese systems, these constituents of the body were also held to be components of the psyche and of the world outside. The four humours were yellow bile (fire, summer), which was the opposite of phlegm (water, winter), and black bile (earth, autumn), with its opposite blood (air, spring). This neat, quadrate diagram of the universal opposites proved an extremely tough and rigid defensive system that was used to strangle empiricism for two thousand years. Its very brilliance and intuitive power ensured this. This is the case with all neat quaternities. In their negative aspect, they are rigid and defensive. For the systematists, health was a balanced state at the centre of this quadrate arrangement, just as for the Hippocratic ideals, it represented a golden mean between extremes of this or that.

Naturally, no two doctors using the humoral theories could agree as to how they should be applied either in the diagnosis or treatment of one person or with patients in general. This led to the formation of numerous schools of medicine, for example, at Alexandria, where the doctrinal quarrels remind us of the doctrinal quarrels among the early Christians.

Asclepiades, Cicero's personal physician, apparently irritated by the pretensions of the systematists, found the humoral theory insufficient. In addition to, or instead of, imbalances of the four fluids being the cause of illness, he postulated that the solids of the body were chiefly responsible, illness occurring if the body is too constricted or too relaxed.

In medicine, what works in practice is usually a threat to the systematist. Suggestion and faith being the most important ingredient for success, bad medicine tends to drive out good. The standing of doctors therefore diminishes until a new canon emerges, reincorporating successful practice. The physician of Marcus Aurelius, Galen, and the Arabian physician Avicenna, several centuries later, together provided the classical learning and the sense of authority that maintained the status of the physician until the Renaissance. Christ's miracles of healing, and the importance of faith, also had an enormous influence on the medicine of the Middle Ages. The mediaeval hospitals gathered together the sick and the indigent, provided for the exercise of Christian mercy and charity, and discouraged purely medical discovery. From the time of Galen until the anatomical discoveries of Vesalius, the dissection of the human cadaver was anathema. Vesalius was a contemporary of Leonardo and Michaelangelo, and all of them profited from the knowledge they obtained from the dissection of human cadavers.

But the leader of the revolt against the established authority of Church and canon in medicine at that time was undoubtedly Theophrastus Bombast von Hohenheim, who styled himself Paracelsus, Celsus being a Roman physician of Hippocratic leanings whose encyclopaedic writings had been discovered in a Milan church in 1443.

For Paracelsus, medicine rested on four pedestals. First was astronomy, the macrocosm after which man the microcosm is modelled. Second was geography, which yielded knowledge of important regional variations in disease. Third was chemistry, or rather alchemy, learnt from the Arabs throughout the Middle Ages; and fourth was love and unselfishness. He replaced the Galenical humours with an alchemical triad of mercury, sulphur, and salt, and he taught that therapy depended fundamentally on the life force emanating from the character and creative imagination of the physician. Psychiatry and psychotherapy owe a great deal to the liberating effect of this courageous bombast. He sought to replace superstition and received wisdom by personal discovery, and so he made an inevitable enemy of the Church.

Paracelsus and Vesalius and their enlightened colleagues made little impact on medicine as a whole. Galenism, Christian doctrine, superstition, and envy of innovative colleagues continued to prevent change for the most part. At the time of the founding of the College of Physicians of London in the time of Henry VIII, physicians, surgeons, and apothecaries were at each others' throats, and the granting of permission to practice physic was in the hands of the Bishop of London and the other bishops. The art was practiced, it was said, by "illiterate monks and empirics" at that time. New discoveries increased in geometric progression. Let me mention a few.

The correct theory of how the blood circulates was published by William Harvey, physician to James I and Charles I. The discovery of vaccination in the early eighteenth century led to the gradual elucidation of the role of the microorganism and of cellular pathology in disease which unfolded over the next century and a half. The invention of the stethoscope by Laennac in 1816 helped to further the development of diagnosis based on accurate use of the senses and of scientific instruments. Claude Bernard, in 1830s, had very influential thoughts about the self-regulating properties of the body which maintain the internal environment of the body, the body chemistry, blood pressure, body temperature, etc., at a reasonably constant level. The discoveries of the negative feedback mechanisms that underlie self-regulation were very powerful in medicine at the turn of the century when Pavlov, Freud, and Jung were formulating their ideas. The concept of the compensatory functions of the unconscious and of the self must owe a good deal to the prevalent physiological thinking of that time.

There is insufficient space here to trace the evolution of all the polarizations in medical opinion and theory throughout history. However, the tendencies are clear enough. Let us take one line of development and, for descriptive purposes, suggest the following stages:

(1) The yin/yang pair of opposites

(2) The four humours

(3) The idea of separate body fluids, each with tendencies to regulate themselves

This last implies, at least nowadays, a concrete sensing mechanism that detects whether the level is too high or too low, and by how much, and brings about compensating mechanisms on a graded basis.

In the three stages of the doctrine of bodily humours, we see decreasing universality and decreasing literalness of the crude, archetypal idea with increasing respect for the material facts. The archetypal, dualistic tendency is still at work in us, still admittedly at a relatively unconscious level providing, nowadays, creative hypotheses, quasi-mathematical models, and technology for investigation. For example, we have computers working on a plus-minus principle. The yin-yang opposites explain the heavens, the earth, the human body, and human psychology; the four humours are less all-pervading but have their cosmic analogies and correlates. With the Renaissance, the Promethean investigator dares to question these projections, and the unitary, explanatory, Procrustean doctrine breaks down into smaller areas of our universe. The projections are withdrawn and reemerge only in a fragmentary form as far as the science of the body is concerned. But the underlying archetype of opposition, if we may call it that, remains as an internal organizer and as a preferred way of looking at things and thinking about things.

Just as the microcosm-macrocosm conflation is never very far away, so the tendency to observe and experience the inner and the outer worlds in terms of opposites is quite obviously inherent in us.

It has become clear that the late sixteenth and the seventeenth centuries were times of great change in the emancipation of the medical sciences and of the medical profession from the doctrines and the governance of the Church. René Descartes, by many regarded as the father of modern philosophy, lived at that time and played an important role in the differentiation of science, in particular medical science, from theology.

From the cradle to the grave, we balance the need for security with the need to be free, to explore, and to win space. Or rather, these things are balanced in us. This is just as true today as it was when the Church offered greater security at the price of restrictions on scientific exploration. Having a secure means of livelihood undoubtedly helps. Although educated by the Jesuits, Descartes was of independent means. He started to doubt all the alleged truths of his upbringing and education, wandered around Europe in search of his own inner certainties, and wrote of his findings, thereby incurring the displeasure of the theologians, but eventually gaining disciples and admirers, including Queen Christina of Sweden. Incidentally, Queen Christina is said to have made him discuss philosophy with her from five to six o'clock each morning and soon proved to be the death of him; the chill mornings of Stockholm no doubt helped to cause him to succumb from some form of pneumonia.

For Descartes doubt, not faith or dogmatic certainty, was the starting point of his philosophy. However, he could not doubt that he could think, and that in order to think he must exist. He also seems to have further concluded that what can be clearly thought must be true, thereby allowing himself to be certain of the existence of God as the Perfect Being, because the idea of the Perfect Being can be clearly thought, and God must be the originator of such an idea.

From the point of view of this essay, Descartes's importance lies in his insistence on the essential difference between spirit and matter, between mind or consciousness and matter. Matter is mere extension. The human body, like the bodies of animals, is a mere machine. The human being differs from animals in knowing consciousness.

One attribute of the machine aspect of the body is the response to external stimuli. Descartes is credited with developing the hypothesis of the nervous reflex, whereby certain external or internal stimuli produce certain given responses, the pathway between stimulus and response being the nervous system. The fundamental ideas of the body as machine and of the nervous reflex were used and developed by the "iatrophysicists" during the next three centuries. The idea does not, of course, exclude studies of body chemistry and of the analogues of the ancient humours, but there was a polarization between the so-called "iatrophysicists" and the "iatrochemists" from the time of Descartes onward. The secure state of mind of the one-sided stance seems to account for the schismatic, polarizing result of any new discovery or of any new hypothesis. One is more comfortable when for or against.

Working in the late nineteenth and early twentieth centuries, Ivan Petrovich Pavlov saw himself as owing to Descartes the fundamental idea, namely, that of the reflex activity of the nervous system, which informed his own approach to physiology – and to psychology, too, it is fair to add. At the same time he completely rejected Descartes's dualism of mind and body, according to which "the brain is a piano, a passive instrument, while the soul is a musician extracting from this piano any melodies it likes" (Pavlov's words, extracted from a stenographic record made on September 19, 1934, of a Wednesday departmental meeting at which Pavlov was attacking the "idealist dualism" of Charles Sherrington). In spite of, or perhaps partly because of, being the son of a priest, educated at the local theological seminary, Pavlov espoused a thoroughgoing philosophic materialism whereby psychology and psychiatry were to become one with neurophysiology.

The chief discoveries of Sigmund Freud were also made in the last decade of the nineteenth century, about the same time as those of Pavlov. Freud was attracted to medicine by force of circumstances rather than by inclination, his preference being toward scientific research rather than the medical profession. He regarded psychoanalysis as a science following naturally upon his research work on the central nervous system, his specialism in neurology, and his discoveries of the cathartic method and his work under Charcot. His project for a scientific psychology was a heroic but rather unsuccessful and abortive attempt in the last years of the century to unify psychoanalysis and neurophysiology.

Freud's father's family was Jewish and immigrated during the nineteenth century from Lithuania via Galicia into German Austria, coming to Vienna when he was four. Almost as soon as he could read, he found himself deeply engrossed in "the Bible story" (as he puts it), and later, at the gymnasium, he was strongly attracted to the theories of Darwin. In those days Darwinism and established religion constituted opposing camps. Although Freud found rest and full satisfaction for the first time in the physiological laboratory, his interest in religion must have persisted at a deep level. He says in his autobiography (1925, p. 9) that the anti-semitism of his fellow students and medical colleagues made him familiar from an early age with being in the Opposition. He certainly succeeded in arousing the antagonism of both the medical scientists *and* the theologians, which one would have thought impossible at the time. His discoveries of the unconscious basis of neurosis and of repressed infantile sexuality in the fabric of the unconscious seem now to follow naturally from his research interests in hysteria and in hypnosis. He replaced hypnosis as a clinical method of research and therapy with the more satisfying research tool of the technique of free association. His use of hypnosis had never been for the purpose of producing the powerful therapeutic effects of suggestion, but rather for elucidating the unconscious origin of his patients' psychopathology.

Freud's genius and courage were, of course, extra elements that this short history cannot adequately address, but his ability to provoke and to survive bitter opposition is not difficult to understand at least partly.

Freud's stand as a scientist and realist, and his ambivalent attitude to instincts, wishfulness, and religion, are well expressed in *The Future of an Illusion* (1927). Here he defines an illusion as a belief based not on reason and reality but on the irrational and the wish. Religions are illusions in this sense. Illusions may turn out to be true or false, but this does not alter the fact that religions belong to the illusory realm.

For practical purposes Freud was a dualist, as Pavlov was. Pavlov, in spite of his own philosophical scientific materialism, respected his parents' and his wife's religious beliefs. Love and tolerance seem to have informed his family life as opposed to his academic stance. Freud's feelings about religion were positive in so far as one's beliefs are based on love, generosity, and affection, and negative toward the burdensome, repressive, intolerant, and harsh aspects of religious upbringing. As he was a clinician especially skilled in the treatment of neurotic persons, the repressive, anti-instinctual aspects of the institutionalized religions would every day be forcibly impressed upon him.

As with Freud and Pavlov, Jung's interest in medicine was largely pragmatic (as a means of livelihood) and an expression of his scientific and realistic side (what he called his No. 1 personality in *Memories, Dreams, Reflections*). Yet he was painfully aware of his other, No. 2 personality, for whom God was an immediate, often dark and painful experience; his God forced him to think abominations in order to experience His grace. Although there were six parsons in his mother's family and his father and two uncle's were parsons, he experienced these men as learned in theology but as not knowing God. His father urged him to cease thinking and simply to believe, but Jung felt, "No, one must experience and know." His No. 2 personality lived in a transforming realm where the ego is overwhelmed by a vision of the whole cosmos and where nothing separates man from God. And, incidentally, this was a personality sometimes startled by unwanted intuitions and unbid paranormal experiences. The schoolmen left the teenage Jung cold, but the mystic Eckhart was the breath of life. He felt that Schopenhauer and, later, Nietzsche shared this immediate secret experience which compelled him, terrified him, and isolated him from his fellows.

Jung's painful awareness of the dualism in himself, of the clash between his practical No. 1 personality and his secret No. 2 personality, enabled him to elaborate his concepts of extraversion and introversion. But for the present purposes it is worthwhile remarking that he was experiencing in himself not only the age-old clash between personal experience and established "truth," the conflict between Dionysus and Apollo, the conflict between heresy and dogmatism, between Protestantism and the mother-Church, but that between religion and science and one which was polarized in the artistic Europe of the nineteenth century into the romantic and the classical camps. In art, too, the urgency of immediate experience threatens to burst the secure structure of established form.

Part Two

The Interaction of Opposites in the Theories of Pavlov, Freud, and Jung

Pavlov, Freud, and Jung were all late-nineteenth and early-twentieth-century European medical men; as such they, together with their theories, had much more in common than perhaps they themselves, being partly submerged (as we all are) in the polarizations and controversies of the time, would have emphasized. They were all brilliant medical students, and they were all profoundly preoccupied by the study of the nervous system and the psyche. But whereas Pavlov remained an experimental physiologist of genius, Freud's early postgraduate interests lay in neurophysiology and neurology and, after that, in neurosis, while Jung soon found that psychiatry was the logical meeting ground of his No. 1 and No. 2 personalities, and his early postgraduate interests lay in a psychiatric study of multiple personality and in an experimental study of the unconscious complex as revealed in his word-association test. Thus, along the spectrum matter/mind, the three doctors conveniently arrange themselves, Pavlov more at one end, Freud more in the middle perhaps, and Jung more at the other end. Although all doctors no doubt have their favourite position on this continuum, it could be argued that the best doctors move easily to and fro along it and can even locate themselves in more than one place at once.

In the work of Pavlov, the opposites with which we shall mainly concern ourselves in this chapter are neural excitation and neural inhibition, especially in what he termed the higher reflex activity of the central nervous system, a term which dispenses with the notion of the mind and with the need for a separate study of the mind. Experimentally he had found that violent neurotic behaviour in his dogs was due to the explosive clash between conditioned excitation and conditioned inhibition, as we shall see later.

In Freud's formulations, the Eros instincts and the Thanatos instincts are the opposites chiefly to be considered here. The class of Eros instincts has to do with energy, reproduction, creation, and love, while the Thanatos group has to do with sleep, rest, death, and also with anger, hate, and destruction.

It seems fair to say that Jung was concerned more with how we relate to the opposites and how psychic growth and self-realisation result from the laws of behaviour (*enantiodromia* was the term he used) of the opposites in general. The opposites he studied in detail were introversion and extraversion, thinking and feeling, sensation and intuition, masculine and feminine, persona and shadow, ego and unconscious, and the opposites as seen by the alchemists in the texts he studied for the last decades of his life.

Pavlovian Excitation, Inhibition, Irradiation, and Induction

The terms *irradiation* and *induction* have not been introduced so far in this essay. They are terms used by neurophysiologists generally and were not introduced by Pavlov himself. The spread of excitation from a focus of excitation in the central nervous system to neighbouring areas is termed irradiation. But an area of excitation at certain strengths, instead of spreading, may induce inhibition rather than excitation at its boundary. This is the process of induction. A sort of induction in time rather than in space can literally be seen in the visual phenomenon of the afterimage, where a bright object leaves a dark, negative version of itself in the visual field. (The reader is advised to check this using a bright object, not a bright light.)

In his book, *Conditioned Reflexes* (1927), written to summarize his work until 1924, Pavlov says that his work on the nervous system developed out of his investigations into the activities of the digestive glands. "I had to inquire into the so-called psychic secretion of some of the glands" (p. 6). He soon formed "an unqualified conviction of the futility of subjective methods" (ibid.). He started to record all the external stimuli falling on his experimental animals at the time of salivation, at the same time recording all other changes in the reactions of the animal.

Summarizing the subsequent twenty-five years of research in his laboratories in 1924, he uses Descartes's idea of the nervous reflex as his starting point. This, he says, is a genuine scientific conception, since it implies necessity. An external or internal stimulus activates a receptor, which responds by initiating a nervous impulse then transmitted along nerve fibres to the central nervous system. This is a network of nervous connections that responds with a fresh outgoing impulse, which in turn excites the cellular structures of the active organ. Stimulus and response are related in a definite way as cause and effect. The animal must respond in a manner that is appropriate or it would obviously perish. Reflexes are the elemental units of an equilibrating system that enables the animal to maintain stability in spite of environmental changes and threats. Instincts, in Pavlov's view, are simply complicated reflexes, probably chain reactions whereby the reflex response to one stimulus becomes the stimulus for the succeeding reflex. One of his mentors, the Russian physiologist Sechenov, in a pamphlet published in 1863, had gone so far as to postulate that all the "higher activities" of the nervous system could be viewed as reflexes. Sechenov regarded thoughts as reflexes in which the effector path was inhibited, while great outbursts of passion he regarded as exaggerated reflexes with a wide irradiation of excitation. (This idea is echoed in a less oversimplified way by Freud in his project, and in the earlier chapters of the present book.)

Reflexes, for Pavlov, are of two kinds, positive and negative, excitatory and inhibitory. The mechanisms for inhibition were at that time obscure. Likewise the mechanism of the interaction of reflexes in potentiating or negating each other was not clear.

A reflex crucial to his theory of conditioning was the investigatory reflex, whereby animals (including, of course, man) are alerted and become ready to respond to the slightest change in the environment. The animal pricks up its ears, looks in the direction of the new stimulus, and becomes generally more alert. Another reflex important in Pavlov's ideas was the freedom reflex, whereby the animal responds violently to restraint and overcrowding. The freedom reflex would be the biological forerunner of the explosive projection phenomena described in Chapter Five.

Developing a technique he used in his early work on digestion, he had perfected a minor operative technique whereby a salivary duct was diverted away from the mouth to the exterior of the cheek or neck of the animal. Using a suction cup and a system of tubes, he could measure the response of salivation to food and other stimuli in drops secreted during any particular period of time.

Salivation is brought about by an inborn reflex when food is introduced into the mouth. For this the cerebral hemispheres are not necessary. Salivation also occurs at the sight of customary food or at the sound of its preparation or approach. This is brought about by a conditioned reflex for which the cerebral hemispheres are necessary. The stimulus thus used by the animal as a signal for food is called the conditioned or conditional stimulus. The sound of a metronome, if followed by the reinforcement of actual feeding, could be used as a conditioned stimulus. This had the advantage that the frequency of the metronome beats could be varied in an experiment if desired. For example, some frequencies might be reinforced, whereas others could be left unreinforced by actual feeding. The latter frequencies might then acquire conditioned inhibitory properties, i.e., a negative influence on conditioned salivation.

A neutral stimulus could never cause a conditioned reflex to be formed when it followed rather than preceded the unconditioned stimulus. A strong conditioned excitatory stimulus could be linked with a further neutral stimulus so that the second stimulus acquired excitatory properties. Such "secondary conditioning" is possible under some circumstances.

A conditioned excitation could also be set up as a result of the regular repetition of an unconditioned reflex such as regular feeding. The salivation commenced when the next feed was due.

Coming now to the sources of inhibition, there is the direct inhibitory effect of certain nervous pathways, or of chemical changes in the blood, and there are indirect sources, which are of greater interest to us. For example, a sudden external stimulus might elicit the investigatory reflex and inhibit the salivation reflex. This effect might last for some time, so the work had to be carried out in quiet, uninteresting surroundings and conditions to which the animals were well accustomed. New people and other dogs could ruin an experiment for this reason.

A second source of inhibition was the nonreinforcement of a conditioned stimulus, which led to inhibition by what Pavlov termed experimental extinction. If a second conditioned stimulus such as a hooter is sometimes used to accompany conditioned stimulus such as a metronome, and the combination is never reinforced while the metronome continues to be reinforced, the hooter acquires inhibitory properties and is called a conditioned inhibitory stimulus. This type of inhibition is known as conditioned inhibition.

Another type of inhibition is that caused by a delay between conditioned stimulus and its reinforcement. If an animal is trained to salivate say five minutes after a metronome stimulus, it will manifest signs of inhibition when it hears the metronome, such as dropping its head, ears, eyes, and tail, and perhaps even becoming drowsy. However, when the time for reinforcement draws near, it will become alert, apparently expectant, and will salivate at the appropriate time.

Pavlov and his colleagues made a detailed study of the spread or irradiation of excitation and inhibition to neighbouring areas of the cortex (i.e., the central representations of neighbouring skin areas, or of neighbouring frequencies in the case of a tone or beat). They also demonstrated the phenomenon of induction in the cerebral cortex, a phenomenon that had been discovered already by Hering and Sherrington in the nervous system. A point in the cortex (i.e., the cortical representation of a particular locus on the body surface or a particular frequency) could be made to acquire excitatory properties, and it was often found that surrounding points thereby acquired inhibitory properties (negative induction). Conversely, points surrounding a negative point would acquire excitatory properties (positive induction).

Finally, it is important to mention Pavlov's insistence that the phenomena of generalised inhibition in the conditioning sense and that of sleep are one and the same process with the same fundamental physiological mechanism. All the examples of inhibition we have mentioned, when repeated, prolonged, or intensified, lead on to sleep, usually rapidly. Pavlov at that time knew nothing of the physiology of arousal and sleep and the role of subcortical centres in this, but he was, of course, fully aware that subcortical centres were probably involved, and that his irradiation of excitation and of inhibition might not be a simple spread along a sheet of neurones in the cerebral cortex.

In some animals inhibition manifested itself in what looked like an intermediate form. The animal would look alert and erect. The eyes would be open but unmoved, not responding to food or other external stimuli. Pavlov found this cataleptic type of response in a fleeting form in all animals prior to sleep, but in some it was a marked feature. He postulated that cortical centres were inhibited but that the subcortical centres involved in producing wakefulness were not yet being reached by the inhibitory process. He also described states in which normally stronger conditioned stimuli produced weak conditioned responses, and normally weak stimuli produced strong responses (paradoxical phase). This was often followed by the phase of equalisation, when all conditioned stimuli produced an equal effect. Sometimes a state was observed when positive stimuli became negative and negative stimuli positive (ultraparadoxical phase). Pavlov thought quite correctly that these different states were important in the pathological physiology of nervous illness in humans.

The Collision Between Excitation and Inhibition

Pavlov succeeded in actually producing certain pathological changes in his animals by the use of conflicting stimuli, excitatory and inhibitory effects competing with each other at points too near in time or space. Another method of producing disturbance was the use of stimuli, such as electric shocks, conditioned to produce strong alimentary responses and perhaps increased in strength so as to produce strong defensive reactions. He found that temperamentally alert, excitable dogs showed pathological changes related to overexcitability of the nervous system, whereas quiet, depressive dogs who are better at forming inhibitions show pathological changes related to pathological inhibition and unresponsiveness.

Pavlov summarized his findings on experimental neuroses as follows: "The underlying cause of their development is in every instance the same. Broadly we can regard these disturbances as due to a conflict between the processes of excitation and inhibition which the cortex finds difficult to resolve" (1927, p. 302).

For our purposes, however, it may be important to emphasize that conflict, leading to neurosis, violent escape behaviour, or pathological inaction, may be of two distinct types:

(1) The conflict between conditioned excitatory effect and conditioned inhibitory effect at the same or neighbouring points. For example, an excitatory frequency and an inhibitory frequency may be brought closer and closer together in frequency until successful differentiation is lost and replaced by neurosis.

(2) The conflict between two kinds of response (alimentary and defensive, for example) to the same stimulus. Shocks of increasing strength and painfulness may be used as conditioned stimuli for the alimentary response to food. As the pain is increased, explosive or other neurotic behaviour may suddenly or gradually supervene, the reaction depending partly on the temperament of the animal. Furthermore, active or violent behaviour in an animal might take the form mainly of panic and attempts to escape, or of rage and destructive behaviour. It is interesting that Pavlov, Freud, and clinical psychotherapists find that the differentiation between these three negative responses (inactivity or depression, panic and escape, and destructive behaviour) is clinically often rather difficult and unimportant. Freud therefore grouped them together under the general term *Thanatos* or death instinct as opposed to the clearly positive responses which are manifestations of life or Eros.

According to W. Horsley Gantt, who worked with Pavlov and translated his classic lectures on conditioned reflexes, Pavlov often spoke of "a collision between excitation and inhibition" as being the phenomenon responsible for disturbed behaviour in his animals (Gantt 1944). Gantt himself lists five kinds of experimental situations producing explosion or inactivity.

1. A conflict between two emotions, or subcortical centres, or two unconditioned reflexes (depending on the terminology preferred). For example, the responses to food and to pain.

2. A conflict between conditioned excitation and conditioned inhibition. This may be brought about in space or in time, as in imposing differentiations which are too difficult, or in producing excitation and inhibition too close together in time.

3. Changes in daily routines.

4. Excessive intensity of conditioned reflexes.

5. Methods causing inhibition, e.g., extinction, can sometimes or in some animals produce chronic disturbance. Pavlov had found that inhibitory reflexes were in many cases transformed into excitatory ones as a result of the panic of the Leningrad flood, which trapped many dogs in their cages. His paradoxical and ultraparadoxical states are important in demonstrating how excitation and inhibition may be reversed in pathological conditions of excitement and stress.

It is worthwhile stressing at this point the extremely explosive nature of the transition from inhibition to excitation as the balance of excitatory and inhibitory forces is slowly changes. Pavlov gives many examples of this, but let us take a typical one (Pavlov 1927, pp. 289–290). He was using a strong electric shock as a conditioned alimentary stimulus. The shock was given to other places on the skin and these places produced alimentary responses and no defence reactions. But there came a time when the addition of just one more location for the shock produced the most violent defence reaction. After that, extremely weak shocks produced the same violently explosive behaviour.

Just as these explosions are produced by the use of systematic or accidental cruelty to animals, the partial therapy of these conditions is, in general, achieved by what to the subjective viewpoint of ordinary human beings would be the provision of a quiet, restful environment, by kindness from a trusted person, and by the provision of normal feeding arrangements. Once the conflict has produced the pathological explosion, the level of conflict has to be drastically reduced for recovery to occur.

The Interaction of Eros and Thanatos in Freud's Theory

Writing about 1922, Freud recognized two classes of instincts, corresponding to the contrary processes of construction and dissolution in the organism (1922, p. 258). The death instincts are to do with dying, destruction, and aggression. The life instincts are to do with forming living substances into ever greater unities, thus prolonging and enhancing life. These are the instincts of Eros. The life and the death instincts are present in living creatures as regular mixtures or fusions; but defusions would also be liable to occur, as in examples of regression. Life, according to Freud's view at the time, would consist of conflict and interaction between the two classes of instinct, death being the victory of the destructive instincts and reproduction the victory of Eros.

This generalisation emerged after three decades of clinical work and constant updating of his earlier theoretical formulations, which could now be seen to be incomplete versions of the later one, each stressing certain aspects according to his clinical findings at the time.

In this general statement he is saying that conflict and interaction between these opposing classes of instinct is the stuff of real life. From his earliest clinical writings he had taken the view that the neuroses and psychoses he saw in his practice were due to pathological mechanisms that were exaggerations or distortions of normal neurological and psychological mechanisms. Freud, like so many thinkers, found it easiest to see things in terms of a struggle between opposing tendencies: will versus counterwill or antithetical ideas; discharge versus inhibition; infantile sexuality versus the ego; pleasure versus pain; pleasure principle versus reality principle; oedipal wishes versus castrating father; id versus ego; and so on.

In order to describe some of these antitheses in a little more detail, I shall for the sake of brevity deal with them as if they were separate and as if they had a chronological sequence. This is misleading insofar as the later ideas always had earlier germinal forms. There is also some distortion because of the plethora of ideas and hypothetical mechanisms in Freud's work. Although we know how Freud agonized over his ideas, it seems to the reader that no sooner had he made a clinical observation than he had a theory ready to explain it. This impression is paralleled in his accounts of his work with patients. No sooner had his patients done something or related a dream than Freud was there with a ready and exhaustively detailed interpretation. How far this is a justified criticism, and how far a product of his style of writing, I am not able accurately to judge.

Writing in 1892, on the case of a young mother who was having difficulty breast-feeding her baby, and whom he successfully treated with hypnotism, he observed how often the symptomatic behaviour runs directly counter to the conscious will (Freud 1892, p. 117). In the article he develops a lucid exposition of the relationship between will and counterwill. He describes our various ways of dealing with antithetic ideas which arise counter to the will, and he subtitles the article, "With some remarks on the origin of hysterical symptoms through 'counter-will.'" This was a year or two before the importance of infantile sexuality in the origin of neuroses had emerged in his writings. But already the hypothesis of an active process of opposition and contrariness between conscious and unconscious intent in hysterical cases had been developed. By the end of 1895, in his "Christmas Fairy Tale" to Fliess, he was writing of neuroses as defences (essentially against unpleasure) which are pathological aberrations of normal affective states such as conflict (in the case of hysteria), self-reproach (obsessional neurosis), mortification (paranoia), and mourning (acute hallucinatory amentia) (Freud 1896, p. 220). The reason for the pathological affective state was now felt by Freud to be an infantile sexual trauma damaging to the ego. The memory of the traumatic experience is repressed, together with the formation of the primary symptom.

At the same time, Freud's mind was at work night and day on an attempt to integrate and explain his clinical discoveries with an all-embracing neurophysiological theory of mental function. This was his "Project for a Scientific Psychology," which soon had to be abandoned because it gave rise to too many apparent absurdities at that time (1950, pp. 295–397). For example, he employed an idea of psychic energy, with the buildup of excitation, its discharge, and its binding in ego formation, which he spoke of as properties of the neurone, thus confusing the rather complex properties of the mind, or brain, or nervous system as a network and a hierarchy of functions, with the properties of the neurone. Naturally this overloads the "neuronal" unit with too many functions which could not be compatible with each other. But the same basic ideas could be used perfectly simply and validly without any major absurdities in the theories of psychic function which he developed later. His concepts of excitation, cathexis, repressions, discharge, conflict, pleasure and pain, ego, and so on, are all concepts that can help integrate objective observations of behaviour with subjective introspections and introspective reports, etc. They are not expressed in such concrete physiological terms as to be easily disprovable by naive and simplistic scientific experiments, yet they are useful as tools and are being tested every day as to their usefulness as such, in the workshop or the consulting room.

The basic unit of the project, out of which all the different mental functions are built, is the neurone or group of neurones in a state of excitation or rest. The quantity of excitation is variable. In a simple reflex this quantity is increased by an external stimulus acting on a sensory nerve, and the excitation of the central neurone is discharged by motor activity. But the fact of learning by experience requires some neurones that (unlike those subserving the reflex) retain excitation and are not immediately permeable, but with a permeability which is increased by repetition of the stimulus and by facilitation. Bodily needs, such as hunger and sexual needs, cause a buildup of the quantity of excitation that is not immediately discharged but which sets up processes leading ultimately to a reduction of the quantity of excitation (satisfaction). On the other hand, increase of the quantity beyond a certain level corresponds with pain.

Proceeding in this way, Freud builds up a plausible theoretical edifice explaining consciousness, the ego, judgment of reality, sleep and dreams, inhibition by the ego, and many of his pioneering clinical findings. But even in the initial stages of the theory, which I have already outlined in a rough and ready way, Freud was already beyond and outside (in a different world from) the neurophysiology of the time. His attempt to encompass so much can only be thought of as heroic. Whereas Pavlov, on the whole, worked with those processes he could observe and assumed that his findings would one day explain the complexities of the mind, Freud tried for a while to bridge the gap between physiology on the one hand and psychology and psychopathology on the other. He was already firmly rooted in the observations of the consulting room and not primarily concerned with the realities of the physiological laboratory. If we regard his project as an attempt to systematize his basic clinical findings to that date, his genius become apparent enough.

We can take the basic opposition in the project as that between the buildup of excitation in the central nervous system and the discharge of this excitation. This is a concept not so very distant from the later formulation I have cited, namely, the opposition between the life instincts and the death instincts. Nor are we so very far removed from the opposition in Pavlov between excitation and inhibition. But we must remember that the excitation and discharge in the Freudian theory is not quite the same as in the Pavlovian concepts. In the present volume I also use similar concepts of excitation and its containment or discharge.

In his "Christmas Fairy Tale" to Fliess, written while he was engaged on the project, the important opposition was derived from his work with neurotic patients, particularly with those suffering from hysterical and obsessional problems. In the former, the problem was the repression of a painful (sexual) memory. He speaks of the memory as of a scene. The problem in obsessional neuroses, on the other hand, is to do with the avoidance of the pleasurable libidinal content through over-conscientiousness and the pain that that brings about. The basic opposition, therefore, might be said to do with that between pleasure and pain. Later, mindful of the phenomena of repression and the many clinical phenomena exhibiting the conflict between the ego and the Eros instincts, he saw the most important opposition to be that between the Eros instincts and the ego instincts. Later still, in "Beyond the Pleasure Principle," he came to grips with the analysis of the ego and the phenomena of narcissism and saw that the ego is, in fact, the object of Eros instincts (self-preservation and self-regard). And so the basic conflict was once again seen as the struggle between life and death and was seen to be present from the cellular, biological level onward and upward in the evolutionary scale. Clinically, in the human, the basic conflict was now seen to be between ego instincts and object instincts, but both of these were of a libidinal nature.

Although not strictly speaking an opposition, but rather an important contrast, there was the distinction between unconscious processes and consciousness, between the instincts in the freely mobile form of the primary process and in the bound form in which they achieve consciousness. It is the function of the mental apparatus to master or bind excitations, not in opposition to the pleasure principle, but independently of it (Freud 1920, pp. 34–35). A failure to effect this binding, Freud states, would provoke a disturbance analogous to a traumatic neurosis, and only after the binding has been accomplished is it possible for the dominance of the pleasure principle and its derivative, the reality principle, to proceed unhindered.

In therapeutic practice, an important example of unbinding or of partial failure of binding is the repetition compulsion. This is the tendency to repeat unconsciously, in actions, emotions, and attitudes, patterns acquired in infancy. The primary process predominates in the repetition compulsion of the neurotic person and of the transference neurosis. This means, says Freud, that the repressed memory traces of the neurotic person's primaeval experiences are not present in a bound state and are therefore incapable of obeying the secondary process. Freud argues that all instincts, apart from the Eros instincts, tend toward the repetition of older patterns and earlier forms of mental activity. The binding of instincts, the evolution from primary to secondary process, and the freeing of the individual from the repetition compulsion are all correlated with each other and can be ascribed to the interaction of the Eros instincts and the death instincts.

In the area of object-love, the opposition between life and death takes the form of the polarity of love (or affection) and hate (or aggressiveness). This polarity is usually discussed in connection with neurotic ambivalence and the existence of sadism (Freud 1920, pp. 53–54). However, after his essay "Mourning and Melancholia" (1917), Freud is concerned increasingly with earlier, psychotic levels of the personality. He affirms the essentially ambivalent nature of the child's identification with the loved and admired parent and its "cannibalistic" basis (I love you, I want to eat you. I eat you (introject you). I both assimilate you as part of me and destroy you). In melancholia Freud observed an ego divided into two parts, both of which could be regarded as parental introjects, one raging at the other. The one that rages is the introjected critical parent or conscience, and the one raged at is the lost bad part of the lost loved-and-hated parent. This bad part is now experienced as oneself.

I have described some of the oppositions and polarities used by Freud in understanding the clinical observations with which he was concerned. He described himself as a dualist, certainly as far as the basic structure of the mind is concerned. He was, on the whole, impressed by the conflict between opposing tendencies and by the pathological aspects of opposition and of ambivalence. Although he felt that a creative outcome of these oppositions is vital in the building up of normal mental structure, this positive aspect of the interaction of opposite functions and between opposing parts of the personality is not very clearly formulated and described. The vital conflict and interaction between love and hate, and the importance of a creative outcome in the building of mental structure and of an ego that can cope with ambivalence and indeed multivalence, are discoveries of Melanie Klein and others who followed Freud in the use of the psychoanalytic method. The Kleinians were not the first to understand the value of beauty, unselfishness, and concern for others, but they reunited psychoanalysis with the traditional valuation of beauty, unselfishness, concern for others, and other ageless human values. The reflex machine, the search for pleasure and avoidance of pain, the need for gratification and for security – they are all still there. They are not exactly superseded but built upon and worked with, by an I who can survive conflict and feel guilt, concern, and sadness on behalf of both oneself and others. In the words of Donald Meltzer, the baby moves from pain-and-fear to love-and-pain (1973, Chapter 4). As we all know, we do not continually move in the one direction, but most of us find some way of bobbing to and fro along this particular dimension, and, on the whole, we can feel grateful rather than destructive toward people who show unselfishness and concern for us.

Jung, the Self, and the Union of the Opposites

Writing *Memories, Dreams, Reflections* in his early eighties, Jung clearly saw himself as a man acutely and painfully aware of the conflict of opposing attitudes and feelings in himself, of the paradoxical nature of God and man, and of the potentially creative results of uniting these opposing tendencies or at least of becoming aware of them. Moreover, it seems fair to assert that he saw himself as a person uniquely blessed – and condemned – in his ability to resolve these mighty conflicts within himself. In this respect he seems to have taken his clergyman father as a negative model. He saw his father as taking a bland, orthodox attitude toward religion, avoiding painful conflict within himself for the sake of a peace of mind which he never, in fact, experienced and never really deserved.

As a child and young man, Jung felt almost as if he were two different persons. For example, he knew that he was an ordinary school-boy but at times felt he was an important old man from antique times. He sometimes felt he lived in two completely different worlds, the outer world of everyday life and commonsense reality, and a mysterious, dark, and shining secret inner world of dreams, revelations, and intuitive knowledge. The person living in the everyday world he called his No. 1 personality, the other person was No. 2. He does not write much of the conflicts between these two subpersonalities, but the fact that No. 2 was completely secret and, for the most part, the thinker of forbidden thoughts is sufficient indication of awareness of opposition, if not of conflict within himself.

Unlike that of his father, at least as far as he knew him, Jung's experience of God was all-important, authentic, and paradoxical if not actually ambiguous. He wrote of a dream at the age of three or four of a great underground phallus on a sort of altar. This strange deity was associated with death, burials, the devouring of men, and dark aspects of Jesus. Several years later he was intensely troubled by a visual image of God on his throne above the local cathedral. For days he was tormented by a conflict between a feeling that he had to let himself experience the image more fully, and a feeling of horror and fear of the consequences of so doing. He finally decided that God wanted him to dare to see what happened next, and what he saw was God shitting a great turd, which shattered the sparkling new roof and the walls of the cathedral he loved. This vision was followed by profound relief as well as a feeling of ineffable grace. He wept for happiness and gratitude to God for revealing

His wisdom and goodness to him now that he had yielded to His command to dare to see the vision. The experience was an illumination whereby many things became clear. For instance, it became clear to him that his father had not experienced the will of God, but had, in fact, opposed it for reasons of the deepest faith. Jung felt afterward at times that the experience had been evil and sinister. It had to remain a secret, like the vision of God as underground phallus.

For Jung these experiences were crucial ones of his life. He was sure that it was God, not the Devil and not Jung himself, who had 'invented' these images and issued these commands. He had a sense of destiny to be fulfilled. It did not have to be proved; it proved itself to him. From this sureness he had an inner security, a strength to go his own way. In all decisive matters he felt he was not among men, but alone with God outside time. But these encounters were a bloody struggle as well as supreme ecstasy. From then on he felt that no one could rob him of the conviction that it was enjoined upon him to do what God wanted and not what he himself wanted. Yet it was also this that gave him the strength to go his own way. Again, paradoxically, he felt that he must take the responsibility for the outcome of it all.

This personal relationship with the non-ego, the God who was the ego of the universe, led the young Jung to explore the traditional nature of God and to read widely in theology and philosophy. At the same time, the demands of school, the need to earn a living rather than opting out in nervous illness or living his No. 2 personality, eventually decided him to seek the light of consciousness, go forward with his No. 1 personality, and study medicine. In the profession of psychiatry and above all in his later experiences of the self and what he referred to as individuation, he felt that the main streams of his personality were once again flowing together.

The tension between the needs of his No. 1 and No. 2 personalities, and the tension between his ego and his non-ego experienced as "thou" or "Other," i.e., as objects, can easily be seen to be at the roots of his later work on extraversion and introversion. His intimate accord with the Other as God, with all the moral imperatives of that encounter, can equally be seen as the root of the essentially optimistic view Jung had about the possibility of creatively reconciling the opposites. But the creative work is, in its most urgent form, an agonizing struggle as well as a supreme ecstasy. The human instinct for perceiving and understanding both inner and outer realities in a polarized way, and the sublime feeling surrounding the achievement of reconciliation, permeates Jung's work on the opposites. I think it fair to say that this need to reconcile is absent in the theories of Pavlov and Freud, although not in the theories of post-Kleinians and other post-Freudians. For Jung, the Self, his term for the non-ego centre, is where the opposites meet, the heart of the paradox and of the creative mystery of life. The term *Self* is, of course, paradoxical and profound, and its implications are vast when we consider how closely his Self is related to what we experience as God.

Writing in 1950 about his first major work, known in English as the *Psychology of the Unconscious*, Jung said that the whole work "was the explosion of all those psychic contents which could find no room, no breathing-space" in the narrow outlook of Freudian psychology, an outlook termed by Jung one of reductive causalism (Jung 1952, p. xxiii). Jung saw his own outlook as one of awareness of the teleological directedness of everything psychic.

The issue between Jung and Freud at the time concerned the interpretation of the unconscious material brought by patients and others in dreams, symptoms, fairy tales, and myths. Both agreed this material had strong links with incest motifs, the Oedipus complex, and pregenital infantile sexuality. Jung accused Freud of taking too much of a deflating, "nothing but" attitude to all this rich cultural, religious, and mythological content. To take an everyday example from modern psychoanalysis, an analyst who felt irritated and overwhelmed by so many grand archetypal dreams from a patient that patient and therapist could not together derive any value from them might offer a causal reductive interpretation such as, "You are trying to make sure you produce plenty of poo (or whatever word was used for faeces by the patient in his infancy) because you don't want the mummy-analyst to be angry with you for not being able to do anything, as your mother was." This sort of interpretation does not address the actual intellectual, emotional, or forward-looking content of the material, but reduces the material to the infantile, the past, and the putative cause of the transference aspects of the patient's behaviour. I have seen Jungian analysts walk out on colleagues who reported interpretations of this precise sort, although I myself did not feel that the interpretations had been at all reductive in the sense of diminishing or devaluing the child in the patient. My "reductive" colleagues seemed to be able to validate and value the child in the patient and his infantile sexuality so that accusations of reductive causalism seemed rather irrelevant. However, analysts of all persuasions sometimes infantilize their patients just as employers and teachers and administrators do, and this has changed very much for the better in the last twenty or thirty years. In short, looking at the infantile sexual aspects of material and behaviour is only reductive when the infant and his sexuality are seen as small and unimportant, in other words, when the magic, the beauty, and the omnipotence, as well as the horror, the ugliness, and the impotence of the child's world are not fully respected by the therapist. Full respect usually includes paying respect and attention to the content of the material.

On the other hand, the teleological directedness of the unconscious needs to be constantly kept in mind. Witness the scientist friend of mine who had trouble producing scientific papers in connection with his profession and who dreamt of shitting in a public place. He did not need any interpretation and thereafter he began to be able to write. Insensitive, reductive interpretation might have put him back years, depending on the strength of the infantile transference. Jung's own dreams are themselves good examples of the forward-directing, integrative aspects of the unconscious. Unfortunately not everyone has such a good working relationship with his unconscious, and blocks may have to be worked on in therapy.

The clash with Freud and the resulting professional isolation brought about Jung's next great work which was essentially about opposites, namely, *Psychological Types*, published in German in 1921. In his memoirs Jung wrote that this work arose from his need to define the ways in which his own outlook differed from those of Freud and Adler. The attempt to answer this problem brought him up against the problem of personality types and their respective attitudes and perspectives.

Introducing the book, Jung remarks that in the course of his practical work with patients he noticed that besides individual differences there are also typical differences, which he terms the introverted and the extraverted types. We notice how the fate of the introverted type of person is determined more by his own inner self, by the subject, while the fate of the extraverted type is determined more by the things and persons who are the object of his interest. Everyone possesses both mechanisms, but one or the other usually predominates. The energies of the extraverted person, or the person who is for the time being extraverting, seem to be drawn as if by a magnet toward the external object, whereas the opposite is true of the introverted or introverting person. Every human being tends to move from the one attitude to the other and back as an expression of his natural life rhythms, but the demands of our lives seldom permit undisturbed flow.

In addition to the mutually antagonistic nature of these two attitudinal opposites, stemming from the fact that when one's energy is flowing outward it tends to be not flowing inward at the same time, Jung describes four functions of the mind that in his opinion are arranged as pairs of opposites. When we are using our feelings, we tend not to be also using our thinking faculty, and when we are using our intuitive function our awareness and use of sensations or matters of fact is being inhibited. In other words, thinking and feeling are opposites, and sensation and intuition are also opposed to each other.

Jung uses these hypothetical pairs of opposites to examine a wide range of historical and religious movements, controversies, and political polarisations. He is using an essentially biological view of the opposites and of the clashing, the polarisations, and the schisms that have gripped men throughout the ages. The sort of opposites that his interests led him to study were: clashes in the ancient Christian Church, especially theological disputes, such as the problem of transubstantiation; nominalism versus realism; the Apollonian versus the Dionysian attitudes; Prometheanism versus the cautiousness and timidity of Epimethianism; rationalism versus empiricism; idealism versus materialism; monism versus pluralism; and dogmatism versus scepticism. These are the types of polarisation and controversy that are better understood when also looked at in terms of the mutually inhibitory properties of the extraverted and the introverted attitude.

More than this, Jung devotes some attention in this book to the reconciliation of opposites, to the uniting symbol which may emerge out of the conflict of opposites if these are each given full value by the individual human person, or if each of the opposites in a pair is given up in equal measure. Brahman is an example of the latter type of uniting symbol. In the *Mahabharata* we read, "he who does neither right nor wrong, renouncing the merit and demerit acquired in former lives, whose soul is tranquil when the bodily elements vanish away, will be liberated." In this state the identity between divine being and the self of man becomes a living experience. The symbol of the middle way in Chinese philosophy is another example Jung uses of the uniting symbol emerging from the conflict of opposites. Yet another example of the uniting symbol as an experience arising out of the splitting of libido into opposing halves is the "god-renewal" of the poet Spitteler, the symbol of the dying and resurgent god who mediates between the opposites, the Messiah.

In this book Jung writes as thinker and scholar, but during this period we now know from his memoirs that he was engaging in a very intense intrapersonal struggle with inner forces and subpersonalities which I need not describe in detail here. Out of these personal conflicts of opposites arose his own personal uniting symbols and concepts, subsumed under his concept of the Self and of the individuation process, symbols of which were thrown up into consciousness by his own unconscious processes but which he found he shared with mankind in general, oriental and occidental alike. These symbols of transformation and of the union of opposites he found to be particularly rich in old alchemical texts, and in the latter part of his life he devoted much of his research to this field. He found that the alchemical philosophers had made the opposites and their union one of the chief objects of their work. The symbols they used had much in common with dream symbolism and were useful tools for understanding the dynamic changes in the unconscious for the very reason that the philosophers were unhampered by the knowledge that they were dealing with the unconscious, but thought that they were dealing with the properties and changes of matter.

Jung compared the alchemical quest with the dialectical relationship of analysis and the human search for wholeness. In so far as either is successful, the unconscious changes are the same. He compared the process of the analytical relationship with the sequence of changes described in the alchemical text known as the *Rosarium Philosophorum* (see Jung 1946 for sources), "on the true way of preparing the philosophers' stone, containing the precise way of advancing in its knowledge." The sequence of changes pictured in this work is envisioned as the mystical alchemical union between royal brother and sister, or mother and son, or sun and moon, materially embodied in their chemical equivalents in the alchemist's vessel. This vision is essentially the same as Kekule's vision of the dancing couples which preceded his discovery of the benzene ring (presuming on the indulgence, even the willing effort, of the reader to make this all-important conceptual bridging effort).

The union of the opposites takes the form of a sexual union and merging of the couple in the liquid of the bath. Before the miraculous birth of the divine child, the stone, there is a stage of blackening or putrefaction, and in some texts this is seen as the raw material at the beginning of the work. Hence the vulgarization of the description of the philosophers' task of changing base material or lead into gold. (No doubt the alchemists themselves varied in their "vulgarity!" Here I am using *vulgar* as synonymous with the term *concrete*, as I have used it throughout this volume.)

"Psychology of the Transference" was first published in 1946. Jung elaborates and comments upon the pictures of the *Rosarium* in an effort to describe his view of what is really happening, mostly unconsciously, in an ongoing, more or less successful analysis, with its vicissitudes and with the necessary bad times and the dark aspects of the transference. More than that, it describes in metaphorical or poetic language the creative interaction at the nucleus of the successful mother-child relationship (the "good feed" in Kleinian language) but also the creative union of opposites which is the bright side of the nucleus of the I (the dark side being seen as the explosive annihilation which is even more basic than putrefaction in my opinion). The creative aspect of primal scene excitement is also an important manifestation of this mysterious union within the self. The forbidden or fearful, dark side of the approach to the union is to do with the overcoming of the incest taboo or more generally, the "Thou shalt not." So the desirable outcome is both a freeing from the maternal bond as well as a metaphorical fulfillment of the regressive wish to merge with the mother or get back into the womb.

In using the theme of the mystic marriage of opposites as the best way of hinting at the most important transference phenomena, Jung was aware that he was describing a classical transference evolution. Sometimes the transference is purely destructive and sometimes, to put it crudely, nothing happens. In other words, it is partly a matter of chemistry, although I think we now know much more than Jung or Freud knew about the work on the transference which is involved in character analysis and the healing of narcissistic wounds in general, and of the generalised and localised hardenings and need to project which they entail. For Jung, as for countless others, the mandala was the symbol, the description, albeit a cryptogram, and even a living experience, of the self in this sense of the creative and harmonious union of the opposites. It is "the wholeness of the personality, which if all goes well is harmonious, but which cannot tolerate self-deceptions" (Jung 1963, p. 187). It is "Formation, transformation, Eternal Mind's eternal recreation."

Jung painted his first mandala in 1916, after writing his Seven Sermons for the Dead, a cathartic outpouring of antique, arcane, intuitive parts of himself not successfully contained by his commonsense everyday self. This particular mandala was an attempt to express Jung's whole world at the time in a harmonious balancing of spirit and instinct, mind and matter, conscious and unconscious.

In 1918 he began to understand his mandala drawings as statements about his state of being at the time. For example, when he felt at one with himself, the mandala would be a harmonious, symmetrical, intact whole. Another day, for example, after being shaken and disturbed by a letter from a woman he thought he had successfully extruded but who was clearly still "under his skin," the attempted mandala had a burst periphery and had lost its symmetry. This is Jung's description—I have not seen this one.

It is clear that Jung's mandalas, like all those done by my patients, had their defensive and self-delusory aspects. The nonharmonious, chaotic, destructive experiences are not in consciousness at the time. It is a time of the successful union, the good feed, the healing of the I. We need to experience this self or I time and time again in order to establish an I that can take knocks, putrefactions, shatterings, and disillusionments, and an I that can allow the multitude of persons within us each to have their say.

The defensive aspect of the mandala is the city wall, the temple, the church, the stage, the secret lovers' meeting place, the secure marriage of the nursing mother, the magic circle keeping out the evil spirits. Within this sanctuary the union of opposites is given space to unfold and eventually be experienced creatively. The protective defensiveness and, in a sense, the self-deception are a necessary part of the conditions under which it can proceed. In the temporal sphere, a time set aside for prayer, meditation, worship, or recreation subserves basically the same potentially therapeutic end.

Jung's last book, *Mysterium Coniunctionis: An Inquiry into the Separation and Synthesis of Psychic Opposites in Alchemy*, was finished in his eightieth year and was the final statement of his twenty-five years of research into alchemy. The factors conceived by the alchemists as coming together in enmity or love were seen by Jung as manifestations of the psyche's intrinsic nature—its propensity to polarize. The psychological view of opposites introduces a new viewpoint that is outside the concomitant religious, philosophical, or political polarizations in which, as acting or reflecting persons, we may be gripped.

This statement does not, Jung submits, subvert the validity or the point of religious, philosophical, or political debate or controversy. Polarization, separation, differentiation, and synthesis are how our minds work. They *have* to work like that. Yet the fact remains that these polarizations are psychic. The reality underlying the psyche is another matter; there is no reason to suppose it is polarized—at least I think that is what Jung is saying.

Returning to alchemy, the list of opposites conceived as coming together in enmity or love includes dualisms such as moist/dry, warm/cold, upper/lower, spirit/body, heaven/earth, fire/water, bright/dark, active/passive, gaseous/solid, precious/vile, good/evil, open/occult, east/west, living/dead, masculine/feminine, and sun/moon.

Often the dualisms are arranged two by two, producing a cruciform arrangement, as we have seen in our historical survey of medical controversies and theories. The mandala usually has a fourfold arrangement of this sort, or the bipolar arrangement may be extended to the third dimension producing a cruciform arrangement in space.

The mandala can be said to include other elements apart from the balancing and creative combining of opposites. These include (a) the successful establishment of boundaries, in particular that between self and not-self, and (b) the achievement of wholeness and harmony combined with resilience. Boundless states of all-pervading oneness may even be included if the mandala and the cosmos are brought together in a person's experiential state.

Again, the opposites in alchemy are often seen as real or mythical animals, or as human or divine persons. Their interaction may be seen in crude, basic quasi-chemical terms appropriate to the alchemical laboratory, such as love/hate, separation/merging, solution, sublimation, and the many products of chemical action.

In the epilogue of this work, Jung asserts that the entire alchemical procedure for uniting the opposites could equally well describe the process whereby a single individual attains autonomy and wholeness, though with the not unimportant difference that no single individual attains to the richness and scope of the alchemical symbolism. Hence the thanklessness of the task of describing the individuation process in human case material.

We might differ from Jung in this view. If his own memoirs are any guide, more case histories would have been less repetitive, less recondite, and more humanly moving than his scholarly masterpieces. But this is largely a matter of taste.

We could, of course, easily take the reductive-causal view that his entire work on the *mysterium coniunctionis* was nothing but a way of satisfying his forbidden curiosity about his parent's intercourse and their lack of true intercourse. We have his own dreams to support such an interpretation.

His work on the *coniunctio*, he says, was heralded by a dream of a house. It was his house, his own self one might say, and it contained a large wing which so far he had never visited. However, he finally resolved to enter it. It contained a laboratory which was his father's work room and which contained hundreds of specimens of all kinds of fish. Further along was a haunted room, his mother's. It was very large and contained two rows of five suspended pavilions each of which looked like chests or gardens. Each pavilion had two beds each. This was the room in which ghostly couples visited her for the night; each couple used one of the twin-bedded pavilions.

Opposite his mother's room was one full of ostentation, jollity, and bonhomie, even with a brass band playing; this was a caricature of Jung's extraverted side, he thought.

Jung commented that the reception room for spirit couples expressed in a farcical fashion the *coniunctio* and that the fish laboratory indicated his preoccupation with Christ, who is associated with the fish symbol. Both were subjects that kept him busy for more than a decade. In one way we cannot gainsay this interpretation, because this was what happened.

The reductive view would, of course, lead to a more personal analysis of Jung and his parents, on the split in Jung and in his internalized primal scene, and on the evasive and defensive purpose of the father's and mother's sublimations of their flesh-and-blood drives. But we know, again from Jung's memoirs, that he would probably have eschewed such lines of association as distasteful and banal.

This dream explains to me why the world-destructive, evil aspects of the *coniunctio*–the nuclear bomb aspects, as it were–have not been fully explored by Jung. The work on the *coniunctio*, the mandala, the Self, and the individuation process perhaps quite rightly emphasize wholeness and harmony. Blackness, darkness, putrefaction are acknowledged fully by him but the insane, bombing destructiveness that we perforce have to address, not only in some of our young people but in ourselves, is not. This has been left to our generation. Jung had visions of the blood and filth of war but he projected that onto the canvas of history, as I am saying in this book that we all have done.

Forms of the *Coniunctio*

The archetype of the union of opposites is, like all archetypal phenomena, protean in its manifestations. To Jung's breadth of vision we owe our appreciation of the small and large ways in which archetypal images and archetypal experiences underlie and inform our lives and our behaviour.

The archetypes all have positive and negative forms. The good mother is twinned with the bad, if not even identical. It may be abhorrent to experience this undoubted psychological fact, but it is nevertheless unwise to derive good and evil from altogether separate instinctual or separate psychic or divine sources.

As an archetypal image, the *coniunctio* sometimes exists in an autonomous or free-floating form. Jung's speculations on flying saucers serve as an illustration of the power he discerned in such an image of the detached, free-floating *coniunctio*. I have speculated in this volume on the subject of how bits of the Self may become entirely split off from the I and seem to have, or in fact have, an entirely real, outside, material existence.

The positive *coniunctio* may be experienced in an important form, not entirely split-off from the I, but with a delusory connection with the I, in the form of the ideas of influence and ideas of reference of the psychotic person. The mysterious meaning, the "revelation" that ties things together, the knowledge that an item on the television news refers specifically to oneself, all these phenomena, experienced as either positive or negative feelings and convictions, are forms of the archetype of the *coniunctio*.

The negative forms of *coniunctio* include explosions and collisions and form the main subject matter of this book. Bombs, in common with all archetypal phenomena, come in all shapes and sizes, in all degrees of personalisation/depersonalisation and all degrees of sexualisation. The image of the explosion may take the form of sparks bringing life, showers of rain, eruptions, the bursting forth of new life, the ordinary bomb or the nuclear bomb.

As an autonomous, negative, *coniunctio* bit of the Self, the explosion may be delivered by phallic, anal, face-to-face, or insinuating means. The gun, the aeroplane, the bomb, placed in the place of concourse or inside the maternal body of the building, are all imagined or actually used as means of delivery for both positive and negative forms of free-floating, disembodied *coniunctio* images or material entities.

In the long term, Jung took the optimistic view of these phenomena. The fact that they are activated and envisioned so powerfully in the psychic atmosphere of our present times means that these autonomous subpersonalities of the self are capable of being integrated with the collective I. But the magnitude of such psychological work means that the possibility of integration is an open question, by far the most important of our times.

Consciousness, Adaptation, and the Opposites

In his essay "On Psychic Energy," first published in 1928, Jung gives a fairly precise, biologically oriented account of how he sees the relationship between adaptation, progression, regression, the experience of conflict, and the emergence of new adaptations resulting from the mobilization of the unconscious (Jung 1948, par. 60–76).

Adaptation to environmental opportunities and demands, he says, normally proceeds fairly smoothly through a consciously directed attitude. This necessarily entails a certain one-sidedness. To the extent that adaptation fails, the progression of libido ceases. The libido activates psychic contents which conflict. Subjective contents and reactions press to the fore and the psyche is ripe for explosions. This state of affairs indicates a damming of libido, in which the unity of the pairs of opposites is broken up. During the progressive phase, the pairs of opposites had been "united in a co-ordinated flow" (ibid.). Such balancing and coordination is seen in the process of reflection and the kind of decision-making that ensues therefrom.

The damming of libido, however, causes even more energy to be invested in each of the conflicting opposites, resulting in splitting or dissociation, alienating part of oneself from another. Uncoordinated acts based on repression of one of the opposites tend to follow. This may hinder further adaptation, and the fruitless struggle would result in neurosis if a regressive movement of libido did not supervene, in which the opposites are deprived of their energy and the conflict is deprived of its conscious importance. The direction of libido is now more inward, increasing the value of those elements not concerned with outward adaptation. The activated unconscious contents may cause a disturbance of consciousness, possibly with neurotic or symptomatic acts characteristic of the activation of the complexes and unconsciously determined phenomena of the Freudian literature, i.e., of an infantile-sexual nature. But if one can refrain from passing judgment on these slimy or abhorrent elements, it can be seen that they include the possibilities of new life. This is the empirical finding of psychotherapy in general and of psychoanalysis in particular.

By activating the unconscious elements, regression confronts consciousness with inner psychic needs as opposed to the ostensible demands of outward adaptation. But just as outward adaptation may be too one-sided or imbalanced, inward adaptation may likewise be one-sided and may become pathological, rigid, and fixated. Normally, once inward adaptation is achieved, progression can be resumed. But progression should not be confused with the enrichment and differentiation that constitutes true development. Progression and regression are like the flow of the tide and may take place in a natural ebb and flow without the enrichment and deepening of consciousness and awareness involved in psychic development.

This latter requires a certain attitude toward the activated opposites and to unconscious material, which Jung calls the symbolic attitude. The conscious confrontation and holding of the opposites generates a living third thing, not a logical stillbirth, not a mere compromise or grey average, but a living birth that leads to a new level of being and of adaptation. This "transcendent function" manifests as a new quality of conjoined opposites that have not been kept apart for the purpose of avoiding subjective disturbance or subjective explosion. The present volume can be regarded as an elaboration of this theme in various practical and theoretical directions not all by any means unfamiliar to Jung or his followers. One of the main differences in emphasis here is on the importance of the structure of the I, on its holding capacity (of conflict between the opposites) and its ability to relate to the apparently destructive aspects of the not-I (usually projected, of course). Jung saw the I as a kind of complex but did not study it to the same extent as that to which he interested himself in the not-I or, in his terminology, the Self considered as a centre of organization outside the I.

Jung's concept of the breakup of the pairs of opposites when adaptation and progression are blocked is quite similar to Freud's concept of the unbinding of the (opposing) instincts or the failure to bind the instincts together. This, in Freud's view, was a failure of the ego, a view more in line with that taken here.

Conclusion

One thing is clear from the work of these three men, and that is that man is a polarizing animal. From the lowest spinal level of organization to the highest spiritual level, we are built to polarize in order to act, react, adapt. Each level has its own ways of dealing with the various kinds of conflict or imbalance that must occur. Sometimes, as in the case of many motor reflexes as well as in the higher nervous system, imbalance has to be accentuated by mutually inhibitory mechanisms or by the processes subsumed under the heading of induction. The phenomena of boundaries in dynamic psychology are related to processes of this sort. "Do" and "do not" have to be clearly differentiated in the first instance.

At the same time, the internal environment has to be kept fairly constant within certain limits of chemistry, temperature, and physical tolerances in tissues. In this entire sphere of keeping the body's functions going, opposites and extremes are avoided by stabilizing systems which bring the bodily state, the internal environment, back to a "middle way."

Polarizations of attitude and of behaviour historically become ethical dualities and are appropriated by what we think of as masculine elements of the personality. On the other hand, the middle way, the needs to reconcile and contain, tend more to be linked with the parts of ourselves we call feminine. But containing, mothering, merging, and mating all have to do with dissolving and/or enjoying differences and transcending boundaries and are not at all confined to female animals or humans.

The fact that humans are polarizing animals needs to be assimilated along with the fact that humans are pluralistic animals, in that, in common with animals, they have many drives, behaviour patterns, and complex reflexes which are subsumed under the heading in the present volume of subpersonalities. And finally we must recognize that humans are also both monistic and monotheistic at times, and this is true whether we are talking of the self or of society. I am not talking simply of monism as a denial of dualism or pluralism, e.g., Pavlov's assertion that material reality is the only reality that matters, but of monism as a profound experience and a profound insight into the nature of our universe.

Another thing is clear, and that is that nature has invented many ways of resolving conflict and of avoiding explosive and catastrophic behaviour. These ways have of necessity evolved *pari passu* with the level of organization and with the specific nature of the competing or clashing "opposites." In Pavlov's dogs, cruel and ingenious ways of exacerbating the tension between the opposites were needed before violent explosive behaviour, based on fear or the desire to burst out of the intolerable restrictive situation (Pavlov's "freedom reflex"), could be made to occur. In human beings, it is clear that comparable explosiveness and tension can be built up by social movements, and in the course of the building of our personalities and character, threat or hurt to the early I is preeminently important, as we saw in the first part of this volume. Freud's concept of Eros, covering the drives of mothering and mating, seems to summarize and encompass those parts of the self which are concerned with ensuring a creative outcome. With Jung, the idea of the *coniunctio* is extended into the general situation of the marriage and subsequent creative outcome of the potentially conflictful meeting of incompatibles.

CHAPTER 12

The Democratization of the Divine Self

In therapy the client's actual behaviour, and in particular his patterns of repeated behaviour which are unwilled, self-destructive, or unconscious, give the therapist the first clues as to the discrepancies between his I and his unconscious. The second line of evidence comes from the feelings the therapist has in the emotional relationship between himself and his client, and the third set of data comes from the dream and fantasy content, as well as from those slips and leakages so well described by Freud in *The Psychopathology of Everyday Life* (1901).

Only if the life behaviour, the transference behaviour, the therapist's feelings about and toward the client, and the dreams form a consistent and meaningful whole does the therapist try to link it all together for the patient in an interpretation of what it may all mean. Of course, I am describing an ideal or principle; for much of what is actually said in therapy does not come under the heading of interpretative work. But the general principle is worth formulating because I think that I am following a similar principle in trying to understand and formulate what the human race is up to at the present time. In therapy one hardly ever makes unilateral interpretations but tries to work together with the patient toward interpretations, having each others' views modified by the dialectic exchange as one goes along. This book is, of necessity, a relatively unilateral affair, a very tentative foray into interpretative work with an imaginary patient consisting of present-day humanity. How much of a dialogue will ensue remains to be see. Incidentally the picture of oneself, Joe Redfearn, conducting a dialogue with the human race is a grandiose, omnipotent fantasy of godlikeness which constitutes the main topic of the present chapter. Let us all have such harmless omnipotent fantasies, provided that we can allow the next person to have them, too, and can moreover maintain our sense of humour about our godlikeness.

Returning again to individual therapeutic practice, I would like to convey a more detailed picture of how some of the main subpersonalities emerge into the mutual understanding of therapist and client. The unconscious figures or subpersonalities at work in an individual, as I have repeatedly said, determine his behaviour in a choiceless manner until they emerge into consciousness and become integrated into the ego, when a modest degree of choice becomes possible. I sincerely believe that the same applies to group behaviour. When the subpersonality becomes conscious, it may be integrated as a living symbol around which controversy and dialectic can eventually move toward conscious choice rather than the fateful unconscious tides of history that otherwise sweep us helplessly to and fro.

For our individual therapy case, let us again use the example of the timid son with the father complex. Having perhaps been somewhat bullied or overpowered by his actual father, he behaves in a timid way and tends to perceive father figures as overpowering and frightening. He may well behave in such a way toward the therapist, who may point this out from time to time. From the patient's timid behaviour toward him, and from his own feelings in response to the patient's behaviour and apparent feelings toward him, the therapist imagines that there is a frightening or bullying parental subpersonality at work distorting the relationship. A dream may give more precise information about the nature of this figure and what causes this figure to become activated. The therapist may feed these data back to the patient, and gradually patient and therapist learn more about the frightening parental figure, how this figure dominates his life and relationships, and how the figure can be related to in a new way perhaps. It may happen that a benign parental, grandparental, or divine figure may emerge at some stage and, while at first being used to contrast with or defeat the bad father, may eventually help the bad father to change.

The therapist must learn to allow himself to respond in a feeling way to the patient and to pay attention to his own feelings, impulses, and emotions in relation to the patient. The therapist's subjectivity, in other words, is in a sense an objective datum that is nowadays an essential part of therapeutic practice. Experience, supervision, and the comparison of one's feelings and reactions toward one patient as opposed to others enable the therapist to learn more and more about his own complexes and biases in his therapeutic interactions, although it is always necessary to be open to being proved foolish or mistaken.

The nuclear bomb is a real threat to mankind. Mistakes, mistaken preemptive escalating moves by opposing factions, and increasing panic could turn the threat into a reality. It may even be that the human race would have blown itself up long ago if it had had the technical means to do so. Regarding the nuclear bomb as a human subpersonality seems reasonable in view of the undoubted fact that it has been created by human beings. In this it is at first sight unlike a so-called "natural" disaster such as an earthquake or a flood. But looking at natural disasters more closely, we see that the extent of the human disaster and the number of casualties, etc., can vary with the carelessness and the self-destructive forces at work, almost as if a malign human subpersonality (malign earthquake god or whatever) is unconsciously at work.

If actions really speak louder than words, or conscious beliefs, it follows that many "mistakes" are the result of unconscious motivation. If we allow

(1) that, for at least three thousand years, there has been a powerful apocalyptic wish in the religions arising out of the Middle East and hence in the unconscious actions of the Western world, and

(2) that the unconscious works more through apparent mistakes than in any other way, although unaware acting-out may also often occur,

then we should beware of trusting our ability to build up real safeguards against "mistakes."

Treating the nuclear bomb as a shared human subpersonality, then, what sort of a subperson are we dealing with? This would seem clear enough. It is an all-powerful, all-destructive, humanity-hating "person." Most of us can perhaps recognize such a person, however fleeting its appearance, as a part of ourselves. Many of us might recognize the angry omnipotent male god of the thunderbolt – some moods or periods of the god(s) of the Old Testament, or the god of the punishing or ignorance-shattering thunderbolt. Or we can diagnose this subpersonality as our impotent rage manifesting itself as a childish omnipotent fantasy. A mad, cruel boy in a temper tantrum.

Using these psychological diagnoses may encourage us to smile in condescension at the superstitious idea that the coming apocalypse is God's punishment and God's millennium. That sort of passive complacency is probably an important factor in our present predicament. A moment's thought will remind us that such a god really exists, if we would only take seriously the evidence of our behaviour, of the infantile and often omnipotent, compensatory nature of our unconsciousness, of the fact that the mass of mankind for all practical purposes believes concretely in such a god or gods – unless it believes steadfastly and blindly in a one-sided God of Love and blinds itself to the dark side of reality.

It is a commonplace finding in therapy that the more a person derides and denies the irrational, infantile, omnipotent parts of his personality, the more likely it is that these parts will burst or break through in mistakes, illnesses, criminality, neurosis, or psychosis. The buildup of such natural pressures undoubtedly occurs in groups with one-sided mythologies. The God of our present-day mythology may well be one-sidedly male, loving, and creative. The cruel boy with his omnipotent temper tantrum would perhaps be the Satanic subpersonality threatening to emerge in order to counterbalance this idealizing state of affairs.

For the mass of Western people, God is God and man is man (or woman) and the divine is different from the human. There has been a basic split between God and I. As God is all-powerful and all-loving, good has to be found, and usually is found, in all that occurs. There is psychological soundness in this view, of course, or it would not be so persistent. The concrete apocalypse is not very far from such concrete and simplistic theology. Our mass religions are at this primitive level. It would be interesting to know what people would make of the question, Does God exist? Most people, I think, would say that a simple yes or no would suffice to answer it.

In the theology of the all-loving Father God, the behaviour pattern of God the Destroyer can never be far away. As a sophisticated, interpreting therapist-observer of the human race, I am saying it is *as if* an omnipotent, sadistic, infantile God were at work causing the human race to explode. The rub exists in the fact that the majority of people, at least in Western civilisation, behave as if there were no "*as if*" in the previous sentence. Such a God is therefore a reality in the only sense that matters – the reality that makes people behave in the way they actually behave. Such a God would not be consciously believed in by thinking people, but especially because He is unconscious and shows Himself in our behaviour and emotions, we must give all due weight to His importance *in practice*.

So in order to start the therapeutic dialogue with our patient, the human race, let us suggest that there is an angry, destructive, omnipotent God subpersonality at work in our patient, an angry male subpersonality to be more precise.

Why is God angry and destructive? Usually the reason for this sort of omnipotent anger is narcissistic hurt – hurt feelings. Why are God's feelings hurt? We have suggested several possibilities already:

(1) The development of order, thinking, and depersonalisation, now robotisation – a robot universe. This makes feeling and emotion more unconscious and ever more primitive.

(2) The reemergence of the importance of the mother goddess and of the feminine side of the personality. A male chauvinistic god (human subpersonality in projection) would be extremely put out at this cultural phenomenon, just as He was in the time of the Old Testament. I am not speaking of the childishness of God, but of the God we, on practice, worship.

(3) The undermining of His omnipotence as a concrete person outside the I, i.e., of the naive Western (Levantine) belief of the pre-Reformation, Church-dictated sort – as a result of the Reformation, the growth of science, and now of psychological understanding. Prometheus has been a threat to God and has angered God since the presumptuous growth of science and psychology.

We are talking here of a polarisation between a scientifically enlightened and psychologically insightful humanitarian consciousness (a minority in demographic terms) and an anti-Reformation backlash of superstition and infantile emotions, backed by technological power of awesome creative and destructive potential (the demographic majority, the unconscious, the Way We Behave, the Dark Side of God).

The rise and fall of Nazism in Germany should be proof that I am talking about real forces of shattering magnitude that we should realize are present in our depths and that cannot now be lightly dismissed or denied. A course in psychology or a psychoanalysis will not solve this problem.

The Democratization of Omnipotent Subpersonalities

In his brilliant and seminal book, *Lord of the Four Quarters* (1966), John Weir Perry studies the myths of celestial and terrestrial kingship, particularly in the ancient world, when the god-king of the realm was one with the king-god myth. He embodied, as we have seen, the principles of order and of law in the human and sacred realms. The orderly division of society into four functioning groups (priests and scholars, warriors and administrators, merchants and tradesmen, craftsmen and labourers), the design of the city, the differentiation of person from tribe, ego from unconscious, go hand in hand as projections are progressively withdrawn until at last the fulfilled democratic state is reached where every man is king. Understanding the order and experiencing it in himself, the democratic individual agrees with the ordering and does not need either to project the ordering principle onto an external god-king or king-god, or to have the order imposed on him.

This simple but hopeful description of the evolution of democracy is applied by Perry to the role of the Father archetype in presiding over the fourfold ordering of the mind, and by projection, of society and the view of the cosmos. The quadrate organization of the Self-image has received very full attention by Jung and Jungian authors. Moreover, it is a truism, worth repeating again and again nevertheless, that the growth of the personally responsible ego and the democratization of society go hand in hand, and each cannot exist without the other. But, by the same principle of opposites and polarity enunciated by Jung and by Perry, as well as by the philosophies of millennia, order (including the quadrate), contained order of the self, or the cosmic model, it has its opposite in explosion or chaos, which may catastrophically liberate all the energy that, as civilisation and order have laboriously evolved, has been stored and bound in the orderly, responsible, civilised ego, the inner counterpart of our modern civilisation.

The withdrawal of the projection of divine omnipotence and its incorporation into the ego carries with it the danger not only of psychotic inflation but of social explosion. But it is clearly a continuous, Promethean process in the culture of the West. The adventurous, truth-seeking I is always in a dangerous, loggerheads relationship with the jealous and envious monomania of the God out there; winning or losing are both catastrophic.

Impotence and Irresponsibility

In individual therapy it is usually possible to find and successfully relate to the hurt, impotent I hiding behind the omnipotent delusory fantasies or omnipotent rage of the patient, which, as we have seen, are often encountered in the form of a projected subpersonality of the Self. An omnipotent God who will not decide to destroy the world, or an omnipotent, all-loving God who may decide to let the world destroy itself so that something better may emerge, or who can be relied on to prevent catastrophe, amount to an abrogation of personal and collective human responsibility, at least at first glance. The plain fact that, collectively, we are responsible for the nuclear threat and that, consequently, we are not powerless to effect a change for the better, makes it much easier to deny than to accept at an individual level.

In individual therapy, the pain and suffering involved in assuming personal responsibility for one's destructive rage and infantile criminality are avoided almost at any cost and sustained in projection onto others.

I am sure there has always been much truth in the psychological-humanistic view I have just put forward, but we must not forget that the faith in a loving parental figure may give us the confidence to behave far more responsibly and effectively than might be the case in the absence of such a creative "illusion." Reliable internal parental subpersonalities are not, for practical purposes, illusory and are partly what, in a sense, we are aiming for in therapy and in life. In other words, we may *behave* more responsibly when we do not feel *too* responsible.

The considerable strides we have made in understanding our children and our parents must surely be doing something to diminish narcissistic hurt feelings and impotent rage, and thereby our omnipotent robotic destructiveness now threatening us.

The conscious philosophical standpoint is not much to go on, the behaviour much more important. The dreams indicate the effectiveness or, on the contrary, the powerless diminutiveness, of the ego relative to the unconscious instinctual, conditioned, or bodily forces. Dreams of earthquakes, cosmic storms, or wars indicate a relatively powerless-feeling ego. A lover whose beloved is all the world to him will dream of an earthquake or a volcanic eruption when about to quarrel or after a quarrel with her. At this level, the beloved, the Great Mother, the world, and the emotions are coidentical, the ego diminutive as far as control is concerned.

If the nuclear bomb is the dark opposite side of the God of light, truth, and order – the Levantine God of Zoroastrianism, Judaism, Christianity, and Islam, it is also the dark, opposite side of the painful suffering of love and the taking of ultimate responsibility for the world's sins exemplified by the Christ subpersonality. The blanket symbolic gesture of being crucified for the sake of the whole of humanity is in itself an inspiration but, as a fantasy, is sometimes used as a way of avoiding the painful detail of the actual taking of responsibility in real life, the nitty gritty of helping with the washing up or of mending the broken toy. This defensive use of the archetypal image is analogous with our use of the image of the universal apocalypse in order to avoid the painful nitty gritty of the un-grand personal confrontation with the seamier side of oneself.

We are using the nuclear threat to avoid taking responsibility for our omnipotent narcissistic destructive wishes in two ways:

(1) by not taking responsibility for the threat itself, but blaming others for its existence and for the need to have it and possibly use it;

(2) by displacing onto the bomb image the conflict in ourselves – of a mundane, ordinary character – which we are not facing but which we are just about ready to face.

We can use, in a creative way, the example of Christ's self-sacrifice for the many, in a spirit of love, which is just the opposite of avoiding responsibility. The partial and humble identification with the innocent yet responsible victim, for example, through the ritual of the Eucharist, may help us do what we can in our small way to take up our cross of purposeful and meaningful suffering for the sake of others. I am stating this all-too-obvious fact in case it be thought that I was of the opinion that the Christ symbol was always, or more often, used in a defensive, pain-avoiding way as a "blanket" symbol.

Contrast Between Eastern and Western Democratization of the Divine

In the West, then, it can be argued that the tempering of Levantine monotheism with Greek rationalism and aesthetic polytheism, with European paganism and individualism, with the ideal of personal love, and finally the growth of genuine democracy and the flowering of the Renaissance, have produced a strengthening of individual resourcefulness and responsibility and a gradual secularization and democratization of God.

However, the basic separation or split between "God" and "I" has meant that this has only occurred at the cost of the idealization and inflation of the I with the incorporated but unassimilated infantile, omnipotent parts of the self previously projected onto God.

It can also be argued that in the East this basic split between "God" and "I" has hardly taken place. Although the masses have, as it were, used the various divinities as if they were out there, to be worshipped and propitiated accordingly, the wise and the religious have always known that God, the gods, are inseparable from the self. Yet this can be known without the danger of madness, explosiveness, or inflation, as indeed it has from time to time been knowable by Western mystics, gnostics, Rastafarians, Jungians, and similar minorities. In the typical Eastern creation myth, the original One, the original self, becomes two (the origin of the opposites). Also, saying I is the origin of desire and fear, nullifying the division between the I and the not-I, wards off all temptations and dangers and causes the world to bloom. This is the omnipotent fantasy of the East, and it is quite different from the omnipotence of the Western not-I who is God, to be differentiated and distinguished from the obedient I. Humbly aspiring to learn God's will is one thing; knowing God's will, i.e., sharing the omnipotence, is what is socially explosive.

Partaking of the omnipotent or divine is, of course, safe when the next person is allowed equal measure of access to the divine. Political democracy does allow this, and so does religious tolerance. If we try to imagine how far we have progressed since the times of god-kings in sharing out the power and the divinity among ordinary people, we can appreciate both the blessings and the dangers of what I call the democratization of the omnipotent subpersonalities of the Self. Our fate will depend on how near we are in practice to realizing effectively that the nuclear threat is *our* doing and our personal, democratic responsibility. The same applies to the other dangers of biological extinction we are now causing.

CHAPTER 13

The Healing Apocalypse

Destroying the World

It is perfectly possible to be in touch with the part of oneself who would at times wish to do away with the outside world and everything in it, and perhaps with oneself at the same time. It is perfectly possible to be aware of such wishes without actually wanting to carry them out in reality, or being anything but properly horrified at the idea of doing so in reality. It would be better for the prospects for mankind if more people were aware of such manic wishes in themselves. For in that case there would be much less danger of its happening "accidentally."

But there is also an important sense in which it is, and throughout the ages always has been, a spiritual necessity to destroy, lose, or be able to give up, the world and one's body in their material sense. If the world is well lost for love, or for the salvation of one's soul, it is necessary to learn to do so, to learn to die to the world, or allow the world to die to oneself.

In order to live fully with oneself and others, it is necessary to be willing to accept or embrace one's mortality. To face the personal apocalypse may be a more accurate way of referring to this spiritual necessity. This may happen in a single personal crisis, but for many of us the necessity is repeated time and again in varying degrees of fearfulness and importance.

As we grow older and our hold on the outside world has to be progressively relinquished, the I must learn to disidentify itself from the body image and from material reality. I say must; perhaps I should say it is better do so. This independence of the I from the body and from the world can be regarded as a healthy manic defence or denial, and hope-fully can be experienced as a journey toward the Light that is God. But it does entail the destruction of the world in a subjective sense. As ever, we need to distinguish carefully between the mental experience and the concrete destruction of the world. Again, as ever, there is always the danger of conniving unconsciously and entirely unintentionally with the concrete enactment of the inner necessity, if the subjective, spiritual experience does not have a positive relationship with the I. If the spiritual experience is feared, it will assume a negative, even a nightmarish, aspect.

At the psychic level with which these experiences are concerned, an early stage of ego development, the world, the body image, and the mother are not differentiated from each other. So one's baby rage often entails the fragmentation of self, world, and mother together. Deep analysis or other experiences of profound regression in the course of therapy, in which the rage is to some degree experienced in relation to the analyst, who unexpectedly (from the baby's point of view) survives these explosions, should enable one to get in touch with these partial wishes that are a part of all of us (but not the major part, of course).

The Concretized Belief in the After-Life

Is death the end or is it a gateway to new life? Is the death of the world the beginning of a new spiritual era or of new life in a dimension outside time? Is atomic warfare the apocalypse that is to be followed by a second coming of a Messiah? Is death suffered in a righteous cause a guarantee of eternal bliss in the next world?

Many ordinary people throughout the world would give an affirmative answer to one or more of these questions. A belief in the death and subsequent resurrection of a divinity, coupled with a hope of an after-life in some sense, is both ancient and widespread in humanity. If we suspend judgment about its historical aspects and refer to it as a powerfully moving mythological theme or religious truth, or as a profound psychological truth, we are faced with a story or truth that, with variations of a relatively unimportant degree, grips all human beings in some way and is, in fact, a truth for all human beings, a fact about the human psyche. That light follows darkness is perhaps the simplest form of this law of the psyche – and it just happens to be true literally on this planet. The literal, astronomically founded physical truth is not as universally valid as the psychic truth that says, "Every dark cloud has its silver lining." (That every silver lining has its dark cloud is probably not so true, or not true in quite the same way.) All healthy human beings make the best of bad situations, work through failures, grief, and catastrophes, and may come through to acceptance, wisdom, or happiness. They often manage to see the good or hopeful side of natural disasters and personal death. We tend to recover from loss, grief, depression.

This being the case, it would seem to follow logically (but we should by no means accept it as a fact for that reason) that if we answer any of the above questions about life after death with a confident affirmative, then we are not, or should not be, mortally afraid of atomic war.

If this were true, it might well further follow that we would not devote as much energy to avoiding atomic war as we would if death were the end of everything. We might devote relatively more energy to spreading our faith or preparing ourselves psychologically for the coming physical end and relatively less energy to avoiding that end, than if our faith were not so secure. We would expect, then, a tendency, in a time of extreme danger, toward the infectious spread of apocalyptic cults or beliefs – we might call the phenomenon large-scale death-bed conversions. Death-bed conversions are possibly not so common as death-bed avoidance or denial or nonacceptance of death, but in the case of the atom bomb, apocalyptic ideas and even more, attitudes of denial, are common.

It may be that I am unduly worried by these thoughts. We must allow human beings a strong instinct for self-preservation. I do not think it can be true, for example, that an elderly convinced Christian who is not unduly afraid of death would step any the less smartly out of the way of an oncoming bus or motorcycle, if that emergency were to arise in the course of crossing the road, than would an unbelieving person of similar age and agility. Surely optimism about the future, including optimism about one's existence in some way after bodily death, and the instinctive avoidance of danger are both characteristics of the normal human being. Arguing along similar lines, a belief in an after-life should not necessarily make us any less afraid of or horrified by the prospect of the hideous deaths of ourselves or of loved ones that atomic warfare would cause. But if an individual or a group of people were to lose hope of avoiding the catastrophe, or were to feel personally or corporately powerless to help avoid it, we can imagine that people would find solace in the religious interpretation of the death-and-resurrection motif in larger and larger numbers. If a significant proportion of the population were carried away in a fervour of this sort, it would, I suppose, hasten rather than help to avoid the fateful outcome of the real bomb. If I were very worried about the real possibility of my government using the bomb, I might choose to follow the teachings of some apocalyptic/saviour cult rather than the example of people engaged in hopeful political actions aimed against the use of the real bomb.

The fact that we are now in the last years of the second millennium of the Christian calendar is a powerful boost to these deep-seated motivations to take part in a mythical death and rebirth of the human race. It is a sad fact that the hope or conviction of a new world seems to result, in communities possessed by such fantasies, in large-scale neglect of present concerns and dangers. If we consciously dismiss such feelings as blatantly illogical and superstitious, let us reflect on how widespread is the observation of the death of the old year (old self, etc.) and the birth of the new year in all the calendars of the world. These feelings stir us to our depths: those who are *consciously* unsuperstitious about such things are in a small minority. We are, every one of us, unconsciously affected by such ideas in a very powerful way.

The proliferation of apocalyptic cults I would take to be a rather dire and baleful sign that masses of people were giving up contact with the realities of political life and international relationships. Even more so would be a large increase in individual and mass suicidal tendencies, in addition, that is, to the main suicidal outlet of the enormous pile-up of nuclear weapons for which the superficial, conscious motive is self-protection and deterrence.

Let us suppose that we deny the evil in ourselves and attribute it to "enemies" who are sufficiently distant not to be known personally. Then to learn, to really accept and assume moral responsibility for this denied or rejected part of ourselves is a depressing experience, a "dark night of the soul," followed by the day of greater insight and greater ability to live with others in peace. This is suffering that is very worthwhile. But if we attempt to short-circuit this painful and careful personal growth, we may become possessed by the mythical motif of death and resurrection or collective war and victory, or collective suicide and rebirth. There are many ways of short-circuiting the painful path of growing up, and this is an important one.

In our own particular Western version of the creation myth, which I take to be a collective myth of the evolution of our collective consciousness, one of the first steps is the differentiation of light from darkness. Darkness is evil, light is goodness. We learn to distinguish right from wrong, goodness from evil, and do what is right.

This is difficult enough, even if it were that simple! To succeed in doing right immensely strengthens the ego, the will, and the potency of a person. To face the darkness of one's core is another thing, often undermining to one's actual physical health, honour, short-term welfare, and self-respect. Can our leaders, on our behalf, engage in this moral conflict? Would they survive as our leaders if they attempted it? We do not choose leaders of this calibre. We persist at the level of moral development of the Dead Sea Scrolls, identifying with the Sons of Light in their struggle against the Forces of Darkness, at least once war has been declared. Our material survival depends, however, on our being willing to struggle in the dark, our own darkness and blindness, before we emerge into the light of awareness and humility.

The apocalyptic vision consists of more than simply the idea of death followed by resurrection, suffering followed by its reversal, or the despised and rejected becoming the headstone of the corner. It contains the idea of war, the clash of armies or the explosive devastation of the world as we know it. It is the thesis of this book that this explosive and destructive psychic energy is the energy of conflicting opposites at the core of the I, which if faced successfully in a containing situation liberates energy for creative purposes. These opposites are quite separate from each other in the archaic psyche, when no conflict or opposition is felt to exist. In the archaic psyche, I simply love or I hate. A person is either good or bad. Indeed, the same person is good at one time and bad at another, depending on what instincts he is triggering off in me at a particular time. If my beloved (usually Mother) is loving me and pleasing me, she is good, and more than good; if she is withdrawing from me, she is a witch, a murderess, she ought to be got rid of. And at this level I cannot conceive how I could think otherwise, I cannot understand how anyone could see her in any other light. So in one compartment of my mind she is wholly good, in another she is wholly bad. It is the bringing together of these two parts of my mind that is the source of the tremendous apocalyptic energy, for good or ill. This energy corresponds psychologically with the chemical or nuclear energy brought about by bringing the appropriate chemical or physical substances together in the chemical or physical container in which the energy is to be generated, for creative or destructive purposes.

If I hate my enemy and discharge my hatred by acting out some destructive act, I cease to feel the tension and the frustration which I would feel if I were prevented from, or if I prevented myself from, discharging my hatred in this way. The bad feelings are discharged out of myself onto my enemy. I may feel physically better and more relaxed if I am able to do this. I unburden myself of my hatred.

What is the nature of this energy of the clash of opposites? This is a very important question. It is the energy of the clash of the Titans, the energy of the apocalypse, the pent-up energy of the volcanoes existing in so many of us, perhaps the energy visualized or imagined in terms of the unfaceable primal scene of the psychoanalysts, the meeting of sacred and profane love, the face of the God that is too bright for us to face, the energy of the yin and yang synthesis, the energy of the experience of cosmic unity. If we try to answer the question neurophysiologically, we merely come up with the banality of the concept of Dostoyevski's or Saul's sublime experiences being a massive critical neuronal discharge or epileptic fit.

None of us can surely face the face of God. For each of us, subjectively at least, it is a matter of life and death, for each of us the ultimate deterrent. For each of us, it is the trigger of the energy in an epileptic fit (or many fits). It is the energy we would expend in repelling our worst enemy, or in fighting ultimate Evil, or ultimate dishonour.

Multiply this by the number of people in the world, or at least by a fair proportion, and we obviously have energy of vast and unthinkable quantity. Is there any connection, any relationship at all, between the energy of people or in the subjective lives of people, and the energies of nature? Of one thing I am reasonably sure. There is so much subjective energy in the clash of psychic opposites that world destruction would be an appropriate outward expression of its internal image. This being so, we also take very seriously the fact that *internal images seek outward realization.*

It might profitably be questioned: What possible connection could there be between people's images, dreams, and fantasies about explosions, when these images are clearly related to personal conflicts which are not being faced rather than to the real political situation?

But are they unrelated to the political situation in the world, the world of international relationships? Certainly the present international situation and the development of the nuclear threat are responsible for the fact that unbearable or unfaceable internal conflict is so represented in the dreams, fears, and fantasies of a large proportion of the people of the world nowadays. But supposing a person has an unbearable conflict that is represented or symbolized in his dreams, etc., by nuclear warfare, what can we say about that person contributing to the international tension in a positive or negative way? Will he act politically in a way that will exacerbate or will ease the external political situation? I do not think that there is a simple answer to this question, but I do have some relevant findings on the matter.

First, in the course of psychotherapy these fears and these images of cosmic destructive clashings tend to ameliorate and gradually assume a more positive character, and usually a more human character. This seems to result from the repeated meetings and clashings with the therapist, provided that the therapist maintains a basic attitude of goodwill and continence and keeps an analytic attitude of watchfulness and a proper degree of involvement and noninvolvement. There is an evolution in the interaction such that both patient and therapist become more helpful and mutually creative. Concomitant with this, the interaction of opposites in the dream life of the client changes in a positive way, i.e., it becomes more creative and less catastrophic and cosmic. So it is clear that changes in personal life and relationships can diminish the destructiveness and terror in those images and symbols of the clash of opposites.

Second, there is on the whole a positive correlation between the personality of the dreamer and his dreams. Thus a sadistic person will tend to have sadistic dreams, a paranoid person paranoid dreams, a depressed person depressed dreams, a murderous person murderous dreams, a destructive person destructive dreams, a good person good dreams, a loving person loving dreams, and so on. But often the dreams refer to things that are capable of change, or are being given up or sacrificed, for example, dreams of smoking when giving up cigarettes. The same applies to dreams with murderous or destructive content. The dream, then, can represent a beginning of awareness about oneself. A destructive dream can occur when one is beginning to be aware of, and perhaps (one argues) able to take more responsibility toward, destructive tendencies in oneself, while before having the dream, one simply *behaved* destructively in an unaware, unconscious way.

The key event in ceasing to behave sadistically or destructively is a reaction of caring, concern, remorse, or responsibility for the destructive thing. For example, a destructive and self-destructive patient of mine, violent toward her children and herself and spoiled and hysterical toward her husband, dreamt of a woman pouring boiling water on a little black girl. Another woman was present but did not know the act was deliberate. Three years later, when she was behaving in a more caring way toward herself and her children, she dreamt first that she was being chased and that she hid in a cupboard. Next she dreamt that her unfavourite child had done something and was hiding in a cupboard. She found him and kicked him in the head. Now she was able to identify with the child and to become aware of her violently murderous feelings toward this child.

The transformation of a destructive or apocalyptic clash into its opposite, for example, a flash of illumination, a vision of heavenly bliss or splendour, is hardly any more than a swing or a change of mood. Often it is a merely temporary reaction to love or attracted feelings, a sort of honeymoon manifestation. Transformation of this sort is no substitute for a personal, responsible relationship with the depressive, omnipotent, or powerful impulses or feelings or behaviour of which one may not be fully aware as part of one's personality.

The night of darkness, destructiveness, degradation, and doom followed by the daytime of wholeness, happiness, and apotheosis is not a once-and-for-all happening. Death and resurrection, apocalypse and rebuilding, are not once-and-for-all events in human history. They are but opposite sides of a single coin, and they need each other all the time.

A patient of mine dreamt of escaping from a dangerous situation, a dark wood, in fact, by murdering her three male companions. As she awoke from this dream, instead of horror and revulsion she had a feeling of wholeness and saw a vision of two suns, one above and one below a kind of horizontal dividing line. After that she fell ill, and it was not until several years later that she was able to integrate her loving feelings and her hatred toward the same person – originally her mother. When she started to be able to do this, she had a vision of opposing quadrants in a circle combining in the centre of the circle with immense energy and light. This ushered in a period of intense creativity in her, but there were times when the conflict of opposing feelings was felt to be of shattering intensity, like an explosion.

The Energy of Warring and Combining Opposites

This image of opposites combining or clashing with the liberation of immense energy is the key image and the profound psychic truth behind my thesis. The atom-bomb image is only one example of this image. In psychic life the most important opposites are good and evil with their corollaries, acceptance and rejection, love and hate, inside the subjective self and outside the subjective self. Light and darkness are related opposites, too. High and low, yin and yang, mind (or spirit) and matter, male and female (e.g., meeting or clashing in the immense event of the primal scene) constitute a second subfamily of related opposites. We can see how learning to contain, resolve, and use the energy of these primal encounters is a daunting personal and cultural undertaking not only for one person's lifetime but for generations of humankind.

Opposites that are particularly pertinent to my thesis are action versus containment. There are many kinds of action; in this book I have compared action based on conscious decision and choice with the conscious sacrifice of the alternative course of action, to action based on the unconscious, unthinking, acting out of instinct or unconscious fantasy. The "man of action" need not be unthinking or unaware, but he makes decisions and acts on them easily and may prefer action to reflection and contemplation. In order to act efficiently, it is necessary to have clear boundaries between positive and negative, both of which may have to be emphasized or accentuated – in other words, the boundary between the opposites has to be clarified by employing contrasting devices and tactics.

There are many who have agonized over conflicting or mutually incompatible alternatives, for example, whether to fight or face loss of honour. To support one view may lead to action that necessitates taking sides in arguments or struggles which further polarise belief and sharpen the blackness or whiteness of one point of view as opposed to the other. This may lead to pain and destructive behaviour, of course, but at the same time reduces mental conflict and anxiety. What a relief it seems to all concerned when at last war is declared after a period of uncertainty and soul-searching! Action is now not only possible but necessary and applauded. Activity itself discharges tensions, polarisation of attitudes likewise. Balance, tolerance, awareness, judgment are now antisocial in the particular area or world of the war, if not in other areas of communal existence. Those who are not with us are against us.

I am, of course, deliberately contrasting spiritual or mental conflict – intrapsychic conflict subjectively experienced – with action leading to external conflict and clash.

Psychotherapists are very familiar with the phenomenon of the externalization as opposed to the internalization of conflict (pain, hate, love, etc.). Others may regard the idea as oversimplified, the sort of idea that is too obvious to be true to nature.

To illustrate the point, let me take an example of a mother who loves her two sons who, however, hate each other. A dispute arises over some question of ownership, let us say. The quarrel causes anguish in the mother who sympathizes with the point of view of both her sons and cannot and does not wish to take sides. Each son, on the other hand, "knows" that he is in the right and the other in the wrong. Each expresses his rightness and the other's wrongness in actions that exacerbate the conflict and lead toward mutual harm in the familiar escalating way that disputes have.

If I, as one of the brothers, am right and my brother is in the wrong, there is no internal, moral conflict within me. The conflict is in the real, external world, in the "realities" of the facts of the situation, in my brother's hostile acts and the injuries he is inflicting upon me, and in the measures and actions I can devise and pursue in the "real," external world to further my aims and thwart those of my brother.

In psychotherapists' jargon, I am splitting off the badness or wrongness in me and my point of view and my actions from myself and my feelings about myself, so that I feel wholly in the right. And I am projecting this split-off badness or wrongness that I cannot accept in myself (for obviously I could not, in fact, be wholly right) onto my brother. I am white and he is black. So the externalization of conflict goes with the mental mechanisms of splitting and projection.

If the mother loves one son and hates the other and sees one son as wholly in the right and the other as wrong, then the psychotherapist would say that she also is splitting. She is splitting off and denying the faults of one son and splitting off the virtues of the other. She is denying those qualities (the goodness of the one and the badness of the other) and this term *denial* does not mean the same as denial in the ordinary everyday sense, because it means that the mother is not even consciously aware of the split-off truths – they are obliterated from her awareness, rather than known but consciously repudiated or denied.

So splitting reduces the internal sense of conflict or anguish or moral conflict, but increases external damage or conflict. It produces disintegrative changes in groups or societies that are afflicted with it, and this applies to the family, the community, and the international community, too.

Now suppose that one brother loves the other and can see his brother's case in the dispute as well as his own. He sees rightness and wrongness in his own position and in that of his brother. Subjectively he feels torn or split in two. From the point of view of winning his case, he may be at a considerable disadvantage compared with the brother who is sure he himself is wholly right. He is quite likely to be less whole-hearted in his fight, although the psychotherapist would say that he is morally and psychically the more whole, the more integrated a personality, than his more primitive brother. Thus *subjective* feelings of integrity and *actual* moral integrity do not necessarily go hand-in-hand – rather the reverse, in fact. Yet the wholehearted, splitting individual may be much more likely to be clear-cut and efficient in his prosecution of his own interests.

The subjective bomb – the bomb of my patients' dreams – is the chance to heal splits in the personality in the moral and psychotherapeutic sense in which I have used this concept of splitting. The healing of the split is experienced as a shattering disintegration of the subjective self or of the whole of one's world, but actually it is only the ego that fears being shattered, and this sort of shattering can be a spiritually rewarding and morally strengthening event. The psychological situation is completely paradoxical. The subjective shattering is the necessary condition of a moral healing and a healing in relationships, a coming-together or a confrontation whose energy is capable of being contained in the relationship or the therapeutic situation.

But suppose we make the elementary and primitive mistake of confusing *subjective* integrity, wholeness, harmony, and peace with *actual* moral and personal integrity, and suppose we seek our own subjective peace and security. Then we are in danger of splitting and projecting in the psychotherapist's sense, and this produces real external conflicts and real enemies. The person who *feels* at peace, right, and whole is the least likely person to be socially and morally valuable and helpful, whereas the person in subjective conflict or turmoil has at least a chance of acting in a helpful and constructive way. He may feel split or torn, but this is because he is emotionally alive and able not only to see more than one side of a conflict but to feel for both sides, too.

The bomb of our patients' dreams betokens the paradoxical possibility of healing – through being subjectively shattered – whereas the objective bomb is the result of a morally disintegrated situation in which subjective security, peace, and harmony are sought and in which objective destructiveness and enmity are in fact directly caused by the fear of the subjective shattering that is the healing potential of the individual and of God (in the sense of the not-me part of the psyche). Unless we understand the paradoxical nature of the subjective/behavioural relationship, we cannot begin to behave in a morally responsible, socially healing manner. If Jesus said, "I bring you not peace, but a sword," he was expressing the same sentiments, I think, as I have done here. I do not think he was talking of putting infidels to the sword.

CHAPTER 14

The Task of Healing

As we become more mature we become more able to contain our anger and pain if and when necessary, either for our own sake or for some other worthwhile purpose.

"If and when necessary" is a very important qualification here. Depressive people do too much undiscriminating containing, and often the first stages of the therapy of depressive people result in outbursts of somewhat undifferentiated spite or anger.

In therapy there tends to be a progressive change in the relationship between oneself and one's anger and other emotions. At first these emotions do not *feel* as though they are within, but more like outside forces, elemental or cosmic forces over which one has no control whatever. If the therapist is able to stay with and eventually feel in sympathy (while not simply siding) with the hitherto repudiated anger and destructiveness of the patient, the anger becomes more and more "owned" (rather than disowned) by the patient's self. He or she feels less helpless, more responsible in relation to these instinctual, emotional forces within. Figure 1 illustrates how these dream images of emotions

FIGURE 1. The Mental Representation of Anger and Related Emotions

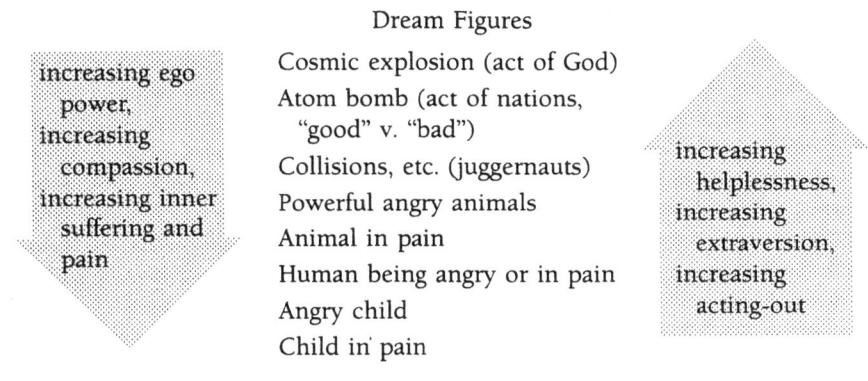

Dream Figures

increasing ego power, increasing compassion, increasing inner suffering and pain

Cosmic explosion (act of God)
Atom bomb (act of nations, "good" v. "bad")
Collisions, etc. (juggernauts)
Powerful angry animals
Animal in pain
Human being angry or in pain
Angry child
Child in pain

increasing helplessness, increasing extraversion, increasing acting-out might change with increasing or decreasing ego strength in relation to them.

As therapy progresses, these images of affect become more humanised. They may pass through stages where they are felt as animal forces taking possession of the self. If not felt consciously in this way, they are often represented in dreams in this way. The dream representation of the energy or instinctual force gives the therapist a notion of the degree of contact, the degree of working relatedness, between the self and the emotions in question. Cosmic and divine forces (winds, tidal waves, floods, volcanoes, explosions, fires, etc.) indicate a very helpless ego in relation to the anger or whatever emotion is concerned.

The energy representation or symbol may, let us say progressively, take the form of juggernaut, monster, animal, hated human adult, angry child, loved child, as the degree of effective compassion and working control of the destructiveness increases (provided that therapy is progressing well). The therapist has to feel his way and help his patient feel his way into the next stage.

All this has to happen mainly in the interaction between patient and therapist for therapeutic change to occur. This means that the therapist has to cope with his own pain, caused among other things by the anger of the patient, before he can see or feel the hurt that the patient, unable to bear, expels outward in directed or undirected anger or destructive act. The important finding here, then, is that if I feel helpless and small in relation to my anger, my anger will be represented in dreams or projections in the "real" outside world by cosmic, divine, or elemental destructive forces.

I have argued already that man-made destructive weapons and forces are, and do not merely represent, the collectively split-off anger and aggression of large numbers of people. I have not argued that natural disasters and the forces of God and Nature *are* split-off (repudiated, alienated) human emotions (although their images certainly *represent* alienated human emotions). But the possibility that matter *is* (and does not merely *represent*) split-off mind or split-off mental experience or split-off meaning or emotion is worth holding in mind at least as a theoretical possibility. A statement of this kind must not be confused with facile and superstitious assertions, e.g., that such and such a natural disorder is a result of human wickedness or (even more superstitious) a punishment for specific human political or social acts. The fact that we split off and act out our dark side so that it behaves as an alien force does not mean that we are forever fated to do so.

For example, if I feel helpless in the face of some moral conflict or conflict of mighty opposing instinctual forces within myself, I may dream of the explosion of an atom bomb when I am potentially able to face this conflict with my mind. The *actual* nuclear bombs are *in fact* largely beyond my powers to influence personally, let alone control, and the statement is not intended to disown our collective responsibility, nor the personal responsibility to do what one can. The dream bomb means that at this stage of the relationships between oneself and one's respective instinctual forces, one has little control. Exhortation and wishful resolutions are pointless at this stage. The I is not powerful enough to be able to carry out what is being asked of it.

No doubt it is *because* the individual has so little control over the actual bomb that the bomb has come to be used to represent the explosive destructiveness in ourselves in the face of which the will or the self feels helpless. In successful therapy, as I have said, we find that when it is experienced in a relationship between the two partners in the therapeutic work, the anger comes to be represented by more and more human and reachable symbols, in relation to which we feel more and more sympathy and compassion. This is the path of increasing responsibility and self-control for both partners in the work. The feelings of the therapist toward the patient's anger *usually* change toward warmth before the corresponding change occurs in the patient.

This progression from the atom-bomb sort of representation to the angry-baby sort of representation of one's destructiveness, with the assumption of the corresponding degree of responsibility and control, represents an enormous moral achievement for an individual. Only those who do therapeutic work can have a practical idea and feeling of how much of an achievement it is, and how much work and strain it may involve to help an individual to achieve it. It is very moving when it happens.

Although the eventual goal of the therapy may be for the individual to bear his own pain, this is not possible in the initial stages, when some form of acting out is the usual outcome of the painful stress on the patient. In this phase it may be necessary for the therapist to bear some of the painful effects of the actions, although this varies from one case to another, and the qualities of a decent parent are more appropriate than those of a saint. Here, forbearance, firmness, and experience are more important than goodness, kindness, and willing self-sacrifice, although saintly qualities may prove necessary sometimes.

I am not idealizing the therapist or indulging in self-congratulation.

It is important to remember that therapy sessions are relatively short and infrequent – even if they are daily, they are still of only fifty minutes duration as a rule. It is much easier to be forbearing for that length of time. Also one is paid for one's efforts, and there are other rewards, too, if one is interested in one's work.

In politics, or at any rate in explosive international situations, similar qualities (of statesmanship) are surely more valuable than those of the fighter, the demagogue, or the saint, at least until the war situation is finally irretrievable and the fighter-leader is called in. The reader will not need reminding that I speak authoritatively as a therapist, but naively as a statesman. However, if we extrapolate from individual therapy to international therapy, we have another area of therapy to call upon for suggestions, namely group therapy. When I speak of the phenomena of group therapy, I am not referring to anything that does not happen all the time in other kinds of groups. But in group therapy one of the functions of the group is to notice what is going on and talk about it, and so the phenomena are perhaps more easily demonstrable.

As an individual, I have a sense of self, of identity, stretching backwards in time from the present, with a lot of feelings, memories, experiences, and so on, and a sense of integrity and cohesion, a feeling of I in my body, seeing out of my eyes and hearing with my ears and moving with my limbs. At the same time, I have to admit that I sometimes feel and behave like one person, sometimes like another. Sometimes I am a good father, sometimes an angry father, sometimes a good child, sometimes a naughty child – I could list dozens of behavioural roles or subpersonalities within myself all competing or acting together at various times.

Every individual can be understood readily in this way. His subpersonalities are derived from normal human instinctual patterns at some times, or from complexes or hang-ups at others. Sometimes they are like the Freudian psychic structures of ego, id, and superego, but these also are like persons or subpersons and are simply Freud's abstractions from the phenomenology I am describing. The priest, the saint, the doctor, the teacher, the criminal, the soldier, the matron, the desirable woman, the angry child, the good child are all common subpersonalities within each of us.

If we look at our own composite personalities in this way, we can see our roles in society or in various groups in clearer perspective. We find that in particular groups we tend to take up particular roles – in other words, we tend to behave like one subpersonality rather than others, and that what we behave as (or who we behave as) depends on the dynamics of the group, i.e., the predominant role- or behaviour-tendencies of each of the others in the group. Even if each member of the group manifests as much as two or three distinct subpersonalities, for each of its members the group represents a superordinate personality, a greater self than his or her individual self, as he or she experiences his or her self.

The family group is, of course, the primary group in which individuals specialize their presenting subpersonalities. One brother may be the good child, another the bad one, one brother the fighter, another the gentle one or the wise one or the peacemaker.

The most probable roles or the most probable subpersonalities that a person tends to take up or be put in by other people describe his character or his persona – the face, dress, or mask he presents to the world. The way in which a child is seen or felt about by his or her parents or by the family as a whole determines, in an important way, how he or she sees himself or herself or feels about himself or herself. (Of course, while these rough-and-ready statements are true, often their exact opposites are true, too, but that is another story.)

The fact that brothers and sisters have a tendency to take up complementary roles or even opposite roles does not necessarily bring about friction or conflict in the family. Brothers and sisters who are quite different may love each other and get on well together. This makes a great difference in any therapeutic work. If I am a peaceful sort of person and I get on well with the fighter-brother hidden in myself, it is very different from having a hated, despised, or feared soldier subpersonality within myself. This in turn makes a great deal of difference to the destructiveness of any confrontation or conflict within myself when those two subpersonalities engage.

In the larger group of the community or nation, we have historically determined specialities of function, largely determined by the economic and religious history and the prevailing myths with their consequent ways of bringing up children. But for the present purposes the tendency for each society to polarize into fighting, tough-minded groups and conciliatory, tender-minded ones is crucial. If we see two major parts of the world engaged in a suicidal arms race (and arms races more often end up in war than in peaceful outcomes) and if we diagnose some sort of acting out of aggression or destructiveness or hurt, with which we attempt to deal along established therapeutic or conciliatory lines, we immediately come up against the situation where the aggression, the hurt, etc., is repudiated and denied. Each individual needs to deny his personal share in the mass suicide because he has a preciously guarded vulnerable core or ego whose feeling of integrity depends on not knowing that it needs to be shattered for the sake of the individual. To be aware of this truth would be to be aware of the deep core of madness in ourselves. So each of us has to deny and project the hurt and the violence to preserve our individual ego. The military man, the tough-minded, the worker whose livelihood depends on armament production are all engaged in the race for defence. It is the enemy who has the aggressive intent or disposition. The tender-minded groups of each society, the therapists, the feeling as opposed to the hard-headed types among us, can repudiate our own hurt and violence by ascribing the arms race to the militarists and politicians of this world. We provoke the militarists into more extreme positions by our self-idealisations. In other words, the societal polarisation into militarists and pacifists would be an unhealthy development.

The obstacle to therapy is not so much in the division of roles itself, but in the alienation and animosity between the various groups. If the men of power feel isolated and misunderstood, the hurt that can give rise to power-made violence is much more likely to possess them. As they control the technicalities of the weaponry, this seems important to remember. The danger of scapegoating the military part of ourselves in the West seems to me the greatest danger of the present world situation. A peace-lover who hates and abhors the militaristic use of power without acknowledging or accepting this part of himself is likely to bring out this subpersonality in others, either in his enemies or his friends.

Differing Degrees of Accessibility to Therapy

It can be imagined that the victim of a destructive action would not be primarily interested in the motive or in the degree of awareness or even in the remorse being felt by the perpetrator of the action, but in the gravity of the effects of the action and whether they can be reversed or remedied. If one were losing one's livelihood, one's child, or one's own life, one would not be *primarily* interested in the degree of awareness and responsibility of the person or persons causing this to happen. But from the point of view of the therapy of the perpetrator of this violence, namely, in this case, ourselves, the accessibility, to awareness and the will, of the feelings underlying the destructive actions is all-important.

One of the therapist's aims may be to help the patient by working toward replacing compulsive behaviour by thoughtfulness. Freud said, "Where id was, there shall ego be." The unconscious (roughly the id) is one's behaviour, when instinctual, conditional, reactive to circumstances, or complex-determined. Let me run through some of the stages by which the unconscious (choiceless behaviour) is gradually brought to awareness (thoughtful choice).

(1) There is usually a stage when there is no problem, either from the patient's or the therapist's viewpoint. Such unfortunate things as may happen seem either like fate or adverse circumstances, and the patient's completely natural or normal reaction to them.

(2) The therapist may discern a pattern. The fateful pattern becomes more discernible. Therapist and patient begin to talk about the pattern and perhaps give it a name.

(3) The pattern may be seen as an interaction between the patient and others or between different subpersonalities in the patient.

(4) The pattern having been discerned and experienced in the feelings of the patient and the therapist, and in the interaction between them at least on occasion, feelings and emotions are discussed from both points of view. Further naming and further images occur. The same pattern and images are discerned where previously "fateful" events had occurred.

(5) The pattern is modified before it reaches the threshold of outward behaviour. This is possible because of the increase in sensitivity and awareness.

While this is going on, it is as if the unconscious is struggling to remain unconscious – the patient is trying to remain oblivious and as free from pain as possible. Instinctive (archetypal) patterns and natural (animal) reactions occupy the life of the patient. Destructive dreams become enacted. If the dream is remembered, we are beginning to make progress – there is a potentiality for awareness of the archetype (instinctual basis for the behaviour) or the complex (the hang-up causing the distortion of the natural pattern) underlying the destructiveness.

Unconsciousness and Instincts

It is far from my intention to enter into theoretical discussion about the nature of instincts, about what the human instincts are, about whether aggressiveness and destructiveness are innate or acquired behavioural patterns in the human being, or about how far instincts can be modified, sublimated, or transformed in religious, aesthetic, cultural, or altruistic behaviour and experience. I merely want to present the simple empirical findings of psychotherapy and point out their relevance to our attitude toward outside explosive situations.

If we look around the world of nature, we see apes, monkeys, and other mammalian brothers and sisters of humanity leading their natural, instinct-based lives as well as learning about how best to satisfy these instincts. We see them as babies, being endearing to their parents, we see the parents looking after their offspring and showing signs of affection. We see the youngsters competing for mates, mating, forming permanent or temporary relationships, becoming parents, getting old, and dying. If we look at ourselves and at what we feel is basic to ourselves, we see a more or less analogous set of themes and variations, with very much richer and more complex patterns corresponding with our richer means of communication and of preserving our institutions. Social groupings of humans have their customs, traditions, rituals and a body of history, mythology, and perhaps religion which amplifies and justifies the present organization and relationships. Social coexistence means the emphasis of one instinct over another to varying degrees at different times. The frustration and channelling of basic instincts entailed thereby gives rise to the myths and the culture of each group. For example, the Oedipus myth is about incestuous acts that are not enacted by decent people and that are feared and abhorred, as they would naturally be if they contained strong wishful elements. The myth therefore helps to perpetuate the existing social pattern of interinstinctual conflict and preponderance, and, at the same time, the existing social pattern tends to perpetuate the myth as a living part of the unconscious of the people in the particular social group.

For people to want to hear a story repeatedly (or a variation of it repeatedly, as in our own story themes), the story has to be latent in those people's minds. This means that the pattern of instinctual emphasis and conflict entailed in the upbringing of the children of those people is such as to give rise to the particular images and fantasies of the prevailing myths of that culture. Our Western culture has not only dreamed up the nuclear bomb but is acting out the fantasy of mutual destruction in a way which suggests that there is something deeply satisfying as well as utterly terrifying in the fantasy. Myths and fantasies are not *mere* fantasies and *mere* myths. They are what motivate great social and historical movements. They are the juggernauts which, once set in motion, are not easily stopped. They are self-perpetuating because they bring about the customs and ways of bringing up children which bring them about in the first place.

What is the false myth in the face of which the counter-myth of the nuclear destruction of mankind is being played out? The material presented here is, of course, inconclusive, but to my mind it amounts in a general way to the myth that the *feeling* of security, harmony, and wholeness is one to which we are entitled and which moreover is a commendable personal ideal or goal. This idea seeks to exclude or escape from chaos, disorder, and feelings of vulnerability and of being invaded, overwhelmed, even shattered by explosion or shock. Of course, feelings of wholeness, security, union with all things, even with God, do occur and can be a source of great strength, but that should not make us feel we have a right to live in the secure womb we long for at times. If we seek subjective peace, harmony, and feelings of wholeness, we are behaving in a way which is sure to be producing chaos, provocation, and explosion in those around us. This seems to me to be the empirical finding of the present volume, and it has exceedingly far-reaching implications, once it has been taken seriously.

With the decline of religion and the idealization of the individual ego have we created more need for such a narcissistic ego to be subjectively shattered in some self-inflicted nemesis? My patients could be helped to face the conflicts which by themselves they would have avoided in the service of their own feelings of security. Who is to help mankind's ego to be freed from its wish to return to the womb without a literal and physical destruction taking place? If God is no longer able to penetrate our narcissism and our namby-pamby need for no-conflict in ourselves, something or someone else will – it will happen from our not-selves in one way or another.

I almost called this book *The Dark Face of God* because of the power and evil and immensity of the disaster which threatens us all. The horror of the extinction of mankind and of much of life on this planet is on a scale and of such an utterly evil character that it is completely the opposite of what many people, whether religious or not, would experience as God or as the ultimate truth or power of the universe, which or who is conceived in the West in terms of infinite power, truth, goodness, light, order, and harmony.

We know from our experience of people that the person who is likely to bring about a catastrophic explosion in his own or other people's lives is not the humble believer in a good God, a believer who is aware of his own personal potential wickedness and of the dark side of himself, but the person who is deluded, grandiose, who thinks he is right, and who identifies himself consciously or unconsciously with an omnipotent God. This latter person is one who not only feels he is in the right but who sees enemies and evil all around himself and in doing so provokes intense anger and hatred toward himself, thus making his erstwhile delusions come true. The knowledge of one's rightness is one aspect of the ego that explosively projects the unwanted, feared subpersonality outward. Such paranoid defences produce real explosions, invasions, or threats. As nations, we are struggling with this primitive stage of psychic immaturity.

The feeling of being right, morally or intellectually, or more fundamentally, the unwillingness to have one's existence, one's honour or sanity or sense of reality put in jeopardy (all these things are manifestations of the primitive, forming self) are the chief causes of explosiveness. They build up irritability, feelings of hurt and pain, tension between people, and bring about interpersonal situations where an explosion is waiting to be triggered. If such people take advantage of humble or depressed people, we have a situation of oppression which is one of latent explosion, but it may take generations to ripen to a triggerable degree of excitability. The humble or depressed person is also potentially explosive and may pass through an explosive phase when undergoing psychotherapy, or when political oppression is removed.

Good people may become irritable or explode on behalf of the oppressed. This often happens, or is contained, in psychotherapy. For example, as a psychotherapist one is often enraged on behalf of one's patient at the injustices being done to him or her. The patient himself may not be angry when talking about a relationship, for example, a marital relationship, in which the patient is unfairly treated or even crushed. It is important that the patient should eventually feel this anger for himself and behave in an effective assertive way on his own behalf. It is important for the therapist *not* to try to fight the patient's battles for him. So the therapist's anger has to be understood and interpreted to the patient and not indulged in or acted upon. Soft-hearted emotional ally-ing with the patient may precipitate explosions within the patient's family, harming all concerned.

Emotional as well as material explosions can be of any intensity but always involve intense energy bursting out of a rigid container or zone of inhibition. In the case of psychological explosions, it is sometimes important not to call the energy by any particular emotional name, as the different emotions share the fundamental energy to which we are referring. For example, in the examples we have given, the explosive energy could be seen as generated by:

(1) primal scene excitement,

(2) a clash of opposites,

(3) war between good and evil,

(4) confrontation with the parent,

(5) confrontation with one's own dark side, etc.

The energy can be experienced as unbearably intense love or light. Schizoid persons tend to be overwhelmed by too much closeness which is felt as unbearable intense excitation – it is overexcitement rather than hate. The energy powering the explosion is always potentially positive and this is no doubt as true of the real nuclear bomb (or the corresponding psychological energy) as it is of the individual patient or group of persons. These then are important therapeutic principles:

(1) The energy is nonspecific and is regarded as potentially creative.

(2) It is a question of containing, harmonising, redirecting, of developing a creative relationship between the ego-consciousness and the sub-personalities involved.

(3) The degree of alienation of the energy and the vastness of cosmic magnitude are a measure of the (usually compensatory) helplessness and alienation of the ego in relation to the mental energy concerned.

The Length of Time Required for Therapeutic Change

How long does it take God, the beloved, the therapist, the enemy to penetrate, shatter, or melt one's hardness, one's defences? How long does it take to grieve, to sorrow, to repent, to find love? A second? A lifetime? Both could be true.

A change of heart from destructive hatred to cooperation and love is much more easily and quickly produced (actually it is not produced, it occurs or it is a mutual achievement for patient and therapist) when the patient has had previous experiences of loving and being loved, of being caring and responsible in some area of his life. This would apply to vast numbers of normal human beings who have been loved, valued, and respected by their parents and family, or by someone else at a formative age.

Is it possible to forgive or feel with the pain of the person who is beating out the brains of one's child or burning one's family to death? In war, this takes many generations as a rule. In therapy it is, roughly speaking, necessary for the therapist to feel for the patient in his angry scream or his hostile acts even against the therapist, in order that the patient can own his anger and be responsible for it. This is not usually possible for the therapist straight away, but may have to be learnt over a lengthy period. Knowledge, experience, and, to a certain extent, faith, professional pride, and financial inducement all help the therapist eventually to feel with or for the patient's pain and consequent anger. This is not conceivable in the uncontained situations of everyday life, and yet, all the time we do see people returning goodness for evil, understanding for hatred. We see families of victims of terrorist murder not taking up vengeful positions toward the people who have murdered their kin. Of course, we see many more who feel angry and vengeful. While it is undoubtedly true that both goodness and evil are self-generating, there is considerable space for knowledge, experience, and even the technical skill of the trained mind to exert a crucial influence at moments of decision.

CHAPTER 15

Summary and Conclusions

My way of looking at human affairs is that of a psychotherapist, although none of us are merely our professional selves. I am reasonably sure of my conclusions as far as they relate to my own experience of psychotherapy, but when I attempt to use this experience to guide me in other fields, my ideas must be treated as extrapolative speculations, which the reader may or may not find helpful or interesting. When I state my conclusions in a clear and forthright way, they are nevertheless advanced with a painful knowledge of their biased and unrounded character. In that sense, they are nonconclusions, but the best that I, a psychotherapist, can offer.

In my work I find it best to take an empirical view of human motivation. For example, when I observe my patient *behaving* repeatedly in a self-destructive way, I postulate that a self-destructive *motive* may be at work, of which the patient and I, but especially the patient, may be only dimly aware. Although it would not be true that the patient on the whole wishes to destroy himself, it is nevertheless true that a part of him does, or might be doing so. Such a part of the self I call a *subpersonality*, because parts of the total personality behave as if they had motives of their own, behave like persons within the total personality, both good and bad, like character in a play. In therapy I help the patient relate not only to the subpersonality who wishes to destroy the patient or his mother, father, or the world, etc., but also to the rest of the subpersonalities in him who do *not* want the destruction to take place in reality. When the partial wish is brought into a living, emotional and moral relationship with the I, conscious pain and conflict, and the boon of conscious choice, become more possible. This is how I understand Freud's hope that as a result of analysis, "where id was, there shall ego be." That is to say, the choiceless behaviour of pure instinct or emotional habit is replaced by a painful awareness of conflict and choice and an ability to make that choice on the basis of practical, moral, and emotional grounds, taking into account the plurality of one's own motives.

If we look at the recent and remote history of human beings with the eye of the psychotherapist practiced in the art of teasing out the human motivations at work, it is not surprising that the same general motives seem to be at work historically as we see in individuals. Indeed we can view history not merely as the fluid enactment of the human subpersonalities of the unconscious, but of their gradual emergence into consciousness, with some increase in awareness and conscious choice of behaviour.

If we view the human world community as, on the whole, gradually emerging from relative unconsciousness into greater consciousness in a somewhat analogous manner to the change that happens in a successful psychotherapeutic relationship, we are again placing emphasis on the nature of the functional relationship between the I, collectively understood as the "we" of the group or the human brotherhood, on the one hand, and our behaviour on the other. Freud would use the terms *ego* and *unconscious* or *id*, and Jung would use the terms *ego* and self or ego and unconscious. I am choosing to stress that for practical purposes our actual behaviour, whether predominantly instinctual or predominantly learned, is largely unconscious, and that the forgoing of previously unconscious behaviour in itself is a potent stimulus to mental activity.

When we allow ourselves to speak of the gradual freeing of our collective we from our choiceless instinctual-and-habitual behaviour, we are obviously taking a very broad and general view of human history. Our observations of groups of primates and of various primitive human societies, our archaeological discoveries, our folklore, myths, religions, and the creative products of our art, science, and religions, all make their contribution to this broad formulation. In this we are taking a linear, time-oriented view of a developing consciousness in humanity. Of course, it is equally possible and also equally fruitful to see ourselves as participants in a never-ending and essentially unchanging cycle of birth and death, and in the endless recurrence of the same human situations and problems. There is an important sense in which the linear sense of time itself has to be understood as a product of our modern consciousness, so the idea of evolution or development itself begs many questions. But there is no doubt, at the ordinary commonsense level, that people change as they grow up, that changes of a similar sort occur as they progress in successful therapy, and that analogous changes have occurred in peoples and perhaps in humanity as a whole in the course of history.

The changes to which I am referring are to do with this increasing awareness of conflict and plurality in the I or collective we, coupled, paradoxically, with the consciousness of greater freedom and choice in the range of possible behaviours and an increase in the room to manoeuvre available to the I. In this space, choice, playfulness, and cultural experience can take place. A person in the grip of an emotion or an instinct has no such space, and there are great variations of the degree to which this is the case, both from one day to the next in the life of one individual, and from one individual to another. A group under the influence of mass hysteria has no such space. A person who has just lost a beloved member of his family may not readily talk about his emotions or feelings immediately, because he is *in* those emotions and feelings. There is no space between him and his emotions. Perhaps after a few days he can talk in quite a different way about his feelings, because his I is once again beginning to surface from its submerged state. It is this depth of submersion or imprisonment of the I in the sea of the instincts, emotions, and absolute necessities to which I am referring as lessening and easing in the growing up of the individual I and the human we.

The well-being of the collective human I is of vital concern in two related ways:

(1) The aware self-conscious I frees us from our behaviour in the way I have just described.

(2) It is the threat to the insecure I that is the cause of explosive and socially destructive behaviour. Clashes of subpersonalities that are felt to threaten the I with disintegation tend to result in the explosive behaviour which characterizes the animal in fear or anger (Pavlov's freedom reflex) and which in the human tends to take the form of the explosive projection of unwanted or feared parts of the self.

The origins and the sources of a healthy I as seen by the psycho-therapist, who is perhaps best qualified to pronounce on the matter, are therefore the issues of most concern to us in this book. I make no apology for reiterating them carefully in this final chapter.

In the development of the individual, at least in Western people, the I seems to emerge gradually out of a boundless state of undifferenti-ated harmonious and nonharmonious mix-up with the rest of one's experiential universe. There is no distinct I at all. The first not-I person from whom one begins to be differentiated, and hence the first person one relates to, would usually be one's mother—she is the first "you." Anger that is tolerated by her, as well as sturdy adventurousness, help the early I to achieve confident separateness without the clinging and the anxiety that occur when the process of development has not been so successful. In the jargon of the analyst, primitive identity is gradually replaced by personal identity with the capacity for relationship. This is the broad view of development taken by the particular school of psychotherapy to which I belong. Others vary somewhat from this formulation.

This emergence from primitive undifferentiatedness to differentiatedness with the capacity to relate (rather than merge or identify) is vitally important in determining the nature of one's relationships. One's I tends to relate to one's not-I in characteristic ways, which differ in different individuals and different groups.

As I said, the general mode of the relationship between I and not-I is laid down early in life. This mode determines not only the general pattern of interaction with other people, but also with internal persons, with external and internal things, and even with abstract principles and mental structures such as democracy, the unconscious, the future, and so on.

Apart from innate characteristics, the main factors I have in mind as determining the patterns of I-not-I relating are the general emotional tone of the parental environment—whether the child is wanted and loved, the way the child is looked at, cared for, touched, fondled, and so on.

My mother and father may (or sometimes may not) continue to regard me warmly and maintain their contact with me (hold me literally or metaphorically) throughout my contented feelings, my loving feelings, my anger and hating feelings, my various bodily states, needs, urges, and expressions. This is the foundation for the possibility that my I can remain a continuous experience and, as we say, contain conflicting, even mutually opposing, feelings.

Naturally there are many variations on this theme. For example, we all know people who have a kind of fiercely held set of values that are the opposite of those of their parents. Their self-regard seems to be founded on being as unlike their parent or parents as possible. But such self-regard may well have a hollow or brittle quality, or a tragic, idealistic quality, or be visibly false in some way. A robust self-regard depends on the survival of clashes with parents, friends, community, and culture in the later stages of the maturation of the I. Indeed, from the first year of life, the differentiation of the I from the maternal matrix evidently depends on such clashes and consequent resilient, autonomous feelings, the sort of feelings originating in activity of the sympathetic nervous system (the system of fight or flight), as long as fear does not paralyse or disintegrate the I.

It is my most important finding here that the bringing together and sorting out of conflicting or opposing wishes (drives, behaviour tendencies, feelings) is *not* usually preceded or accompanied by feelings of wholeness and harmony, but often of the opposite kind of feeling, of shattering, explosion, or conflict, even if such excitation is experienced in a relatively positive form – lightning flash, bolt from the blue, a shock of revelation or realisation. The potential coming-together of parts of the self previously kept apart is thus often presaged by dreams and other fantasy images of explosions, or warfare, including the nuclear sort. This makes sense if one remembers that it is the fear of the subjective threat to the feeling of wholeness of the I which keeps the respective bits of the self apart in the first place – the good inside, the bad outside. The explosive image represents the coming-together of the opposites in feared form.

A strong I is necessary for opposing wishes and feelings to be held together in consciousness and reconciled, decided between, or otherwise dealt with. It takes a strong I to live in conflict, indecision, and doubt. Such coming-together is indeed a threat to the wholeness and continuity of the I, for it generates the intense psychic energy which may be symbolized in various ways. Depending on the ego's standpoint (approach or avoidance), these symbols may assume very positive or very negative forms, some of which I have briefly discussed in this book (Chapters 5, 6, and 7, for example). Jewel, fountain, tree, gold, treasure, divine child, human child, or God-image are examples of positively toned symbolic expressions of this intense energy, while world destruction, nuclear bomb, volcano, cancer, monsters, symbols or personifications of evil, whirlpools, and the abyss are examples of negatively toned, feared symbols of the energy clash of the fateful coming-together.

These favoured positive and negative symbols have been used by the psyche throughout the ages, and the image of the world-destroying bomb is merely the latest of the negative ones. It is unique, however, in two respects:

(1) Enacted concretely, as is happening at the present time, it is a real threat to the whole of mankind; consequently, it is an image that can be used by everyone to symbolize this negatively toned aspect of the coming-together of important opposites.

(2) It is actually being enacted or produced by humanity in a concrete form. It is not a natural or even a God-wrought catastrophe, but something we are creating and have created for ourselves.

The magnitude and power of the real, concrete nuclear threat is a consequence of the relatively minute and helpless feeling of the I in the face of these mighty conflicts of the emotions and instincts. Note that I say consequence rather than corollary or analogue. Such a state of affairs is not new: wars and man-made catastrophes and suicidal behaviour are certainly endemic to civilised man, if not to human beings in general. Inner conflict has always been avoided by overt, explosive concrete behaviour on a mass scale. What is new is the technological ease with which the world catastrophe can be brought about. By avoiding our petty personal confrontations within ourselves and our real loved ones, we can each and all contribute to the catastrophe, which is a very mighty and grand affair, of divine, manic magnitude. We prefer grandeur to pettiness.

The opposites in question, whose coming-together in clashing or creative manner generates intense energy, do not always consist of love versus hate or anger, desires to merge versus desires to confront, or goodness versus evil, although such emotive oppositions and conflicts are the most powerful. Male and female coming-together, as in the Jungian and the alchemical union of opposites within the container of the psyche or the alchemical retort, or as in the Freudian primal scene excitement concerning the actual parental interaction or the sexual coming-together of internalized parental figures, are comings-together within the psyche that also generate intense positive and negative energies.

In history, the conflict between good and evil, subjectively experienced by groups of people in similar, absolute terms, is the most explosive and violent manifestation of this concretely enacted comings-together. The clinical and social manifestation of this need, explosively to project the evil part of the self, obviously needs more urgent elucidation. It is another of those earth-saving studies we need to do. But studying a phenomenon on the one hand and coping with it on the other, even with a single individual patient or loved one, are two very different things. The difference between understanding the present historical situation of mankind and resolving the major problems is, of course, enormously multiplied and complicated compared with the difference between diagnosis and therapy in the individual, but then many more "therapists" and well-wishers are involved.

There is a psychological level, as deep as anyone can penetrate, I think, at which Good and Evil in a bodily, in a personal, and in a world and even cosmic sense need each other and are seen to be opposite aspects of the same fundamental energy. This is the psychological level before one's body image, one's mother, and the cosmos become distinguished and separated from each other. Correspondingly, at this deep psychic level bodily well-being, the Good Mother, and the paradisal cosmos are all the same experience. Terror is the experience corresponding to the threat of the opposite, ultimate experience of Evil, whereas the deepest joy and contentment accompany the experience of the Good. To project this, our deepest personal experience, onto actual political or religious conflicts is to add to the dangerous and explosive ingredient in our present perilous situation. Yet we cannot help doing it.

To experience terror in the face of omnipotent evil, in the above sense, and to experience well-being in the presence of omnipotent love are part of our instinctual makeup. It is easy to understand that the omnipotent evil has to be taken as a projection of one's own destructive instincts, and the omnipotent love has to be understood as a projection of one's own love. Theoretically and in practice this seems to be the case: we just have to grapple with this as a fact. We can never get to the bottom of our own personal destructiveness, any more than we can plumb the depths of our love. We even have to admit that both urges are fundamentally healthy and natural ones.

But at these deep levels within us there is no I sometimes having love and sometimes anger. We have boundless well-being or boundless catastrophe or disintegration (in later stages, wasteland), something quite like nuclear catastrophe in the imagination. These opposite states are experienced at different times, and there is no connection between them. Neither is there a single person called mother even though the actual mother may be, in a sense, the cause of both sorts of feeling-states. These statements are empirical ones derived from observations of regressed patients in therapy. They are not particularly conjectural or speculative.

At this pre-I stage of the self, instead of love we imagine that a better term might be boundless warmth and well-being, and that a better term than hate might be catastrophe, disintegration on a cosmic scale, or wasteland. The nuclear explosion image itself belongs to a later, early I stage, when there is an I or self to disintegrate. Something has to coalesce before it can explode, but we are not speaking of a thing so much as a kind of energy-person.

An important need of the patient, in the kind of therapeutic work I do, is for the therapist to survive the anger and the disintegrated experiences of the patient and stay around, functioning. This seems to enable a continuous and valid-for-oneself self-feeling to develop in the patient who internalizes the therapist's view and feelings toward him. This is an empirical finding in my work as a result of which I can accept with confidence the hypothesis that the infant internalizes his mother's view and feelings toward himself or herself and that this becomes a chief foundation of his or her self-feeling and self-regard.

The other primary source and foundation for the I are the sensations and experiences from the surface and the interior of the body and, especially as far as emotions and general state of feeling are concerned, from the sympathetic and parasympathetic nervous systems. The anatomical projection of these sensations in the brain, which roughly corresponds with the topographical arrangement of the body, forms a body-image, which can be understood as a map on which experiences can be located. This is the reason that even before the self and the world and the mother are differentiated from each other, the primal self/world/mother image is a body-image without specific size and without distinct boundaries. Smaller than small and greater than great is an attribute of this Self. No doubt, too, this is the reason why primitive cosmologies consist of projections of the body, and primitive anatomical/physiological schemata are small models of the cosmos.

The differentiation between I and not-I may have its origins in the need to preserve health and well-being, taking in what promotes well-being and rejecting or ejecting harmful stimuli. This might be said to develop into a kind of pleasure principle with love and hate and the good and the bad as still-later stages, with very major reservations, of course – no one would say that that with which my I is associated is all good and that with which it is not is bad, but there is a tendency for a healthy person to feel a little that way.

The early I cannot contain or own opposite or conflicting emotions at the same time. When mother is being good to me, I love her and she and the world are lovely and lovable and so am I. The hating I and the hateful mother and awful world do not exist.

But, as we have seen, the parent's ability to sustain benevolence throughout conflicting or opposing states of mind in the infant gradually enables an I to develop which can have mixed feelings without splitting or disintegrating. The weaker I may have a to maintain well-being by means of a degree of splitting and projection. The good is kept within the I, together with the loved aspect of the other person or thing concerned, and the bad is ejected into the unconscious and denied, usually reappearing in a projected form, that is, projected onto a suitable stranger or enemy.

I must apologise for spelling out what is nowadays obvious to everyone, but it is worth remarking that it is mainly because of the work of the psychotherapists that we can admit that we all split and project.

We all claim the good and reject the bad. We all have to learn right from wrong and fight for the right. But in a mixed community or with mixed cultures, black-and-white moralities form explosive mixtures, and this form of infantile omnipotence now has to be given up. In times of illness or stress, we again regress to the single-mindedness and subjective peace that is the boon conferred by splitting and projection, if we blessedly escape from the torture and turmoil of subjective conflict and disintegration.

Well before the end of its first year, the robust baby is able to let us know what it wants, at least in the important areas of life such as food and bodily care, and to make us comply with these demands, more or less successfully. Clear boundaries are being established between the positive and the negative, and these early boundaries, in the healthy child, are firm and resilient, even if not consistent by adult criteria. It is one of the great pleasures of our parenting instincts to know how to reinforce the infant's joys of feeding itself, however messily, and of walking and of doing other things alone, however clumsily. The messiness and the clumsiness are, of course, denied by the omnipotence of the infant and the help of the adult. The affirmative anger of the self-asserting child, and the respect the adult has for it, help to establish a resiliently boundaried I separated out from the you in an independent rather than a hating relationship.

If the mother is clinging, invasive, or possessive, the I-boundary is overirritated, paranoid. Or it may need to break out of its boundaries. The culture and traditions of the group to which the mother belongs may determine in large measure whether the mother behaves in a facilitative or a hampering way. The institutions and rituals of the group function in relation to the individual at all stages of his or her life in roughly the same way as his or her parents did, culture, traditions, mythology, and parental behaviour being somewhat of a piece. But whatever the culture, what may be a helpful container at one stage may become a rigid prison at a later stage. What I take refuge in at one moment I find an unbearable prison at the next. This has to be understood if we are to try to understand our explosiveness, but it is difficult to legislate or to govern wisely because of this.

The mother with a strong and resilient I (and this may involve a strong and supportive family and, in particular, a strong and supportive partner) can affirm both the positive *and* the negative feelings of her baby. She is not shattered or enraged by her baby's fear or anger, but maintains her holding, her closeness, and her warm regard toward her baby. But if she cannot tolerate and hold her baby's anger, the baby's I cannot contain mother-hating feelings and such feelings are denied and displaced or projected. Bad mother-figures are needed to take these split-off parts of the self and the mother. Thus bad figures and shadow aspects of the self need to be maintained as part of the defences of the personality.

When a bad figure, an enemy let us say, does something generous or good, or when a good figure does something mean or bad, this is potentially shattering to one's I and one's self-regard, when one's self-regard depends on such splitting defences. But the truth about a person whom we are defensively idealizing or denigrating in this way will necessarily be shattering to our self-regard if we cease to deny it and cease to need to preserve our narcissistic defences in this particular area. If the truth is ready to dawn on us, or if circumstances change so as to force us to see things differently, we may well, in anticipation, have a dream of explosion, and this may be of world or cosmic proportions if the idealized figure "means the world to us." The idealized figure may be oneself, of course. The truth, if integrated, will rarely in practice disintegrate the I or even the relationship with the person who is idealized (or the opposite). But sometimes it does involve breakdown of the person or the relationship. A breakdown of a relationship with an idealized person may produce an atom-bomb dream, which, in the absence of a sufficiently holding I and a sufficiently holding situation or relationship, may not be integrated but be followed by mental breakdown, temporary or long-lasting. One should not usually be too frightened by those dreams, however. The health and strength of the person concerned is the main prognostic guide rather than the frightfulness of the dream itself. This is the main thesis of this essay. Having an atom-bomb dream and facing the inner conflict helps the dreamer to avoid projecting one's explosiveness onto the outer world and contributing to the enactment of the actual shared nightmare of apocalyptic world explosion.

If an "evil" person does something good, however, and one integrates the truth and realizes that one's preconceptions about him, or about oneself, or about human nature, or politics, or whatever, need to be modified or even radically altered, one in the process of being shattered becomes a stronger person. This is obvious and elementary, but only when applied to someone else. Applied to oneself, it can only be seen to be true when the situation is in the past, when one's mental space is not being invaded, so as to encroach on our as-if capacities. The passage of time – to acquire distance from grief, anger, or suspiciousness, etc. – is vital in this acquisition of mental space, necessary in order for I strengthening, as opposed to explosion, to occur.

A word is helpful at this point, I believe, that helps to make much more understandable my concept of subpersonalities and their interplaying way of taking over the I and taking over behaviour.

If we can get in touch with (i.e., become emotionally aware of) our own "oral sadism" and also with our fears of becoming a victim of this oral sadism projected onto other persons or things or situations outside ourselves, then we can reach a profound level of the psyche. At this level, there can be an ineffable experience or state where boundless devouring can take place involving both the devourer and the devoured, in which the I is not preferentially located either on the devouring side or on the victim side, but is able to identify with both. How otherwise can we reconcile ourselves to the real world of human beings as they are, and of Nature as she really is? This is a world in which ruthless devouring and being devoured are going on all the time and everywhere. "I eat you and you eat me" can be blissful, matter-of-fact, utterly horrifying, or utterly terrifying, but in any case it can go to the very depths of the psyche and its possibilities. When as an adult I am aware of these depths in my psyche, my I is consciously able to transcend the boundaries between I and you, but in all probability when I was a baby the I and not-I were not differentiated from each other; the boundary had not yet been demarcated, except in behavioural terms, when I was devouring my mother (i.e., her nipple, her breast, her milk, her body) and not vice-versa. But from our experience with psychotic patients or our own psychoses, from the treasures of mythology and from our dreams, we know that to the psyche, "I do it to you" is a sort of equivalent of "you do it to me." If one does not know this, there are many dreams and many psychosomatic symptoms that do not make sense. For example, my first dream during the night may be about an animal tearing at a person, the next about falling down a cliff (devouring and being devoured). Or one dream may be about trying to find somewhere to shit, and the next about being in a prison or box and trying to get out (being the shitter wanting to shit and the shit wanting to get out). Or while afflicted by a "tummy-bug" causing vomiting, I may dream about being sacked (ejected, i.e., vomited) from my work (I am the rejector, the vomiter, and I am the rejected, the vomited). Or a psychotic patient may crunch a piece of paper into a ball and the next instant flinch and cringe in a manner which makes it obvious that he is hallucinating or fearing being crunched into a ball (I crunch, I am being crunched). Or one day I may be profoundly shocked by my realisation that my irritation with an employee is due to an underlying wish-fantasy of tearing him apart, as a wild beast might, and that night or the next day, I may be attacked by inexplicable anxiety or fear, which I trace to a fantasy of being destroyed by cancer or car accident or whatever (I am tearing you apart, you are tearing me apart).

In other words, the mobility of the I and its predilection for crossing the boundaries between the interacting subpersonalities (beater and beaten, robber and robbed, bully and victim, etc.) of our various complexes or hang-ups, is due to the fact that at the deepest level of the psyche, in the boundless pre-ego dream-time of the psyche, these demarcations are transcended, even though behaviourally we are on one side of a future division and not on the other (the baby is devouring, not being devoured; the baby is shitting, not being shitted, etc.).

It is interesting that the examples of boundary-crossing I have just given are to do with anxiety and anger rather than pleasure and love. It matters very much whether my early feeding experiences are mostly to do with love or whether anger and biting come to predominate. If I devour you in love, then it is okay for you. In that case, "You devour me" is okay for me as it is done in love. In that case, it is not an urgent matter for me to establish a boundary between I and you. If "I eat you" is angry, then "you eat me" is to be feared. I need to know that you do not wish to eat me or that you, my food, are incapable of eating me, you are not "a person." It is momentous effort of the I to be able to eat food without fear, if eating is felt to be a negative relationship between eater and eaten.

Exactly the same considerations apply to defaecation (whether done in a giving, loving way) and urination (whether done in a merging, flowing, loving way). For example, grudging, hoarding, fear of change, fear of coming forth, negative self-value, feeling oneself dangerous or explosive, etc., are all difficulties to do with a negative-shit self-feeling as a rule. The atom-bomb subpersonality as a negative, explosive turd-self, a negative but omnipotent piss-self or ejaculate-self, are very important examples of the exploding I in clinical practice. Fear of bursting, desire or need to burst and save the world or destroy the world, are all fantasies belonging to this level of the psyche. The student of psychopathology will be familiar with all this, but I am not sure I am being very intelligible to others. Let us hope it will strike a chord, at least. I well remember my curiosity and astonishment once, for example, when I dreamt that a chicken I was cooking talked and behaved as if it were a person. I had no way of really understanding a dream like that at the time. Perhaps the reader has had dreams or experiences which the present essay illuminates to some degree.

So far so good. By that I mean I am talking of the established therapeutic findings of all and especially of my own actual experience. But what is the connection between those empirically established findings and the historical development of the I, the present sociohistorical situation and the collective narcissistic defences of Western man, or of humanity as a whole, whose continued existence tends to perpetuate real social explosions and in particular the present world dangers?

I think that the value of the present volume depends not on my proposing correct answers to those questions, but on the kind of approach suggested by these established therapeutic and psychodynamic observations, and for the flickering light they may perhaps throw on history, religion, and politics.

The lessons that can be suggested by modern psychotherapeutics for the therapy of the present maladies must depend on the view one takes of the nature of the relevance that psychology has to history. The view taken here is that although, collectively, we wish the world and ourselves to remain intact, our behaviour suggests at least a partial wish to explode, and for the world to explode. At a deep psychological level, one is partially identified with the world. One *is* the world. Furthermore, I am arguing that the fear of the disintegration of the I reflects the pressure on the modern I to let in elements of the total personality that the modern I is trying vainly to keep out and which, if incorporated successfully into the collective I, would result in an enrichment and blossoming of our present-day civilisation (if the analogy of therapy is anything to go by).

With the communication explosion of the present day, we are less and less able to project our own badness onto foreigners and strangers. There is a stirring of the natural, Green Man, in us all, a strengthening of the Mother Goddess, a humanization of the Divine. All these subpersonalities of the Self are pressing for admission to the collective I so as to threaten implosion. It all feels a little too much to cope with. Add to these the hope of a new-world democratic order and a new millennial age, and there is no wonder that our rather fragile, and historically speaking, infantile I feels in considerable danger of disintegration.

In a successful therapy, such conflicts can be contained and resolved, but where the relationship between therapist and patient is not well-enough established, the I may indeed explode with disastrous results either for the individual or his relationships. I have collected several examples of both from colleagues and friends.

Resolved, such conflicts result in an enrichment or new blossoming symbolized by such symbols as tree, baby, divine child, or some image of a result of a successful union. The mandala is a symbol of wholeness and unity in which (it is hoped, at least) the opposites are successfully united. The image of a good god or goddess or of a harmonious world are also good or idealized self-images for which the image of world destruction stands in total opposition. In this sense, we can say that the image of world destruction by explosion is the dark face of, or the opposite of, the good and loving God we would like to believe in, and of personal wholeness, peace, and harmony, the enjoyment of which is such a blessing for us.

The baneful, negative self-images of nuclear explosion (opposite of mandala and utopia), cancer (opposite of baby), and punishing God (opposite of approving or loving God) represent the fear of the subject or the hatred of the subject toward the emerging conflict of opposites, rather than an objective forecast of doom. For God's sake, let us remember this. We find that the result of facing the conflict fully and of fully experiencing the fear is a negation of the fear/wish. Just as the beast when loved turns into the prince, the imagined catastrophe when faced tends to turn into something of an opposite image of union or acceptance.

On the other hand, the deliberate cultivation of states of harmony and wholeness may carry dangers of explosion, either in the form of the buildup of explosive outbursts of irritability or temper, or the causing of explosive feelings or behaviour in others. A friend of mine, for example, practised a kind of meditation which resulted in a pleasant nirvanalike state of relaxation and well-being. He had a dream of being with a group of Buddhist monks and nuns who were treating him very considerately and with some ceremony. Then there was an air-raid warning, the sources of danger apparently being great nondirigible airships shaped like plump fishes, which looked very harmless and endearing. He took heed of the dream and realized there was a danger of explosion as an escape of pent-up anger. In spite of this, he found himself that day calmly making a remark to a friend which caused that friend to explode in a quite devastating way, to the lasting detriment of their friendship. His remark had been incredibly provocative, although enunciated in a calm, considerate, detached voice, and my friend realised that he had in fact unconsciously caused the explosion; thus the danger in the dream had unfortunately not been averted in spite of my friend's correct under-standing of the dream. His "amateur Buddhism" was responsible for producing the explosion in his friend. The unconscious provocativeness and destructiveness of the tranquil, peaceful-feeling, conflict-free person is not widely realised, except perhaps by psychotherapists.

If we see an individual behaving explosively or destructively, we are entitled to look for destructive motives or drives, and the same applies to groups. Often groups seem to behave explosively in order to avoid intragroup conflict or to avoid experiencing moral conflict in individuals. The evil is seen in black-and-white terms in the enemy who is to be destroyed by the explosive behaviour. The present danger of nuclear world catastrophe and the collective avoidance of personal moral conflict could be correlated phenomena associated with the col-lective I and its fear of fragmentation. In any case, the I has a long history which needs to be understood if we are to begin to understand our apparent need to explode collectively. Such an understanding is in a state of infancy, but it is obvious, for example, that the Eastern I is radically different, with a different history, from the Western I.

The wise Western man would differ from the wise Oriental man in the degree to which the divine is experienced as being outside the self more than in or of the self. It seems to me that the Oriental can experi-ence the divine as of the self without so much danger of a disastrous inflation or ego-mania as would a Westerner who experienced God in or as himself. This must be because the Westerner's tradition is to regard the omnipotent subpersonality as outside himself. God is other than myself and is out there, a separate Person. To experience God and myself as one is odd or blasphemous, and people have been burned alive for less. But let us not forget the mystical tradition in Western religion, which has done much to keep God alive in the personal I.

By the same token the apocalypse, in which the world explodes in war and a new world arises, is much more readily seen as referring to conflict and change within the self in Oriental tradition than in Middle Eastern and Western tradition, where the vision and the prophecy are more likely to be taken literally and concretely to refer to historical outside events.

To some extent visions and dreams are self-fulfilling. It therefore matters greatly whether I believe that the vision of war between the opposing parts of humanity, say that between good and evil, is referring to some actual, real, opposing groups to one of which I belong, or to conflict within myself. If I believe the Holy of Holies is located in an actual thing, person, or place, I need to defend that thing or person with my life. But if the Holy of Holies is located within myself or my inner world in some sense, it may be a different matter altogether. For example, for Jew, Christian, and Muslim the Holy Place is in the Holy Land, say Jerusalem. How concretely this is to be taken has varied throughout history, but it still matters a great deal how concretely this is experienced (and I say experienced rather than interpreted) by each individual Jew, Christian, and Muslim. We are all involved in this issue, wherever we live, and however superficially sophisticated we are. When Jewish Jerusalem fell many centuries ago, many wise Jews were able to say, "It matters not. Jerusalem is a place in my heart." Zionism reverses this. It reconcretizes the Holy Place with explosive consequences. Many modern Israelis I have talked to do not understand this.

The nuclear threat is, in my thesis, the concrete enactment of an omnipotent destructive fantasy, the projection into concrete reality of an omnipotent explosion of the I or of the self out of its normal containers and defences. A word is necessary about the terms *omnipotence* and *omnipotent*, especially for those not familiar with the jargon of dynamic psychology. The loving mother can lovingly see the omnipotent, grandiose play and behaviour of the child as a healthy development and as compensating for her child's relative powerlessness. She does not crush the child's omnipotence nor does she inflate or overexcite it unduly, for that will end in disaster, too. The psychologist Donald Winnicott had a kindly attitude toward infantile omnipotence. He was aware that the omnipotent part of oneself contains the magic of childhood and much of our creativity, whereas the realistic, conforming part of oneself feels meaningless and false, although often bringing about success in the real world. Jung had to struggle hard with his own omnipotent subpersonalities, and his psychology is omnipotence-kindly, although he was fully aware of the dangers of inflation. Let us take two powerful images of the divine which Jung envisioned as a child, that of a huge underground phallus and that of God shitting on the local cathedral. It is important to remember that Jung's father was a minister of the church. It is easy for us to see how the phallus must have symbolized Jung's powerful repressed phallic impulses, and that the other vision was an expression of the omnipotent/impotent boyish subpersonality that harboured a malicious wish to shit on his father's Church. Before we belittle these experiences, we must remember what enormous creative work was achieved by Jung in his life in working through these fantasies. I am permitting myself to use these examples of omnipotent subpersonalities in Jung because I truly believe Jung has contributed more than most to mankind this century, whereas it would not be forgivable for me to write so disrespectfully of someone I did not sincerely admire.

When, in my own analysis, I dreamt of a beautiful mandala whose circular boundary consisted of golden trumpets sounding outward, my analyst was able to say to me, "That is your timidity." And I was able to hear what he meant, that the trumpets were an omnipotent compensation for my timidity. If, as a therapist, I say to my patient who brings a dream of world destruction, "That is your impotent rage" (or, more accurately, your fear of your impotent/omnipotent rage), he may or may not be able to hear me, depending on how much he is in touch with himself and his rage. How to say this to humanity so that people hear is a problem whose difficulty can only perhaps be appreciated by the therapist who has struggled with some success with these powerful forces at the core of the early I. He knows with what incredible force these I-endangering subpersonalities are split off from the I, projected onto the not-I, and converted into material as opposed to psychic realities.

For the child, the original container of opposing wishes and impulses, the original arbiter of goodness and evil, the original reconciler in love and unity, is the mother. The mother goddess in her dual or twin aspect of loving and terrible mother in my thesis represents the integration of the mother into the early corporate I of the small community.

For the family group and the small community in which everyone knows everyone else personally, there could perhaps be said to be a corporate I which is the group's self. I am not speaking so much of present Western man, with his historically developed individuality, but of the prehistoric and early historical community and of the present "stone-age" cultures. The degree of *participation mystique* of such groups evokes almost a sense of awe and a surge of rampant fantasy in us. The degree to which groups of animals and primitive men seem to know things about things and about each others' doings is of great and continuing interest to us all.

One obviously cannot know too much about the mind of mankind's cave dwellers and early agriculturalists and about the great and awesome power of their artefacts, their sympathetic magic and their world- and group-perpetuating rituals, needed for the continuation of the astronomical and reproductive cycles of nature and of their own bodies and effective in bringing about the cooperation of their food-prey in its own death and in yielding up the bounty of its flesh. For the farmer, human sacrifice and the magical resurrection of the sacrificed person seem an obvious way of sympathetically influencing seed-time and the next harvest. This magical power was especially necessary when digging and planting required a great effort of what we now call will-power (power at the disposal of the I) very much in its early stages. But this delayed gratification (Pavlov's inhibition of delay) would result in increased explosiveness of the social unit and especially of the most excitable persons in it.

At about this historical period, the circle, line, boundary demarcation, and furrow follow, and follow on from, the need to protect oneself or the valued object from its opposite or from one's own unconscious hostility (in projection) toward the valued object. At the same time, identifying with the encircled object, one or rather a part of oneself wishes to burst out, escape, be born or born again, and so we have here, potentially, an explosive impulse or image. Certainly in my patients' dreams, paintings, and behaviour one might say that the jewel, for example, is potentially explosive, as if it wishes to burst free of one's idealization and hoarding possessiveness and possibly change into a more human or natural entity or burst into worthless powder in order to punish one's greed.

The treasure, the Holy of Holies, the person of the god-king and, more abstractly, one's highest principles and ideal values and persons, can all be said to have the same properties, as far as being surrounded by defences and being prone to give rise to explosions are concerned. Good is kept within the defended boundary of the self (or its projected form such as social group or the walled city or the state) and evil is projected outside that boundary. However sophisticated and abstract this structure may become, the fact remains that it is essentially an archaic, paranoid, fighting form of instinctual pattern and represents only part of the total human repertoire of instincts and behaviours. When the evil penetrates the defended area, by invasion or by appearing as good, or when good appears to be evil, the opposites clash inside the I and either explosion or creative work results. Which outcome occurs depends on a balance of forces that are discussed at length here, but the most important factor for a creative outcome is a strong containing and transforming I based on experiences of loving and being loved. Experiences of this kind should be carefully distinguished from the idealizations and abstractions that are essentially defensive and compensatory.

At the historical period when this early form of I was predominant, when the image of the city, and therefore the city itself, becomes a possibility for the people concerned, a considerable degree of abstraction and depersonalisation has to be possible. The city concretizes a depersonalized representation of the body-image and of the maternal body-image (the two not being sharply distinguished at this level). A split between embodied feeling and disembodied intellect enable this abstraction to occur. The intellect becomes airborne, but should be often alighting to reconnect with the mother-earth of fact, reality, and feeling. Mathematics, astronomy, law, the wheel, and engineered defences and other projects all flourish at this stage of history and by their realization and success sustain the intellectual function which made them possible.

The complex interplay of love and aggression that results in the development of culture and of the mental structures making culture possible is brought about through the holding and validating behaviour of the group, acting largely through the child-rearing members of the society concerned. Explanatory and supportive myths play a vital role in this, but only serve their social and culture-enriching purpose as long as they correspond with the actual unconscious needs of the people. When mental structure and external reality do not support each other, the resulting decoupling of love and aggression results in mental or social explosiveness.

Social compliance entails the forgoing of some infantile omnipotence. The danger of this sacrifice in the service of a realistic I is dullness, falseness, and rigidity. Projecting one's repressed omnipotent subpersonalities onto god-king, god, or king results in a stable group within

limits, especially if the god-king is ritually slain at intervals, but throughout history there has been a steady tendency for mankind to withdraw
those projections as people learn to take responsibility themselves.
There is a tendency for king, and god, to be democratized and for people
to be able to take on more responsibility for their own explosiveness.
The Promethean intellect manifested in Greece, in the Renaissance, the
Age of Enlightenment, the French revolution, and the growth of science,
has steadily democratized omnipotence and increased real power to a
frightening degree. We must postulate that the city-state, at the centre of
which was the ritually sacrificed god-king, remained stable through the
power of the astronomer-mathematician priesthood and through the
identification of each person with the mythological role assigned to him,
including, of course, the king himself and his slaughtered wives and
servants. But as the king struggled free of this identification, he had to
become a tyrant, conquer the priests, identify with an all-powerful law-
giving God. Tyrants and monotheistic male gods now appear, together
with a strengthening of myths pertaining to ethical dualism, the struggle
of good against evil. Apocalyptic mythology begins.

The present world situation being in some ways apocalyptic, in
that destruction of the world as we know it and the people in it is a real
possibility, being brought about by ourselves, it is of particular importance to note that apocalyptic myths of the sort that we are now enacting
originated in our culture with the imaginary wars of good and evil,
which reflected the war between goodness and evil in the minds of those
struggling to be good as a result of the new ethical dualism of the time –
of the millennium before Christ in the Middle East. Although founded
on love and hate, which are both necessary for building up the mind,
goodness and evil have by now been subliminated into semiabstract
motivating principles with the use of allegorical figures and images. I
have not addressed the precise mechanism by which this occurs here;
however, it seems clear enough that crude ethical dualism reinforces
paranoid mechanisms and stokes up the energies that underly intrapsychic and extrapsychic explosiveness.

The monotheistic male divinity of goodness and light came to
dominate by first conquering and incorporating the mother goddess and
second conquering his dark evil twin. The present dangers to our planet
are, first, killing off the mother earth, and second, blowing ourselves to
pieces. It is as if the dark side of the omnipotent male deity were coming
into power. The tragedy is that it is not just "as if." The "darkness of God"
is our own darkness, but we need desperately to take responsibility for

these satanic forces within each of us, acknowledging their historical and psychological origins.

The women's movement, the restoration of the mother goddess, the growth of liberal humanism, and the influence of the oriental religions are symptomatic rather than therapeutic. They do not reach very far into our depths, whence originate the mythological, instinctual forces with which we have to grapple. The conscious pursuit of intrapersonal love, harmony, and peace, even the pursuit of social or cosmic love, harmony, and peace, may well be precisely what is building up the tension. Recognizing our own omnipotent childishness, our own conflictedness, disharmony, and the plurality of ourselves and of our motives, then grasping the real power, which we willy-nilly have, to create and destroy, with all the pain that goes with that power and that responsibility – this, I believe, is the way forward for us.

The gargantuan, alien, and monstrous products of civilisation are a measure of the childish impotence of our egos in relation to our non-egos. A human society on a human scale, with ordinary, human values and ways of bringing up children would promise well for our future, as would one that allows for anger, chaos, and even destructive feelings and behaviour on a human scale – in other words, a humorous, tolerant society that can take a deflating, ironic view of itself and its leaders, with leaders who are human and humane rather than power-mad. I believe the world is a better world in many of these respects than ever before. There is so much that has been potentially explosive in the civilised I for millennia that one might say that the civilised Western ego has simply been waiting for the technical means of destroying itself. Let us hope that this can occur in a psychological rather than literal sense, and that there are sufficient humane and containing forces in us humans to ensure a creative outcome.

References

Campbell, J. 1964. *Occidental Mythology*. Harmondsworth, N.Y.: Penguin, 1976.

———. 1968. *Creative Mythology*. Harmondsworth, N.Y.: Penguin, 1976.

———. 1959. *Primitive Mythology*. Harmondsworth, N.Y.: Penguin, 1976.

Dostoyevski, F. 1871. *The Idiot*. D. Magarshack, trans. London: Folio Society, 1971.

Freud, S. 1927. *The Future of an Illusion*. *SE*, vol. XXI. London: Hogarth Press, 1961.

———. 1925. *An Autobiographical Study*. *SE*, vol. XX. London: Hogarth Press, 1959.

———. 1920. *Beyond the Pleasure Principle*. *SE*, vol. XVIII. London: Hogarth Press, 1955.

———. 1901. *The Psychopathology of Everyday Life*. *SE*, vol. VI. London: Hogarth Press, 1960.

———. 1892. *A Case of Successful Treatment by Hypnotism*. SE, vol. I. London: Hogarth Press, 1966.

———. 1896. *The Neuroses of Defence* (Christmas Fairy Tale). *SE*, vol. I. London: Hogarth Press, 1966.

———. 1917. Mourning and melancholia. *SE*, vol. XIV. London: Hogarth Press, 1957.

———. 1922. The libido theory. *SE*, vol. XVIII. London: Hogarth Press, 1955.

———. 1950. Project for a Scientific Psychology. *SE*, vol. I. London: Hogarth Press, 1966.

Gantt, W. H. 1944. Experimental Basis for Neurotic Behavior. *Psychosomatic Medicine* 3, nos. 3 and 4. New York: American Society for Research in Psychosomatic Problems.

Grof, S. 1976. *Realms of the Human Unconscious*. New York: Dutton.

Inglis, B. 1965. *A History of Medicine*. London: Weidenfeld and Nicolson.

Jaynes, J. 1976. *The Origin of Consciousness in the Breakdown of the Bicameral Mind*. Boston: Houghton Mifflin, 1982.

Jung, C. G. 1921. *Psychological Types*. *CW*, vol. 6. Princeton, N.J.: Princeton University Press, 1971.

_____. 1946. The psychology of the transference. *CW* 16:163-326. Princeton, N.J.: Princeton University Press, 1954.

_____. 1948. On psychic energy. *CW* 8:3–66. Princeton, N.J.: Princeton University Press, 1960.

_____. 1951. The psychology of the child archetype. *CW* 9i:151–181. Princeton, N.J.: Princeton University Press, 1969.

_____. 1952. *Symbols of Transformation. CW*, vol. 5. Princeton, N.J.: Princeton University Press, 1956.

_____. 1955–1956. *Mysterium Coniunctionis. CW*, vol. 14. Princeton, N.J.: Princeton University Press, 1963.

_____. 1963. *Memories, Dreams, Reflections.* London: Collins and Routledge and Kegan Paul.

Meltzer, D. 1973. *Sexual States of Mind.* Perthshire, Scotland: Clunie Press.

Neuman, E. 1954. *The Origins and History of Consciousness.* New York: Pantheon.

Pavlov, I. P. 1927. *Conditioned Reflexes.* G. V. Anrep, trans. Oxford: Oxford University Press.

Perry, J. W. 1966. *Lord of the Four Quarters.* New York: Braziller.

Rosenfeld, H. 1987. *Impasse and Interpretation.* London: Tavistock Publications.

Schreber, D. R. 1903. *Denkwardigkeiten eines Nervenkrassken [Memoirs of My Nervous Illness].* I. Macalpine and R. A. Hunter, trans. London: Dawson, 1955.

Tausk, V. 1919. On the origin of the "influencing machine" in schizophrenia. *Psychoanalytic Quarterly* (1933): 519.

Wagner, R. 1880. *Art and Religion.* Nikolaus Lehnhoff, trans. *BBC*, October 1990.

Winnicott, D. W. 1958. *Collected Papers.* London: Tavistock Publications.

Index

www.ingramcontent.com/pod-product-compliance
Lightning Source LLC
Chambersburg PA
CBHW061716270326
41928CB00011B/2005